UNION INTERNATIONALE DES SCIENCES PRÉHISTORIQUES ET PROTOHISTORIQUES
INTERNATIONAL UNION FOR PREHISTORIC AND PROTOHISTORIC SCIENCES

PROCEEDINGS OF THE XV WORLD CONGRESS (LISBON, 4-9 SEPTEMBER 2006)
ACTES DU XV CONGRÈS MONDIAL (LISBONNE, 4-9 SEPTEMBRE 2006)

Series Editor: Luiz Oosterbeek

VOL. 17

2006
lisboa
uispp
XV congresso

Session C33

The Palaeolithic of the Balkans

Edited by

Andreas Darlas
Dušan Mihailović

BAR International Series 1819
2008

Published in 2016 by
BAR Publishing, Oxford

BAR International Series 1819

Proceedings of the XV World Congress of the International Union for Prehistoric and Protohistoric
Sciences /Actes du XV Congrès Mondial de l'Union Internationale des Sciences Préhistoriques et
Protohistoriques
The Palaeolithic of the Balkans

ISBN 978 1 4073 0305 5

Outgoing President: Vítor Oliveira Jorge; Outgoing Secretary General: Jean Bourgeois
Congress Secretary General: Luiz Oosterbeek (Series Editor)
Incoming President: Pedro Ignacio Shmitz
Incoming Secretary General: Luiz Oosterbeek

Contacts : Secretary of U.I.S.P.P. – International Union for Prehistoric and Protohistoric Sciences
Instituto Politécnico de Tomar, Av. Dr. Cândido Madureira 13, 2300 TOMAR
Email: uispp@ipt.pt   www.uispp.ipt.pt

BAR Publishing is the trading name of British Archaeological Reports (Oxford) Ltd.
British Archaeological Reports was first incorporated in 1974 to publish the BAR
Series, International and British. In 1992 Hadrian Books Ltd became part of the BAR
group. This volume was originally published by Archaeopress in conjunction with
British Archaeological Reports (Oxford) Ltd / Hadrian Books Ltd, the Series principal
publisher, in 2008. This present volume is published by BAR Publishing, 2016.

Printed in England

BAR
PUBLISHING

BAR titles are available from:

BAR Publishing
122 Banbury Rd, Oxford, OX2 7BP, UK
EMAIL   info@barpublishing.com
PHONE   +44 (0)1865 310431
FAX   +44 (0)1865 316916
www.barpublishing.com

NOTE OF THE SERIES EDITOR

The present volume is part of a series of proceedings of the XV world congress of the International Union for Prehistoric and Protohistoric Sciences (UISPP / IUPPS), held in September 2006, in Lisbon.

The Union is the international organization that represents the prehistoric and protohistoric research, involving thousands of archaeologists from all over the world. It holds a major congress every five years, to present a "state of the art" in its various domains. It also includes a series of scientific commissions that pursue the Union's goals in the various specialities, in between congresses. Aiming at promoting a multidisciplinary approach to prehistory, it has several regional or thematic associations as affiliates, and on its turn it is a member of the International Council for Philosophy and Human Sciences (an organism supported by UNESCO).

Over 2500 authors have contributed to c. 1500 papers presented in 101 sessions during the XVth world Congress of UISPP, held under the organisation of the Polytechnic Institute of Tomar. 25% of these papers dealt with Palaeolithic societies, and an extra 5% were related to Human evolution and environmental adaptations. The sessions on the origins and spread of hominids, on the origins of modern humans in Europe and on the middle / upper Palaeolithic transition, attracted the largest number of contributions. The papers on Post-Palaeolithic contexts were 22% of the total, with those focusing in the early farmers and metallurgists corresponding to 12,5%. Among these, the largest session was focused on prehistoric mounds across the world. The remaining sessions crossed these chronological boundaries, and within them were most represented the regional studies (14%), the prehistoric art papers (12%) and the technological studies (mostly on lithics – 10%).

The Congress staged the participation of many other international organisations (such as IFRAO, INQUA, WAC, CAA or HERITY) stressing the value of IUPPS as the common ground representative of prehistoric and protohistoric research. It also served for a relevant renewal of the Union: the fact that more than 50% of the sessions were organised by younger scholars, and the support of 150 volunteers (with the support of the European Forum of Heritage Organisations) were in line with the renewal of the Permanent Council (40 new members) and of the Executive Committee (5 new members). Several Scientific Commissions were also established.

Finally, the Congress decided to hold its next world congress in Brazil, in 2011. It elected Pe. Ignácio Shmitz as new President, Luiz Oosterbeek as Secretary General and Rossano Lopes Bastos as Congress secretary.

L.O.

TABLE OF CONTENTS

LIST OF FIGURES

LIST OF TABLES

THE PALAEOLITHIC OF THE BALKANS

Andreas DARLAS & Dušan MIHAILOVIĆ

The Balkan Peninsula, in the south-east of Europe, is situated on the migration route from the SW Asia to Europe, being therefore, the gate of entrance into the latter. The first inhabitants of Europe (arriving from Africa and Middle East) as well as subsequent human tribes, especially *Homo sapiens* must have passed through the Balkans. As a result, the importance of the investigation of the Paleolithic occupation of this area is obvious. In spite of this, the Paleolithic period in the Balkans is barely known (compared with other areas of Europe), since relevant research remains scarce. However, it must be noted that during the last years, the number of Paleolithic research projects has risen, contributing to the advance of our knowledge on this topic.

One first attempt of reviewing these research projects was the organisation of the 1st Conference "The Palaeolithic Archaeology of Greece and Adjacent Areas", held at Ioannina, Greece, in 1994[1].

Since that Conference there has not been organized a single meeting about the Palaeolithic of the Balkans. From that time information about the Palaeolithic of certain regions are considerably extended. There have been conducted archaeological excavations at many important sites and analyses of archaeological and paleoecological evidences have been carried out making possible better insight into the material culture and way of life of Palaeolithic communities in this region.

The organisation of the XVth UISPP Congress offered a very good opportunity for such a meeting to be realised, in order for new data to be presented and for a global examination of this latter issue, in Session C33-The Palaeolithic of the Balkans.

In this session, 10 conferences and 3 posters presented the results of recent research on cultural, economical and social changes during Palaeolithic in the Balkans.

Except for J. Kozłowski's communication, the subject of which covers the whole of the Balkan area, most of the papers in this volume (8) are concerned with the southern Balkans and especially Greece, while the remaining 5 papers refer to the western Balkans: two papers refer to Serbia, one to FYROM (R. of Macedonia) and one to Croatia.

More specifically, J. Kozłowski records the evolution of lithic industries between 30-20 kyrs B.P., following the

transition from the aurigniacian industries to "industries with backed bladelets" in various Balkan regions. Kozlowski starts with the following questions:

- whether the disappearance of the Aurignacian was synchronous in the various parts of the Balkan Peninsula,

- whether the genesis and the evolution of the industries with backed pieces was monophyletic or polphyletic in its nature,

- to what extent the processes of replacement of the Aurignacian by the Gravettian complex were the effect of adaptation to environmental changes, and how far they were the outcome of shifts of population representing new cultural traditions.

Harvati *et al.* present the preliminary results of a research program at Aliakmon valley (Macedonia, N. Greece) with an attempt of localisation of Lower Palaeolithic findings.

Kotjabopoulou attempts to reconstruct, through a faunal study, patterns of land use and mobility in the mountainous interior of Epirus region (NW Greece).

Apostolikas and Kyparissi-Apostolika bring forward the preliminary results from the field surveys in Thessaly and consider the possibility that the findings of Lake Plastiras relate to those from Theopetra cave, a site in the same broader area.

The Middle Palaeolithic industries from Klissoura cave 1 (Peloponnese, S. Greece) are the subject of Sitlivy's *et al.* paper. The very long sequence of this cave, which covers the entire Upper Pleistocene, make this site one of the most important palaeolithic sites in Greece.

Darlas and Psathi's paper constitutes the first presentation of the Upper Palaeolithic in Mani peninsula (southernmost edge of Peloponnese, S. Greece), through the preliminary results of excavations in 6 caves (only a small part of the numerous caves of this peninsula).

The next three papers refer to the environment of Neanderthals in Mani peninsula, as this comes to light by the study of the data from the excavation at Kalamakia cave. These are the first environmental data coming from Middle Palaeolithic site in Greece:

Lebreton *et al.* present the floral environment, resulting from palynological analyses.

Roger and Darlas, reveal, in two papers, the avifauna and microvertebrates from the Kalamakia cave.

[1] G. Bailey *et al.* (eds) (1999). *The Palaeolithic Archaeology of Greece and Adjacent Areas*, British School at Athens, Studies 3.

Salamanov-Korobar make known the preliminary results from the first palaeolithic research in FYROM (R. of Macedonia), and more specifically from the excavation of the Golema Pesht cave, which has yielded Middle and Upper Palaeolithic remains.

In D. Mihailovic's paper, new data about Middle Paleolithic in Serbia is presented, resulting from four excavations carried out during the last decades. The author attempts to give a general but clear view of the periodisation and cultural differentiation of the Middle Palaeolithic in this area.

B. Mihailovic compares the rich gravettian remains from the excavated cave Šalitrena Pećina (W. Serbia) with contemporaneous sites of Eastern Balkans and Central Europe.

Finally, Brajkovic and Miracle present the data of a new archaeozoological study of the material from Vindija cave in Croatia, a well-known site for the Middle and Upper Palaeolithic remains and famous thanks to the co-occur-rence of Upper Palaeolithic material with Neanderthal remains.

Despite the unequal representation of the different geographical areas in the above papers, the total assessment is that Session C33 offered the participants the opportunity to communicate a plurality of new data and to have a broad discussion on them. All in all, we hope that the present volume will enrich the literature by offering new and important information about Palaeolithic in the Balkans.

We wish to thank all those who contributed to the organisation of the Congress, especially the General Secretary Luiz Oosterbeek, those responsible of the Secretariat who have helped us during the preparation and the holding of this Congress, as well as the volunteers, who were charged with dealing with all the practical matters of our Session. We would also like to offer very special thanks to those who have participated in Session C33 and, in particular, to the authors of the papers of the present volume.

END OF THE AURIGNACIAN AND THE BEGINNING OF THE GRAVETTIAN IN THE BALKANS

Janusz K. KOZŁOWSKI

Universitet Jagiellonski, Instytut Archeologii, UI Golebia, 11, 31007 Cracovie, POLAND

Abstract: *The aim of this paper is to evaluate the role of environmental factors vs cultural traditions in the transition from the Early to the Middle Phase of the Upper Palaeolithic in the Balkans. Three questions have been analysed: 1. the relation between the different facies of the Balkan Aurignacian and the Early Gravettian and the problem of the contemporaneity of the Final Aurignacian and Early Mediterranean Backed Bladelets Industries. 2. The origin of the Backed Bladelets industries in the Balkans, 3. The role of the Middle Danube Centers of the Gravettian in the formation of the Shouldered Point Horizon in the Central Mediterranean zone.*
Key words: *Aurignacian, Gravettian, Backed bladelets, Shouldered points, Upper Palaeolithic*

Resume: *Le but de cette communication est d'evaluer le role des facteurs environmentaux et traditions culturelles dans le passage de la phase ancienne a la phase moyenne du Paleolithique superieur des Balkans. Trois questions ont ete examinees: 1. la relation entre les differents facies de l'Aurignacien final balkanique et les industries a lamelles a dos de la Mediterranee centrale. 2. Origine des industries a lamelles a dos de la Mediterranee, 3. Le role des centres gravettiens dans le bassin du moyen Danube dans l'origine des industries a pointes a cran de la Mediterranee centrale.*
Mots cles: *Aurignacien, Gravettien, lamelles a dos, pointes a cran, Paleolithique superieur*

INTRODUCTION

The problem of the cultural evolution in the Balkans, between 30–20 Kyr B.P., is, first of all, expressed by the replacement of the Aurignacian by the units dennotated as "industries with backed bladelets", or by other industries with backed pieces assigned to the Central European Gravettian. Three questions can be posed in respect of this process:

– whether the disappearance of the Aurignacian was synchronous in the various parts of the Balkan Paeninsula,

– whether the genesis and the evolution of the industries with backed pieces was monophyletic or polphyletic in its nature,

– to what extent the processes of replacement of the Aurignacian by the Gravettian complex were the effect of adaptation to environmental changes, and how far they were the outcome of shifts of population representing new cultural traditions.

In the time span between 30 to 20 Kyr B.P. a number of analogies can be seen between the cultural development in the middle Danube basin and in the Balkans: indeed, it can be assumed that the Balkans functioned as refuge territories for the middle Danube basin during cool oscillations preceding the glacial maximum (LGM).

In terms of taxonomy two types of stratigraphical succession can be distinguished in the Balkans between 30 to 20 Kyr B.P.:

1. the sequences where the Aurignacian is followed by the Gravettian: Willendorf II (Haesaertes *et al.* 1996, Otte, Noiret 2004), possibly also Krems-Hundsteig (Neugebauer-Maresch 2000) in the middle Danube basin and in the Balkans: Bacho Kiro (Kozłowski ed.

1982) and Temnata (Kozłowski *et al.* ed. 1992) in Bulgaria, and the Franchthi Cave in Greece (Perlès 1989. As a rule, at Balkan sites the Aurignacian is separated from the Gravettian by a chronological hiatus (well observable at Franchthi – Perlès 2000).

2. the sequences where the Early Gravettian or the Backed Bladelet industries are followed by the Younger Gravettian or Epigravettian. In the middle Danube basin, besides Willendorf II, these are sites on the slopes of the Pavlov Mts such as Dolní Věstonice, Pavlov, Milovice complex (Svoboda 2004, 2005). This chronological sequence is much more frequent in the Balkans e.g. at Asprochaliko, Kastritsa (Bailey *et al.* 1983, Adam 1989), Kephalari (Reisch 1980).

Recent investigations in the Klisoura Cave 1 in Greece (Koumouzelis *et al.* 2001) point to a possibility that one more type of sequence could have existed viz.: the Aurignacian and the Backed Bladelet industries are interstratified i.e. a level with backed bladelets is sandwiched between the younger portions of the Aurignacian.

ENVIRONMENT AND HUNTING STRATEGIES OF THE AURIGNACIAN AND THE BACKED BLADELETS INDUSTRIES

Pollen diagrams from the Ioannina Lake in Epirus (Bottema 1974) and Xinias in Thessaly (Wijmstra 1969) show a fast drop in the proportion of arboreal pollen in the time interval between 30 to 20 Kyr B.P. When forests shrank steppe with Artemisia and Chenopodiacae became the dominant type of habitat. It was only in mountain terrains that forest communities had been preserved with oak, spruce and juniper. Such tree composition bears witness to stability of climatic conditions with simultaneous presence of a mosaic of environments. The faunal

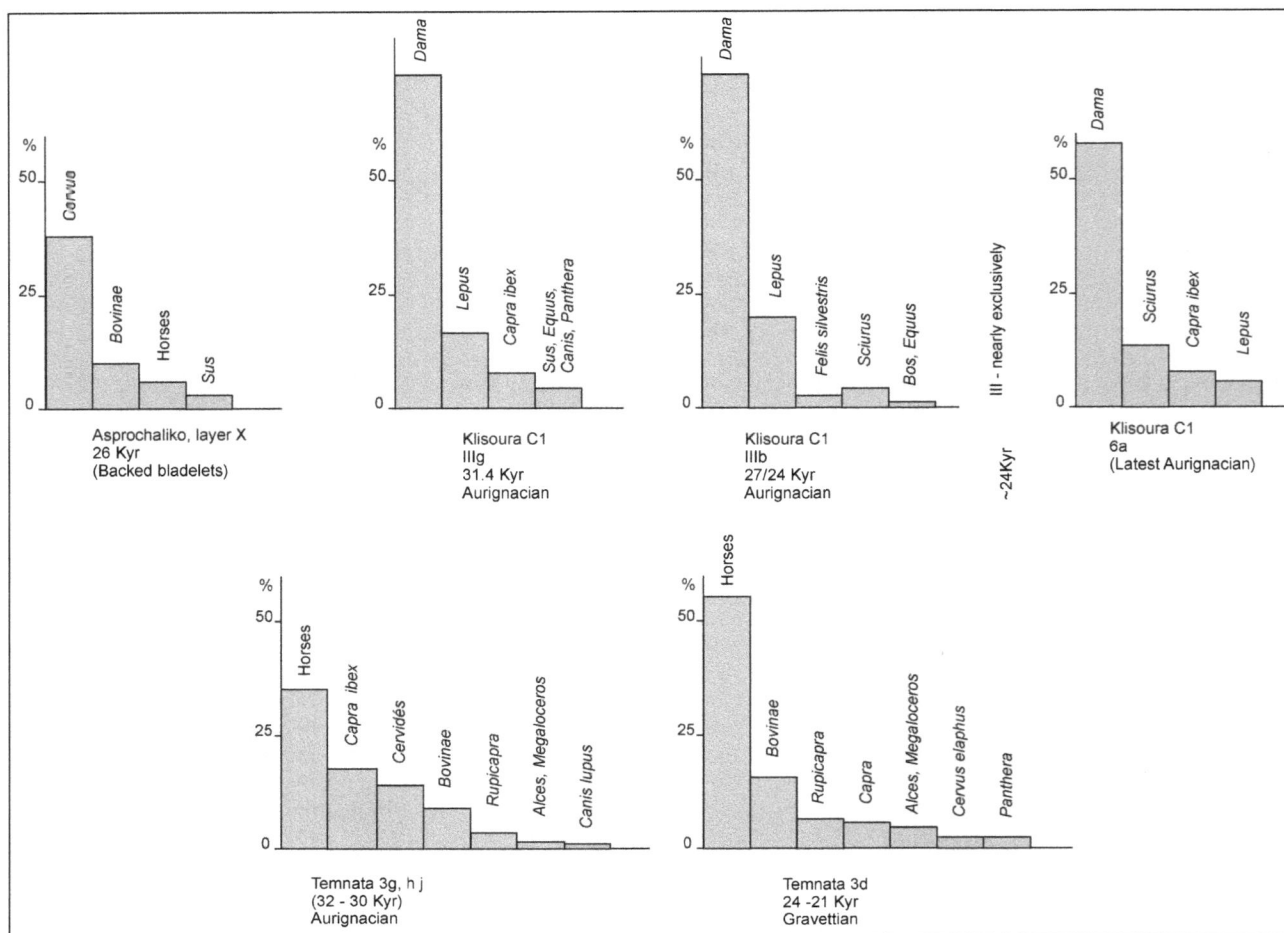

Fig. 1.1. Game structure in selected Aurignacian and oldest backed bladelets/Gravettian layers in the Balkans

composition at sites from this period is proportional to the frequency of species inhabiting the surrounding habitats.

Epirus was dominated by ibex and roe deer (Bailey, Gamble 1990), at the edges of Argolid there were fallow deer and hare (Koumouzelis *et al.* 2001), possibly hare and roe deer (Payne 1982, Reisch 1982) (Fig. 1.1).

In the northern Balkans, for example in Gravettian levels X–IV in the Temnata Cave, dated to 29–20 Kyr B.P., the faunal structure well mirrors the proportions of species in the habitats within a radius of 5–8 km from the site (Delpech, Guadelli 1992). The dominant fauna are steppe species (horse, bison), species inhabiting limestone plateau (ibex), whereas forest species (roe deer, megaceros) are rare, only in gallery forests in valleys (Fig. 1.1).

Thus, we can justifiably assume that the environmental changes in the period from 30 to 20 Kyr B.P. were not all-important for the cultural changes in that period, the changes that are primarily manifested by the replacement of the Aurignacian by the industries with backed bladelets.

THE TERMINAL AURIGNACIAN AND THE BEGINNING OF THE GRAVETTIAN IN THE MIDDLE DANUBE BASIN AND THE BALKANS

In terms of technology-typology three groups can be distinguished in the evolution of the Aurignacian in the Balkans:

1. The Mediterranean Proto-Aurignacian type industries (Fumanian) with highly advanced bladelet production that used two types of *chaînes operatoires*:

   – microlithic single-platform cores for the production of bladelets with straight profiles,

   – cores-endscrapers or cores-carenoidal burins for the production of bladelets with arched profiles.

These technologies co-occur with large quantities of bilaterally microretouched bladelets and Krems points; end-scrapers, blade and flake burins also occur (Broglio *et al.* 2005). Industries like this, frequent in Italy, are rare in the middle Danube basin (Krems-Hundsteig in Austria, Hahn 1977 – dated at ca 34 Kyr B.P.). Microretouched bladelet industries are equally rare in the Balkans where, in fact, the only site assigned to this type of the Aurignacian is the Kozarnika Cave the layer dated to 38.7 Kyr B.P. (Guadelli *et al.* 2005). The Aurignacian with microretouched bladelets from the Kozarnika Cave was confused with the early phase of the Gravettian which was, erronously, claimed to have played a role in the origin and the evolution of the, so-called, Kozarnikian in layers 5a and 3b/c (culture levels VI sup. – IVa, IVb) (Guadelli *et al.* 2005).

2. Aurignacian industries based on bladelet technology, also using specific cores for bladelets and cores-carenoidal end-scrapers, but with a very low frequency of retouched bladelets. At the same time, the proportion of macroblade technique is small, just as of tools on blades. On the other hand, flake tools, mainly denticulated-notched also occur. Splintered technique besides tool shaping, was used for the production of microflakes. Moreover, numerous cores-carenoidal end-scrapers are made on flakes. Industries like this are known first of all, from the Aurignacian sequence in layers IV–III in Klisoura Cave I in Argolide (Koumouzelis *et al.* 2000) (Fig. 1.2, 1.3). Assemblages on the western coast of Greece may approximate this type of the Aurignacian, but these are exclusively surface materials such as e.g. at Spilaion near Preveza (Runnels *et al.* 2003) and Elaiochori (Darlas 1989). The fact that bladelets are absent in these assemblages can be explained by postdepositional erosion which had damaged finer artefacts.

3. Aurignacian industries based on macroblade and flake technology; among tools there are, first of all, end-scrapers (of which some, notably high and carenoidal end-scrapers, functioned as cores for bladelets), retouched blades (also endscrapers on retouched blades), side-scrapers, and denticulated and notched tools.

At the sites that had been earlier explored the frequency of bladelets (both retouched and unretouched) is difficult to estimate because wet-sieving had not been used in exploration. These are sites in the north-western Balkans (Sandalia II – Malez 1979; Lušćić – Montet-White 1996; Vršac-Červenka – Mihailović 1992).

It should be emphasized that in the Balkans short-term camp sites, with individual stone and bone artefacts (the latter often more numerous than lithics) are frequently recorded. This is, for example, the Potočka Cave, or the Aurignacian (post-Bachokirian) levels in the Bacho Kiro and other caves.

None of these Aurignacian groups exhibit phyletic links with the industries with backed tools. Attempts have been made to substantiate:

– continuity of the, so-called, Fumanian in the industries with backed bladelets (Broglio 1996), but a number of researchers questioned this concept while emphasizing discontinuity between these two cultural units (Palma di Cesnola 1996).

– continuity of pre-Aurignacian industries with arched backed pieces (non-Chatelperonian ones) in Gravetoid industries with backed bladelets (e.g. in the Uluzzian or in the industries with backed pieces and leaf points e.g. from Korpach-Grogorieva 1996). In this case, however, an important fact is that early backed blade industries are separated from the earliest Gravettian by the Aurignacian: both in Italian and in Greek sequences (Gambassini 1997).

It should be stressed that the technology of industries with backed blades/bladelets is clearly different than that of the Aurignacian. Layer 10 in the Asprochaliko Cave yielded double-platform cores for blades and bladelets, with the pra-flaking surface prepared from lateral crests; platforms were rejuvenated by detaching tablets (Adam 1989). The lowest levels of the Gravettian sequence in the Temnata Cave, too, display a tendency towards growing importance of the double-platform core technique (Drobniewicz *et al.* 1992).

The Aurignacian and the Gravettian contrast, moreover, in respect of the ways and intensity of site use: at Aurignacian sites the number of repeated occupational episodes is greater, artefacts and evident structures are more numerous – such as most importantly, hearths – or, as in the Klisoura Cave structured hearths of fired clay (Pawlikowski *et al.* 2000, Karkanas *et al.* 2004). In layer IV of the Klisoura Cave, on an area of 6 sq m 14 340 artefacts were discovered (Koumouzelis *et al.* 2000), whereas in layer 10 of the Asprochaliko Cave, on an area of 12 sq m 1335 artefacts were found (Adam 1989). In the lower levels in the Temnata Cave the lowest, Gravettian level (IXb) yielded only 207 artefacts.

The Aurignacian vanished in the Balkans – just as in other parts of Europe – about 28 Kyr B.P., although in some regions, e.g. Istria, it could have persisted somewhat longer. In Istria, in the Šandalja Cave II there are two Aurignacian layers: *f* – dated to 25.340±170 years B.P., and *e* – dated to 23.540±100 years B.P. The industry with backed bladelets appears only in layer *d* – dated to 21.740±450 years B.P. (Malez 1979). Another such region is Argolide where in Klisoura Cave I a series of Aurignacian layers IV–IIa is dated to 34–31 Kyr B.P. (Fig. 1.4); above layer IIIa layers III' and III" contained an industry with backed bladelets (Fig. 1.5) dated to 24.820±820 years B.P. and 23.000±540 years B.P. Overlying these layers Aurignacian layers III and 6a occurred again. From layer 6a organic fraction provided the date of 22.370±270 years B.P., and land snails the date of 23.800±520 years B.P. (Fig. 1.4). Thus, the Klisoura Cave represents an interstratification of Aurignacian levels and levels containing backed bladelets.

The appearance of industries with backed bladelets in the Balkans – on the other hand – is much earlier. This is confirmed by the parallel existance of this industry and the Aurignacian over a long time span. The earliest

Fig. 1.2. Klisoura, Cave 1, layers IIIe, IIIf. Selected artefacts
from the middle portion of the Aurignacian sequence

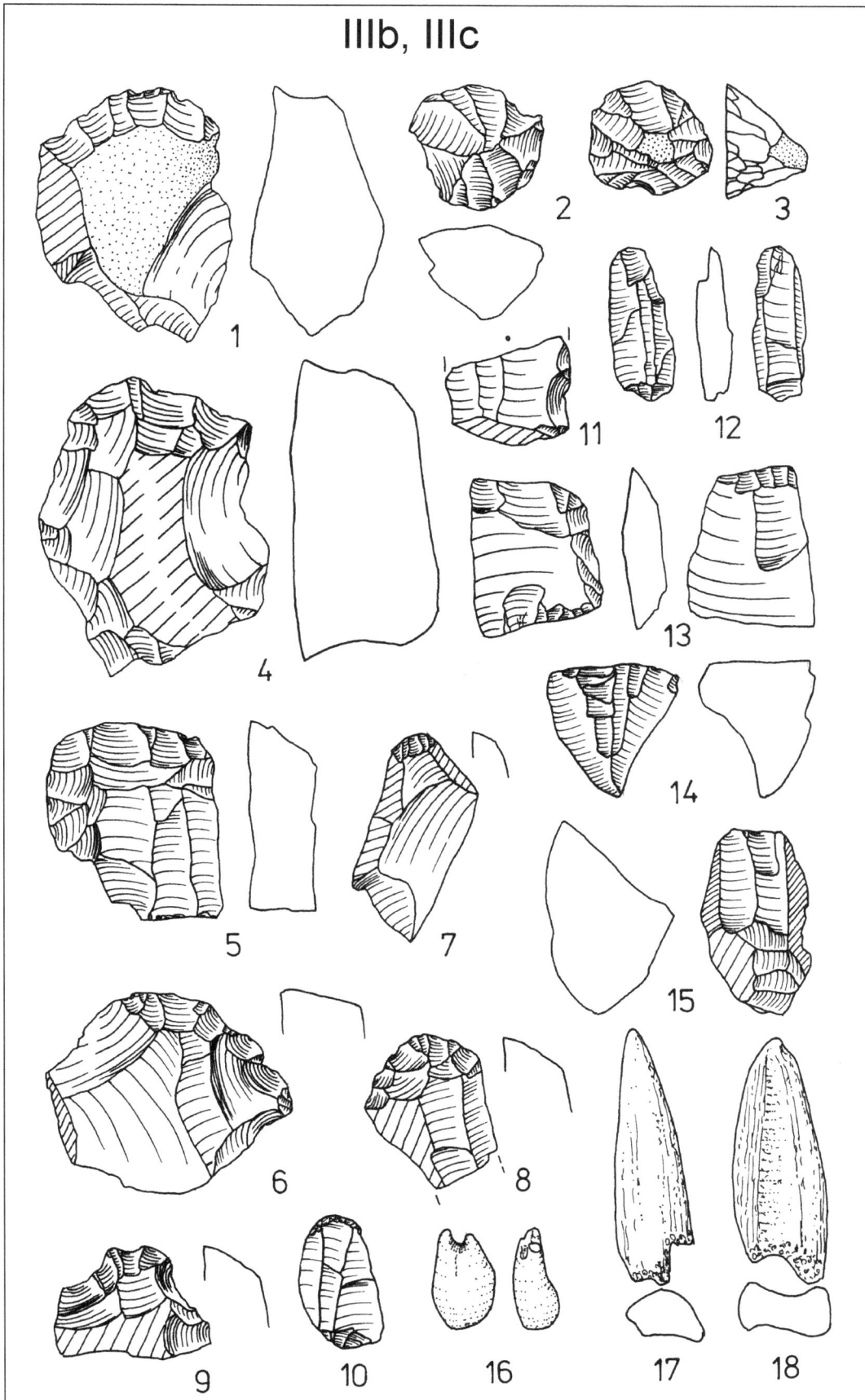

Fig. 1.3. Klisoura Cave 1, layers IIIb, IIIc. Selected artefacts
from the upper portion of the Aurignacian sequence

		AMS	C14 on organic fraction	C14 on shells	C14 on bones	C14 on carbonates
II a	Epigravettian					Gd - 3872 17280±90
II b	Epigravettian					
6a/6	Aurignacian	RTT - 4793 28 600 ± 350 29.150 ± 340 RTT - 4752		Gd - 799 23 800 ± 400 Gd - 7996 27.200 ± 500	Gd - 11546 22.370 ± 270	
7	Aurignacian					
III						
III'	Backed bladelets		Gd - 15349 23000 ± 540			Gd - 3877 21.720 ± 90
III''	?		Gd - 15351 24.820 ± 520			
III b						
III c						
III e						Gd - 12035 26230 ± 140 Gd - 3879 26.770 ± 150
II e'	Aurignacian					
II f	Aurignacian					
II g	Aurignacian	RTT - 4786 30.925 ± 420	Gd - 11300 31.400 ± 1000 Gd - 7892 34.700 ± 1600			Gd -7882 28.270 ± 340
IV	Aurignacian	GdA - 228 31.150 ± 480	Gd - 10562 32.400 ± 600			
V	Initial UP	Gifa A - gg 168 40.010 ± 740 RTT 4791 30.775 ± 410	> 31100 >30800			
VI	Initial UP					
VII	Moust.					

Fig. 1.4. Klisoura, Cave 1. Radiocarbon dates from the Initial and Early Upper Palaeolithic

Gravettian levels from the Temnata Cave, sector TD-I have been dated to 28.900±1400 and 28.900±1100 years B.P. (Ginter, Kozłowski 1992). In the Asprochaliko Cave level X has been dated to 26.000±900 years B.P.; similar dates (between 26 to 25 Kyr) have been obtained for backed bladelets industries from caves in the Peloponese (e.g. Skoini III and IV recently investigated by A. Darlas, see this volume), almost the same as the date for layer III' from the Klisoura Cave.

The parallel evolution of the terminal Aurignacian and the industries with backed bladelets lasted, probably, until 25–24/23 Kyr B.P. Later, as the LGM approached, the Balkans functioned as a refuge territory for typical Gravettian industries from the middle Danube basin.

THE LGM AND THE LATE GRAVETTIAN OF THE MIDDLE DANUBIAN TYPE IN THE BALKANS

In the classical Gravettian sequence in the Temnata Cave in the northern Balkans the early phase, placed between 29 to 28 Kyr (levels IXa, VIII), is separated from the late

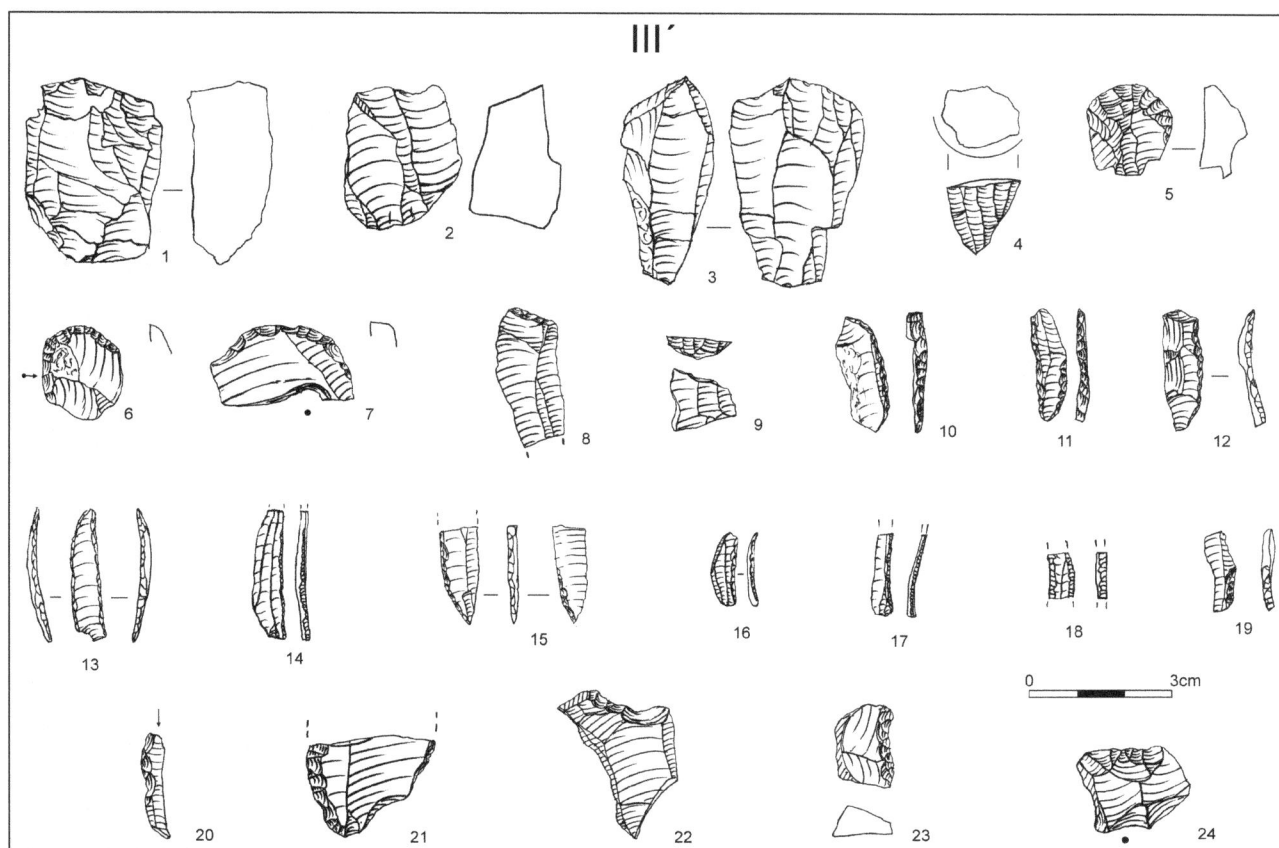

Fig. 1.5. Klisoura Cave 1, layer III'. Artefacts from backed bladelet horizon
sandwiched between the Aurignacian layers

phase, dated to between 24 to 18/16 Kyr (levels VIIb–IVa), by a hiatus (Drobniewicz *et al.* 1992) (Fig. 1.6). The assemblages from these levels show similarities with the classical sequence of Willendorf II in Lower Austria (Felgenhauer 1956–1959, Otte 1981, Otte, Noiret 2004, Haesearts *et al.* 2004), where Gravettian levels 6–8 span the time interval from 27 to 25 Kyr. (Fig. 1.7). It can be therefore conjectured, that during cool episodes and in deteriorating climatic conditions registered at about 28–26 and 23–18 Kyr, the northern Balkans functioned as a refuge territory for the Middle Danubian Gravettian. This hypothesis is grounded not only in the techno-typological similarities of lithic assemblages, but also in the circulation of lithic raw materials, i.e.: the appearance of raw materials from northern Hungary in the Temnata Cave (Pawlikowski 1992, Kozłowski 1999). Recently, the discovery of a rich and interesting assemblage from the Saliterna pečina Cave in western Serbia (Mihailović, this volume, p. 101) has provided another argument in support of the Middle Danubian links of the central Balkan Gravettian.

Another piece of evidence to show that part of the Gravettian population withdrew from the middle Danube basin is the emergence of the shouldered point facies (Fig. 1.8). This facies – deriving from assemblages with shouldered points of the type of Willendorf II layer 9 – Moravany – Banka – Nitra Čerman (Kozłowski 1996) appears in the

Balkans and in Italy in the LGM (21–18 Kyr), persisting until 16 or even 14 Kyr (Kozłowski 1999, Palma di Cesnola 1993). The earliest sites with shouldered points in the northern Balkans occur in Istria (Šandalja II – 21.740± 450years B.P. – Malez 1979), in Slovenia (Ovča Jama layer 3 and 4 – 19.540±500 years B.P., Osole 1962-1963), and in western Greece (Kastritsa level 19 – 19.900±370 years B.P.; Bailey, Gamble 1990). The youngest assemblages with shouldered points occur in Slovenia (Zakajeni spodmol layer 3), Bosnia (Kadar), southern Bulgaria (Orphei), and eastern Greece (Seidi, Kephalari, Klisoura layer IIb) around 16 (possibly even 14) Kyr. (Fig. 1.9).

The shapes of shouldered points in the Balkans are similar to the forms known in the Danube basin. It should be added that assemblages that are richer in these forms (e.g. from Kastritsa) contain, in addition, specific specimens resembling shouldered points from Italian sites. We can, thus, conjecture that in the Balkans and in the Adriatic Sea basin there emerged a specific type of the Late Gravettian/Early Epigravettian with shouldered point – originating from the middle Danube basin (Fig. 1.10). This Balkan-Adriatic culture zone constitutes this part of the earlier Gravettian that derives from the Pavlovian tradition. The groups that in the LGM migrated from the Carpathian Basin to the east gave rise to the Kostenki-Avdeevo tradition.

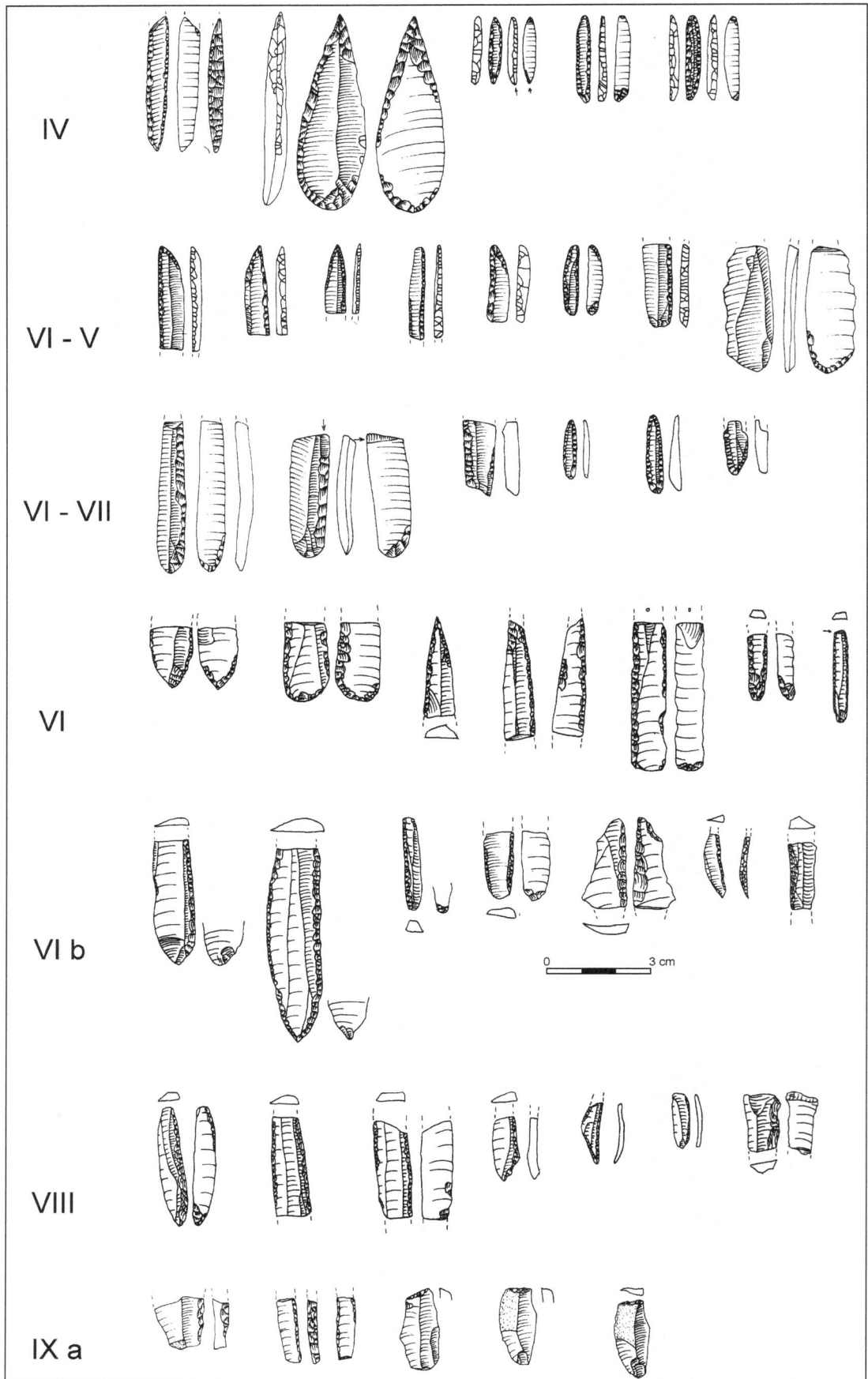

Fig. 1.6. Temnata Cave. Diagnostic tools from the Gravettian sequence

Kyr.BP	Temnata		Willendorf II	
	I	13,6 ± 0,2		
		13,9 ± 0,4		
	IV a			
	IV b			
	V a			
	V b			
	VI			
	VI - VII			
20	VII a			
		21,2 ± 0,3		
	VII b			
		23,4 ± 1,6		
		24,9 ± 0,5		
			9	24,9
			8	25,2 - 25,8
			7	
			6	26,2 - 26,5
	VIII	28,9 ± 1,1		
		29,7 ± 1,6		
	IX a	28,9 ± 1,4		
30	IX b		5	30,5
	X			

Fig. 1.7. Chronostratigraphic relations between Temnata and Willendorf II Gravettian sequences

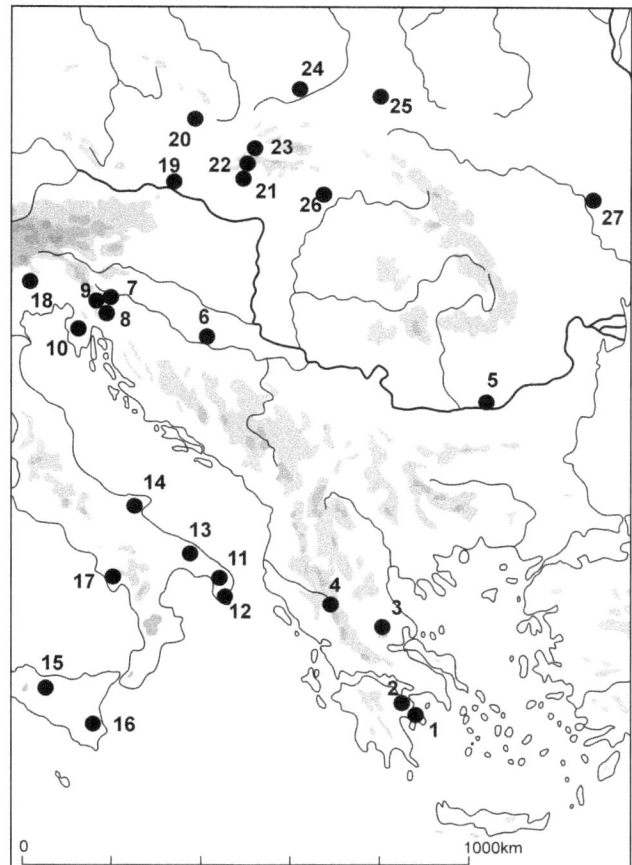

Fig. 1.8. Late Gravettian sites with shouldered points in Central and South Eastern Europe. Greece: 1 – Klisoura Cave 1, layer IIb, 2 – Kephalari, 3 – Seidi, 4 – Kastritsa; Bulgaria: 5 – Orphei (Tchoutchoura); former Yougoslavia: 6 – Kadar, 7 – Ovča jama, 8 – Zupanov spodmol, 9 – Zakajeni spodmol, 10 – Sandalja II; Italy: 11-Taurisano, 12 – Cipolliane C, 13 – La Mura, 14 – Paglici, 15 – Niscemi, 16 – Canicattini Bagni, 17 – Cala della Ossa, 18 - Paina

The elements of the common techno-typological tradition can be seen in both these territories, despite differing adaptations in the economic sphere: in the east of Europe semi-settled mammoth hunters adapted to the periglacial steppe (Rogatchev, Praslov 1982, Sergin 1996, 2002), whereas in the Balkans and in the Adriatic sea basin mobile hunters hunting Cervids and ibex, seasonally exploited the littoral zones and mountain territories (Bailey, Gamble 1990).

References

ADAM, E. (1989). *A technological and typological analysis of Upper Palaeolithic stone industries of Epirus, Noerthwestern Greece*. BAR International Series, 512. Oxford.

BAILEY, G.; CARTER, P.; GAMBLE, C.; HIGGS, H. (1983). Asprochaliko and Kastritsa: further investigations in the Upper Palaeolithic settlement and economy in Epirus. *Proceedings of Prehistoric Society*, 49, 15-42.

BAILEY, G.; GAMBLE, C. (1990). The Balkans at 18.000 BP: the view from Epirus (in) *The World at 18.000 BP*, vol. I, 148-170.

BOTTEMA, S. (1974). *Late Quaternary vegetation history of northwestern Greece*. Groningen, University Press.

BROGLIO, A. (1996). Le punte a dorso del Protoaurignaziano mediterraneo: i reperti della Grotta di Fumane (in) *The Upper Palaeolithic, UISPP XIII Congress, Colloquia vol.6*, 237-249.

Kyr E.P.	Northen Sites	Balkans	Italy
15		Klisoura II b 14.2(?) Kadar 16.0 Zakajeni spodmol 3-17.6 Kastritsa 19 19.9 Ovča jama 3-4 19.5	Taurisano 22 -18-16.0 Paglici 17B -17.9 Paina 14 -18.6 Paglici 17E -19.6 Paglici 18A -20.2-21.6
20		Šandalja II 21,7	
	- Molodova V/7 23.7 (-25.0) - Kraków-Spadzista 24.0-22.9 - Moravany 24.0-23.0 - Nitra-Čerman 23.0 - Willendorf II/9 (24.9 Kyr)		
25			

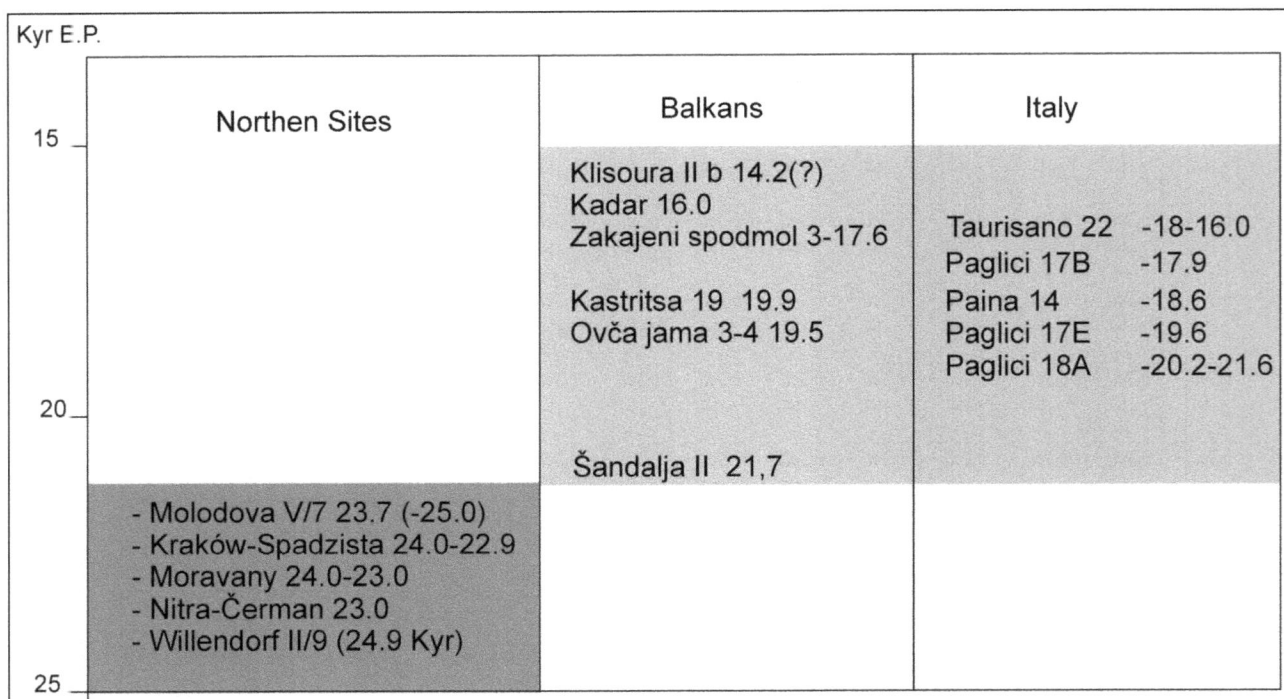

Fig. 1.9. Chronostratigraphic relations between shouldered point horizon sites in Central Europe, the Balkans and Italy

BROGLIO, A.; GIACOBINI, G.; TAGLIACOZZO, A.; PERESANI, A.; BERTOLA, S.; CILLI, C.; DI STEFANI, M.; GURIOLI, F. (2005). L'abitato aurignaziano (in) *Pitture Paleolitiche nelle Prealpi Venete*, Verona, 23-37.

DROBNIEWICZ, B.; GINTER, B.; KOZLOWSKI, J.K. (1992). The Gravettian sequence (in) *Temnata Cave, Excavations in Karlukovo Karst Area, Bulgaria*. Krakow, Jagiellonian University Press, vol. I 1, 295-501.

DELPECH, F.; GUADELLI, J.-L. (1992). Les grands mammiferes gravettiens et aurignacians de la grotte Temnata (in) *Temnata Cave, Excavations in Karlukovo Karst Area, Bulgaria*. Krakow, Jagiellonian University Press, vol. I 1, 141-216.

FELGENHAUER, E. (1956-1959). *Willendorf in der Wachau. Monographie der Palaolith-Fundstellen I-VII. Mitteilungen der Prahistorischen Kommission, VIII-IX*, Wien, OadW.

GAMBASSINI, P. (1997). *Il Paleolitico di Castelcivita, culture e ambiente*. Naples, Electa.

GINTER, B.; KOZLOWSKI, J.K. (1992). *The archaeological sequence (in) Temnata Cave, Excavations in Karlukovo Karst Area, Bulgaria*. Krakow, Jagiellonian University Press, vol. I 1, 289-293.

GRIGORIEVA, G. (1996). Le Paleolithique superieur ancien du sud-ouest de la Plaine Russe (in) *The Upper Palaeolithic, UISPP XIII Congress, Coloquia vol. 6*, Forli, Abaco, 53-69.

GUADELLI, J.L.; SIRAKOV, N.; IVANOVA, S.; SIRAKOVA, S.; ANASTASSOVA, S.; COURTAUD, P.; DIMITROVA, I.; DJABARSKA, N.; FERNANDEZ,

PH.; FERRIER, C.; FONTUGNE, M.; GAMBIER, D.; GUADELLI, A.; IORDANOVA, D.; KOVATCHEVA, M.; KRUMOV, I.; LEBLANC, J.C.; MARINSKA, M.; MITEVA, V.; POPOV, V.; SPASSOV, R.; TANEVA, S.; TSNERAT-LABORDE, N.; TSANOVA, T. (2005). Une séquence du Paléolithique inférieur au Paléolithique récent dans les Balkans: La grotte Kozarnika a Orechets (in) *Données récentes sur les kodalites du peuplement et sur le cadre chronostratigraphique, géologique et paléogéographique des industries du Paléolithique inférieur et moyen en Europe*. BAR International Series,

HAESEARTS, P.; DAMBLON, F.; BACHNER, M.; TRNKA, G. (1996). Revisited stratigraphy and chronology of the Willendorf II sequence. Archaeologia Austriaca, 80, 25-42.

HAESEARTS, P.; BORZIAK, I.; CHIRICA, V.; DAMBLON, F.; KOULAKOVSKA, L. (2004). Cadre stratigraphique et chronologique du Gravettien en Europe centrale (in) *The Gravettian along the Danube*, Brno, Institute of Archaeology, 33-56.

HAHN, J. (1977). *Aurignacien, das altere Jungpalaeolithikum in Mittel- und Osteuropa*. Koln/Wien, Bohlau Verlag.

KARKANAS, P.; KOUMOUZLIS, M.; KOZLOWSKI, J.K.; SITLIVY, V.; SOBCZYK, K.; BERNA, F.; WEINER, S. (2003). The earliest evidence for clay hearths: Aurignacian features in Klisoura Cave 1, southern Greece. Antiquity, 78, 301, 513-525.

KOOUMOUZELIS, M.; GINTER, B.; KOZLOWSKI, J.K.; PAWLIKOWSKI, M.; BAR-YOSEF, O.; ALBERT, R.M.; LITYNSKA-ZAJAC, M.; STWOR-

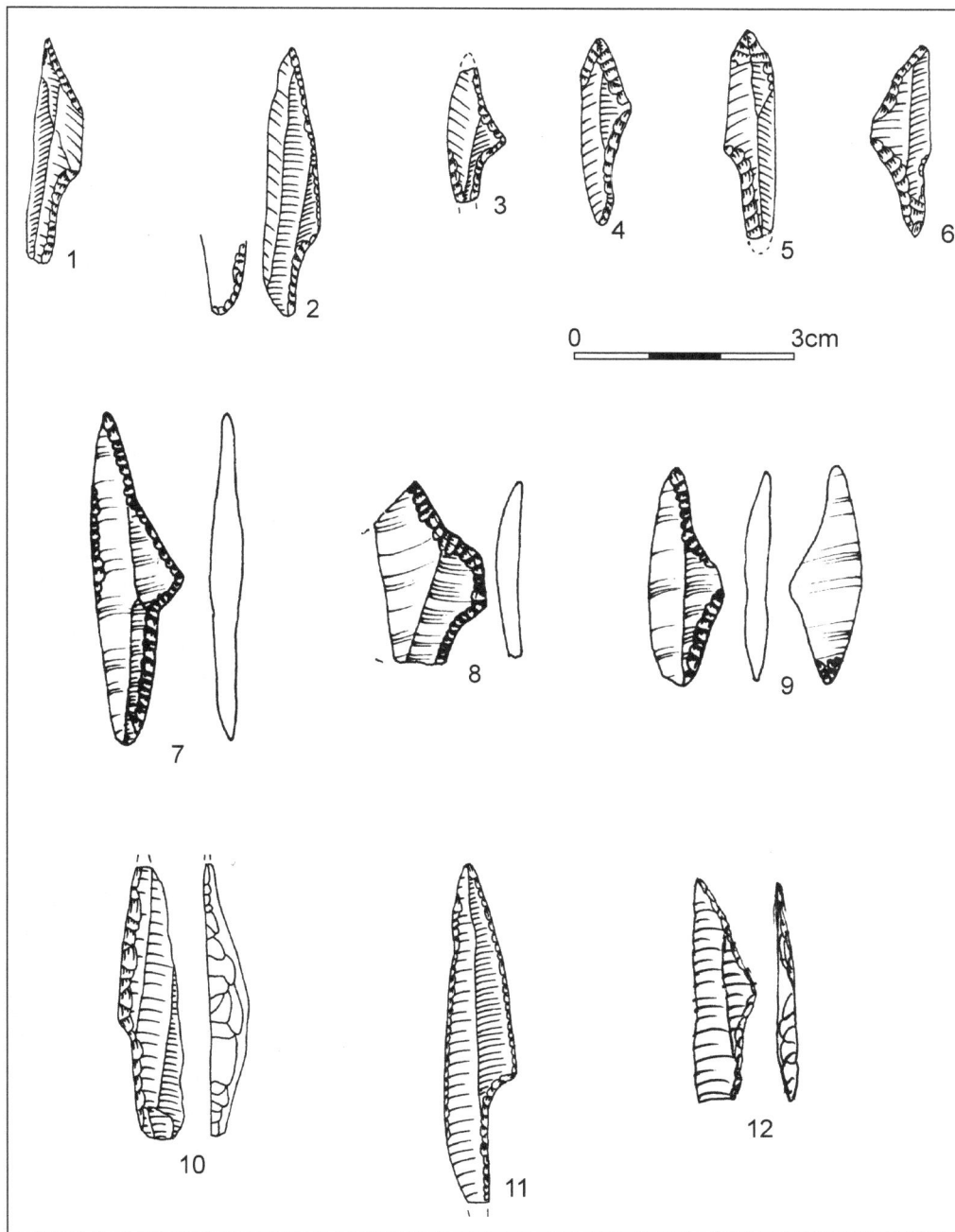

Fig. 1.10. Shouldered points from selected sites in the Balkans: 1,2 – Sandalia II near Pula, Kroatia; 3-6 – Kadar, Bosnia; 7-9 – Orphei (Tchoutchoura), Rhodopes, Bulgaria; 10,11 – Kastritsa, Epirus, Greece; 12 – Klisoura Cave 1, layer IIb

ZEWICZ, E.; WOJTAL, P.; LIPECKI, G.; TOMEK, T.; BOCHENSKI, Z.; PAZDUR, A. (2001).The Early Upper Palaeolithic in Greece: the excavations in Klisoura Cave. *Journal of Archaeological Science*, 28, 515-539.

KOZLOWSKI, J.K. (1996). L'origine du Gravettien de l'Europe centrale (in) *The Upper Palaeolithic, UISPP XIII Congress*, vol. 6, Forli, Abaco, 203-212.

KOZLOWSKI, J.K. (1999). Gravettian/Epigravettian sequences in the Balkans: environment, technologies, hunting strategies and raw material procurement (in)

The Palaeolithic archaeology in Greece and adjacent areas. Athens, British School, 319-329.

KOZLOWSKI, J.K. ed. (1982). *Excavation in the Bacho Kiro Cave, final report*. Warszawa, PWN.

KOZLOWSKI, J.K.; LAVILLE, H.; GINTER, B. Eds. (1992). *Temnata Cave, Excavations in Karlukovo Karst Area*, vol. 1, 1, Krakow, Jagiellonian University Press.

MALEZ, M. (1979). Nalazista paleolitskog i mezolitskog doba v Hrvatskoj (in) A.Benac (ed) *Praistorija Jugoslovenskih Zemalja*. Sarajevo: Academie des Sciences.

MONTET-WHITE, A. (1996). *Le Paléolithique en ancienne Yougoslavie.* Grenoble, Editions Jerome Millon.

MIHAILOVIC, D. (1992). *Orinjasienskja kremena industria sa lokaliteta Crvenka At u blizinni Vrsaca.* Beograd, Centar za Arheoloska Istrazivanja.

NEUGEBAUER-MARESCH, C. (2000). Wege zur Eiszeit. Ein Projekt zur Altsteinzeitforschung der Prahistorischen Kommission der OAW und des Fonds zur Forderung der wissenschftlichen Forschung. *Osterreichischen Akademie der Wissenschften Anzeiger phil.-hist. Klasse,* 135, 31-46. Wien.

OSOLE (1962-1963). Mladsi paleolitik iż Ovce jamy. *Arheoloski Vestnik,* 13-14.

OTTE, M. (1981). *Le Gravettien en Europe Centrale.* Buges, De Tempel, vol. 1,2.

OTTE, M.; NOIRET, P. (2000). Evolution du Gravettien au moyen Danube (in) *The Gravettian along the Danube,* Brno, Institute of Archaeology, 8-32.

PALMA DI CESNOLA, P. (1993). Il Paleolitico superiore in Italia. Irene, Garlatti.

PALMA DI CESNOLA, P. (1996). Le Gravettien le plus ancien en Italie (in) *The Upper Palaeolithic, UISPP, XIII Congress,* Colloquia vol. 6, Forli, Abaco, 227-236.

PAWLIKOWSKI, M. (1992). The origin of lithic raw materials (in) *Temnata Cave, Excavations in Karlukovo Karst Area, Bulgaria,* I, 1, Krakow, Jagiellonian University Press, 241-288.

PAWLIKOWSKI, M.; KOUMOUZELIS, M.; GINTER, B ; KOZLOWSKI, J.K. (2000). Emerging ceramic technology in structured Aurignacian hearths at Klisoura Cave I in Greece. *Archaeology, Ethnology and Anthrpology of Eurasia,* 4, 19-29.

PAYNE, S. (1982). Faunal evidence for environmental/climatic change at Franchthi Cave 25.000 to 5.000 B.P. (in) *Palaeoclimates, Palaeoenvironmnts, and Human Communities in the Eastern Mediterranean Region in Later Prehistory,* Oxford, BAR, 133-136.

PERLÈS, C. (1989). *Les industries litiques tailléees de Franchthi (Argolide, Grece): Présentation générale et industries paléolithiques.* Excavations at Franchthi Cave, fasc.3, Bloomington, Indiana University Press.

PERLÈS, C. (2000). Greece 30.000-20.000 BP (in) *Hunters of the Golden Age,* Leiden, University, 375-397.

REISCH, L. (1980). Pleistozän und Urgeschichte der Peloponnes. Ph.D.diss. Friedrich Alexander Universität.

ROGATCHEV, S.; PRASLOV, N. (1982). *Paleolit Kostenkovsko-Borchevskogo Rayona na Donu.* Moskva, Nauka.

RUNNELS, C.; VAN ANDEL, TH. (2003). The Early Stone Age of the Nomos of Preveza: landscape and settlement (in) *Landscape Archaeology in Southern Epirus,* Greece, I, Athens, American School of Classical Studies, 47-134.

SERGUIN, V.J. (1998). Zhilischtcha na panmiatnikach vostochnogo Gravetta Russkoy Ravniny (in) *Vostochnyi Gravet.* Moskva, 151-176.

SERGUIN, V.J. (2002). Razmiechtchenie kulturnych ostatkov v komplekse I verkhnego sloya Kostenok I (in) *Osobennosti Razvitia verknego palolita Vostochnoy Evropy,* Sankt-Petersburg, IIMK RAN, 42-52.

SVOBODA, J. (2004). The Pavloviana a part of the Gravettian mosaic (in) *The Gravettian along the Danube.* Brno, Institute of Archaeology, 283-297.

WIJMSTRA, T.A. (1969). Palynology of the first 30 metres of a 120 metre deep section in northern Greece. *Acta Botanica Neerlandica,* 18, 511-528.

PRELIMINARY RESULTS OF THE ALIAKMON PALEOLITHIC/ PALEOANTHROPOLOGICAL SURVEY, GREECE, 2004-2005

Katerina HARVATI

Max Planck Institute for Evolutionary Anthropology, Deutscher Platz 6, D-04103, Leipzig, Germany,
harvati@eva.mpg.de

Eleni PANAGOPOULOU, Panagiotis KARKANAS, Athanassios ATHANASSIOU

Ephoreia of Paleoanthropology/Speleology, Ardittou 34B, Athens, Greece,
elenipanagopoulou@yahoo.com, pkarkanas@hua.gr, aathan@cc.uoa.gr

Stephen R. FROST

University of Oregon, Eugene, Oregon, USA, sfrost@uoregon.edu

Abstract: Greece lies on the hypothesized migration route of archaic humans into Europe, and its paleolithic record is critical in addressing issues of timing and routes of dispersal of the earliest European colonization. The Aliakmon Paleolithic survey, conducted on the Aliakmon river terraces in 2004-05, is the first systematic survey for this time period in the region. The area preserves Plio-Pleistocene fluvial fossiliferous sediments and has yielded paleolithic artifacts. We confirmed the existence of the terrace systems at previously proposed levels but with more complex dating than originally proposed. Faunal specimens collected include equids, rhinocerotids, suids, bovids, cervids, rodents, canids, proboscideans, and cf. Hippopotamus. Two possible Lower Paleolithic sites were located. Given the scarcity of such sites in Greece, these findings are pivotal in documenting early human presence in the area.
Keywords: Lower Paleolithic, Middle Paleolithic, South-Eastern Europe, European colonization, archaic humans

Résumé: La Grèce se trouve sur la route hypothétique de migration des hominidés archaïques en Europe et son enregistrement paléolithique est crucial en ce qui concerne le temps et les voies de dispersion de la première colonisation de l'Europe. La prospection d'Aliakmon paléolithique, conduit sur les terrasses du fleuve Aliakmon en 2004-2005, est la première prospection systématique pour cette période dans la région. Cette dernière préserve des dépôts fluviatiles fossilifères et a livré des artefacts paléolithiques. Nous avons confirmé l'existence du système de terrasses à des niveaux déjà proposés, mais avec un système chronologique plus complexe par rapport à ce proposé originellement. Les restes fauniques récoltés comprennent équidés, rhinocérotidés, suidés, bovidés, cervidés, rongeurs, canidés, proboscidiens et cf. Hippopotamus. Deux sites possibles du Paléolithique inférieur ont été localisés. Etant donnée la rareté de sites en Grèce, ces trouvailles sont d'une importance décisive pour la documentation de l'ancienne présence humaine dans cette région.
Mots-clés: Paléolithique inférieur, Paléolithique moyen, Sud-est européen, colonisation de l'Europe, hommes archaïques

INTRODUCTION

The Aliakmon Paleolithic/Paleoanthropological survey is a three-year project aiming to locate new paleolithic, paleoanthropological and paleontological sites in the Aliakmon river basin, Western Macedonia, Northern Greece (Figure 2.1). The ultimate purpose of the project is to help test hypotheses about the earliest colonization of the European continent by adding currently lacking evidence from South-Eastern Europe. It is conducted in cooperation between the American School of Classical Studies at Athens and the Ephoreia of Paleoanthropology–Speleology of Southern Greece (hereafter EPS) and directed by Katerina Harvati (Max Planck Institute for Evolutionary Anthropology and New York University) and Eleni Panagopoulou (EPS).

The timing, routes of dispersal and identity of the earliest archaic European populations are among the most important unresolved questions of European paleoanthropology. Human remains from Spain and Italy have been dated to approximately 800 thousand years ago (Roebroeks & van Kolfschoten 1994; Bermúdez de Castro *et*

al. 1997; Manzi *et al.* 2001; Roebroeks 2001), and the discovery of 1.6 million years old human fossils in Georgia (Gabunia *et al.* 2000; Vekua *et al.* 2002; Gabounia *et al.* 2002) puts forth the possibility of earlier, as yet undiscovered, ventures into Europe. Early colonizers are commonly thought to have dispersed into the continent by a Levantine corridor through Asia Minor and Greece (Darlas 1995; Runnels 1995, 2001; Bar-Yosef 1998). However, early human fossils in Spain and Italy (Bermúdez de Castro *et al.* 1997; Manzi *et al.* 2001) have suggested the possibility of a direct dispersal from North Africa into the Iberian and Italian peninsulas, a significantly more difficult route (Straus 2001).

Greece lies on the hypothesized route of migration of archaic hominids from Africa through the Near East into Europe and is the gateway into the continent through which migrant populations have repeatedly passed (Runnels 1995, 2001; Bar-Yosef 1998). The region's fossil human and paleolithic records are therefore critical in addressing these questions. The Aliakmon river basin holds exceptional promise for paleolithic and paleoanthro-pological research. The region has previously yielded paleolithic artifacts,

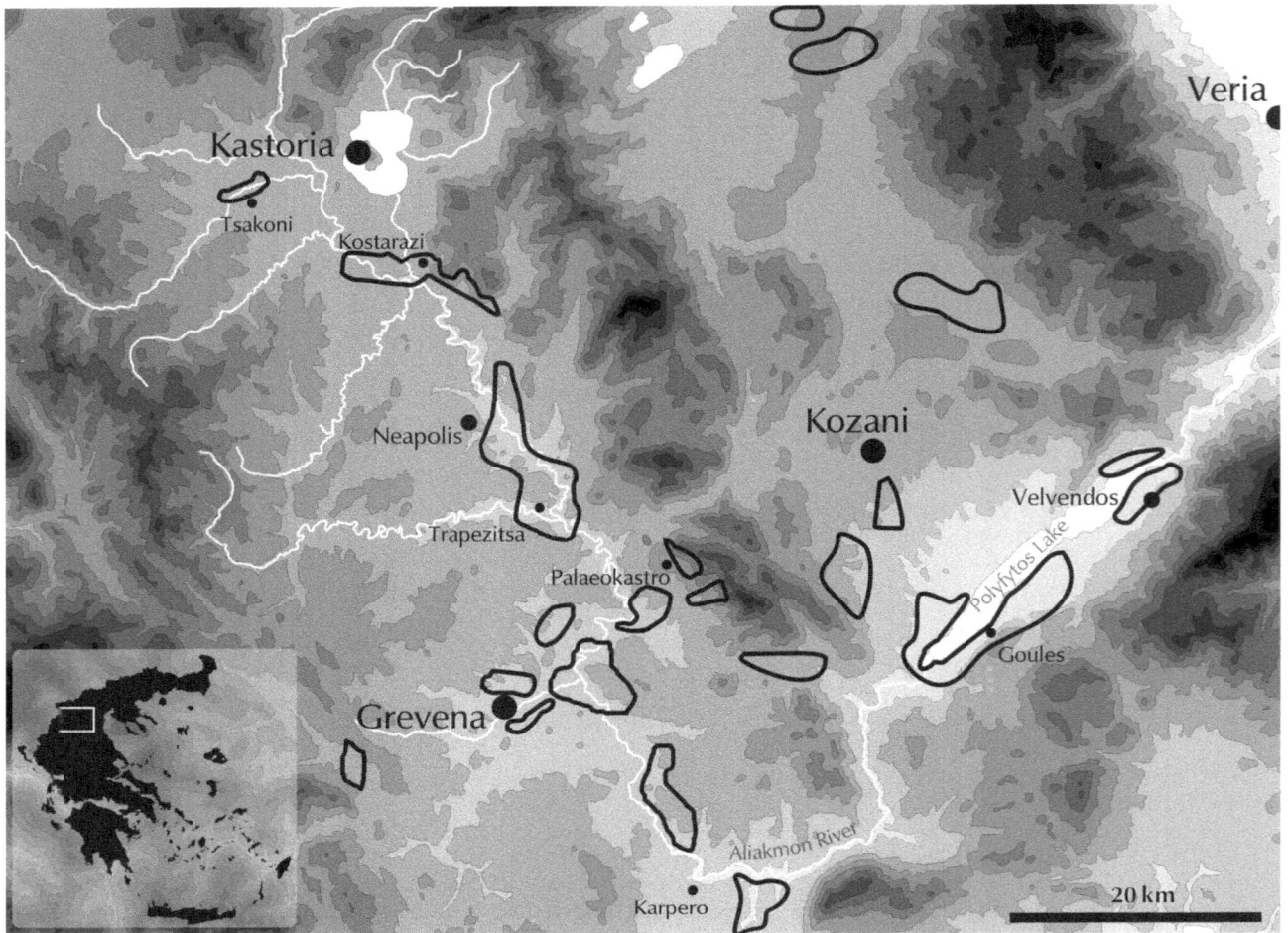

Fig. 2.1. Map of survey area, with localities surveyed outlined in heavy black marker.
Inlet: survey area shown on the map of Greece

including one of only two published Lower Paleolithic bifacial stone tools from the country (Dakaris *et al.* 1964; Higgs 1964), and important Plio-Pleistocene faunas (Melentis 1966; Koufos 1977; Ste-ensma 1988; Koufos *et al.* 1991; Koufos & Kostopoulos 1993; Tsoukala 2000).

The present survey is the first systematic survey for this time period in this area. It focuses on the terraces of the river Aliakmon, which preserve Upper Pliocene to Pleistocene fluvial sediments (Brunn 1956; Eltgen 1986; Rassios 2004).

METHODOLOGY

The survey team was divided into two groups that systematically examined the longitudinal profiles of the terraces found in the survey areas, searching for lithic artifacts or fossil remains. Some terrace surfaces were also explored (although their systematic survey was not possible due to intense cultivation) as well as the shore around Lake Polyphytos. GPS coordinates (WGS 84 datum) were recorded for each search area and for each major archeological and fossil find and plotted on 1:5.000

topographic maps. Field observations were logged for each survey area and photographs were taken of all localities. The survey area covered is outlined in heavy black line on the map of Figure 2.1.

GEOLOGICAL FINDINGS

The existence of the Aliakmon terrace systems at the levels proposed previously (Brunn 1956, Eltgen 1986) was confirmed. However, our geological work showed that the dating of the individual terraces is more complicated that originally proposed, predominantly due to the erosional (strath) rather than depositional nature of most terrace deposits (Panagopoulou *et al.* 2006). Whereas elevation above the current river corresponds with geological age in depositional terrace systems, this is not the case for straths, as the latter are cutting into older sediments. The depositional or erosional nature of the terraces was found to vary from locality to locality due to the complex depositional history of the river. Isolated patches of Pleistocene fossiliferous depositional terraces are preserved as pockets within the main erosional system (Panagopoulou *et al.* 2006). The typical terrace sediment-

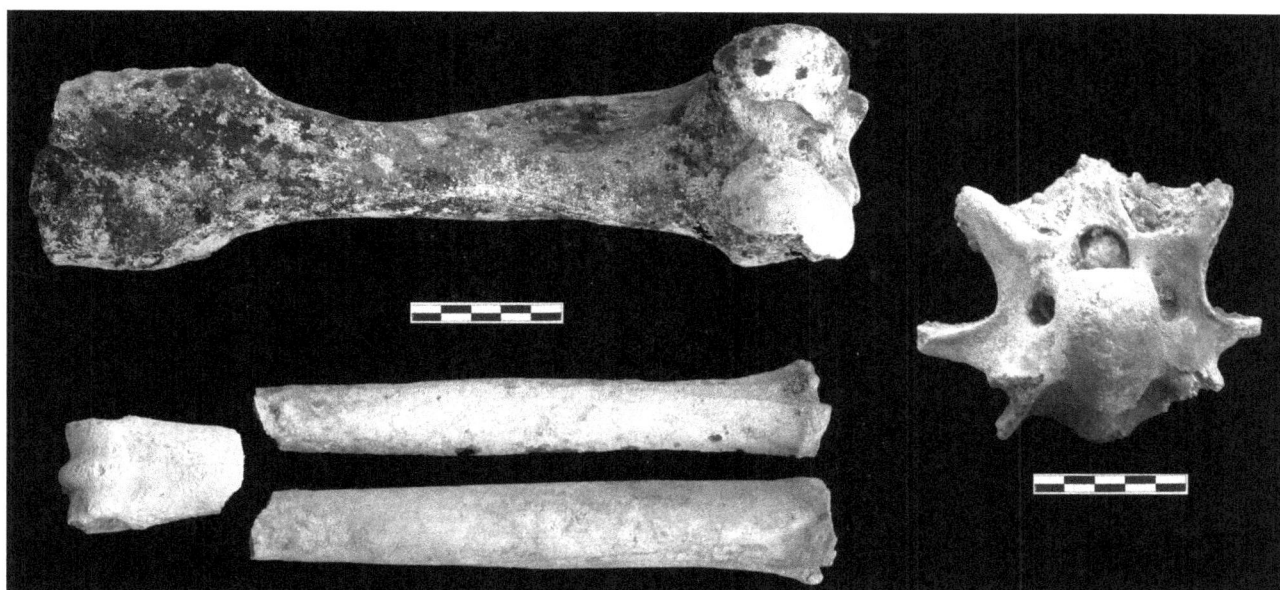

Fig. 2.2. Faunal specimens from the Livakos and Goules localities.
Top left: Equid femur; Bottom left: Equid metatarsal in 3 pieces; Left: Rhinoceros vertebra

tary sequence observed in most localities consist of superimposed cross stratified pebble-rich layers and sandstones banks that most likely represent bars and channels deposits of a braided-type river. Upwards they grade into a series of brownish or grey paleosols formed on silty overbank deposits.

In addition to the terraces, the shoreline around Lake Polyphytos was surveyed. Polyphytos is a shallow artificial lake formed by the flooding of the former floodplain of the Aliakmon at the southern edge of Kozani basin. The Kozani basin consists of a thick lacustrine sedimentary sequence ranging from the Upper Miocene to the Pliocene. Fresh-water limestone and marl, with intercalated lignite seams give way to Mg-carbonate layers in the upper part (Anastopoulos *et al.* 1980; Calvo *et al.* 1995). The margins of the sequence are bounded by faults and the whole plain is being eroded by a subparallel drainage system that flows into the modern Aliakmon River. The latter is flowing along the southern margin of the plain. Alluvial fans consisting of red beds are developed along the western margin close to the contacts of limestone and ophiolite formations. Along the southern coast of the lake a strath terrace 50 m above the former Aliakmon is developed. Nevertheless, patches of fluvial deposits were identified at the same elevation, usually no more that one hundred meter long. On the northern coast of the lake there are no terrace formations except some remnants of dispersed fluvial gravels found on the top of the soft and highly eroded Neogene lacustrine hills.

PALEONTOLOGICAL FINDINGS

Dense accumulations of fossil material were found in Livakos and Kostarazi. Other terrace sequences yielded

little or no fossil specimens, probably the result of erratic deposition of the paleo-Aliakmon river. In total, one hundred and sixty-nine fossil specimens were collected, including equids (*Equus* sp.), proboscideans (*Mammuthus* cf. *Meridionalis*, *Elephas antiquus*), bovids (cf. *Leptobos* sp.), canids (*Canis* cf. *Etruscus)*, cervids, rhinocerotids, suids, rodents and possibly hippopotamids (Figure 2.2).

The Livakos area consisted of several localities along the Livakos stream, a small tributary of Aliakmon River. The fauna collected there included equids, bovids/ cervids, a suid, a proboscidean, a canid (possibly *Canis etruscus*), and a large rodent, possibly *Castor* or *Hystrix*. These findings are consistent with and augment the previous description of the Livakos fauna by Steensma (1988) as Late Pliocene/Early Pleistocene fauna dominated by *Equus*. The predominance of equids suggests open habitats in close proximity to the river.

The Kostarazi locality probably represents a localized depositional terrace within a larger strath, and likely dates to the Middle Pleistocene. The terrace profile consists of sandy gravels and fine pebbles in overlapping cross-stratified beds preserving a wealth of bivalve shells (*Unio*), which indicate a lake (freshwater) environment. Kostarazi yielded several elements from a partial skeleton of a proboscidean, a large ruminant (possibly *Megaloceros*) and equids.

ARCHAEOLOGICAL FINDINGS

Seventy-four lithic artifacts were collected. However, none were found inside the longitudinal profiles. The lithic material covered a range of technical periods from possibly the Lower to the Upper Paleolithic. It was

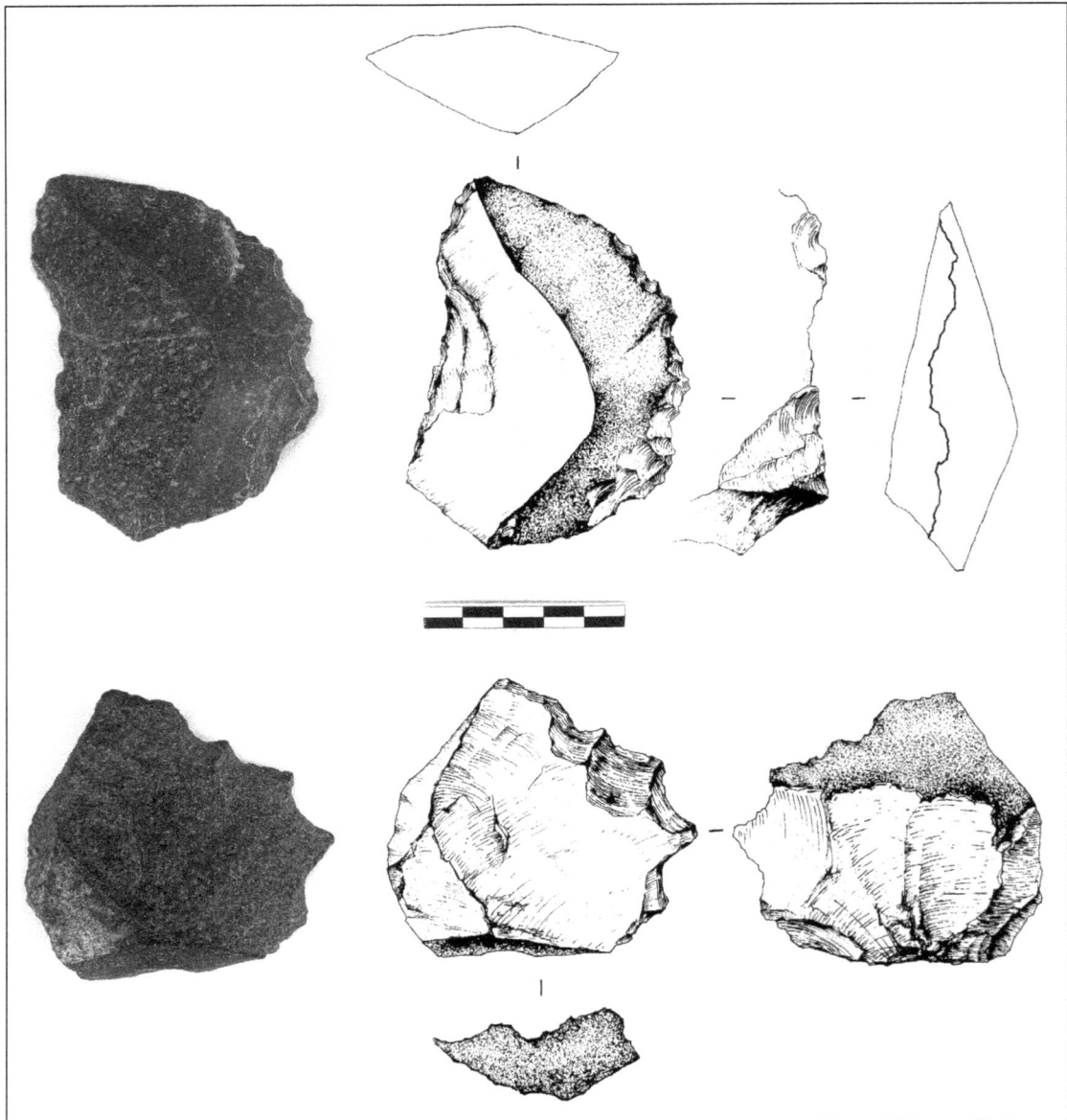

Fig. 2.3. Lithic artifacts from Polemistra

concentrated in two sites, Polemistra and Karpero (Figures 2.3 and 2.4). Both assemblages were surface finds and both probably Lower Paleolithic.

The Polemistra locality is situated on the south-western shore of the Polyphytos artificial lake. In this locality there is a hanging alluvial fill of a stream that flows into the northwestern part of the lake. The fill consists of a sequence of unsorted massive gravelly loams, most likely representing flash floods of hyperconcentrated bedload. Their material derives mainly from erosion of the lacustrine banks of the stream and the hilly area around. Immature brown paleosols separate the different flood episodes of the fill. A total of nineteen lithic artifacts were recovered from the lakeshore among the river pebbles. All lithics were fashioned on river pebbles of a green, coarse-grained volcanic rock. They consisted of large flakes,

several cores, some bifacially worked tools and choppers (Figure 2.3). The type of technology is simple (flakes and chopping tools) and may date to the Lower Paleolithic, although no uniquely characteristic Lower Paleolithic artifacts (such as handaxes) were found.

A second concentration of lithics was found at the Karpero locality, near the future construction site of the new Aliakmon dam. As in most other localities investigated, this locality presented long sequences of cross-stratified pebble-rich layers and sandstone banks (probably bars and channels deposits) grading into a series of brownish or grey paleosols (overbank depostis). Nine artifacts were collected from the terrace surface, comprising several large cores, one chopper and one flake (Figure 2.4). As in Polemistra, the raw material was volcanic pebbles, probably andesite or basalt. The techni-

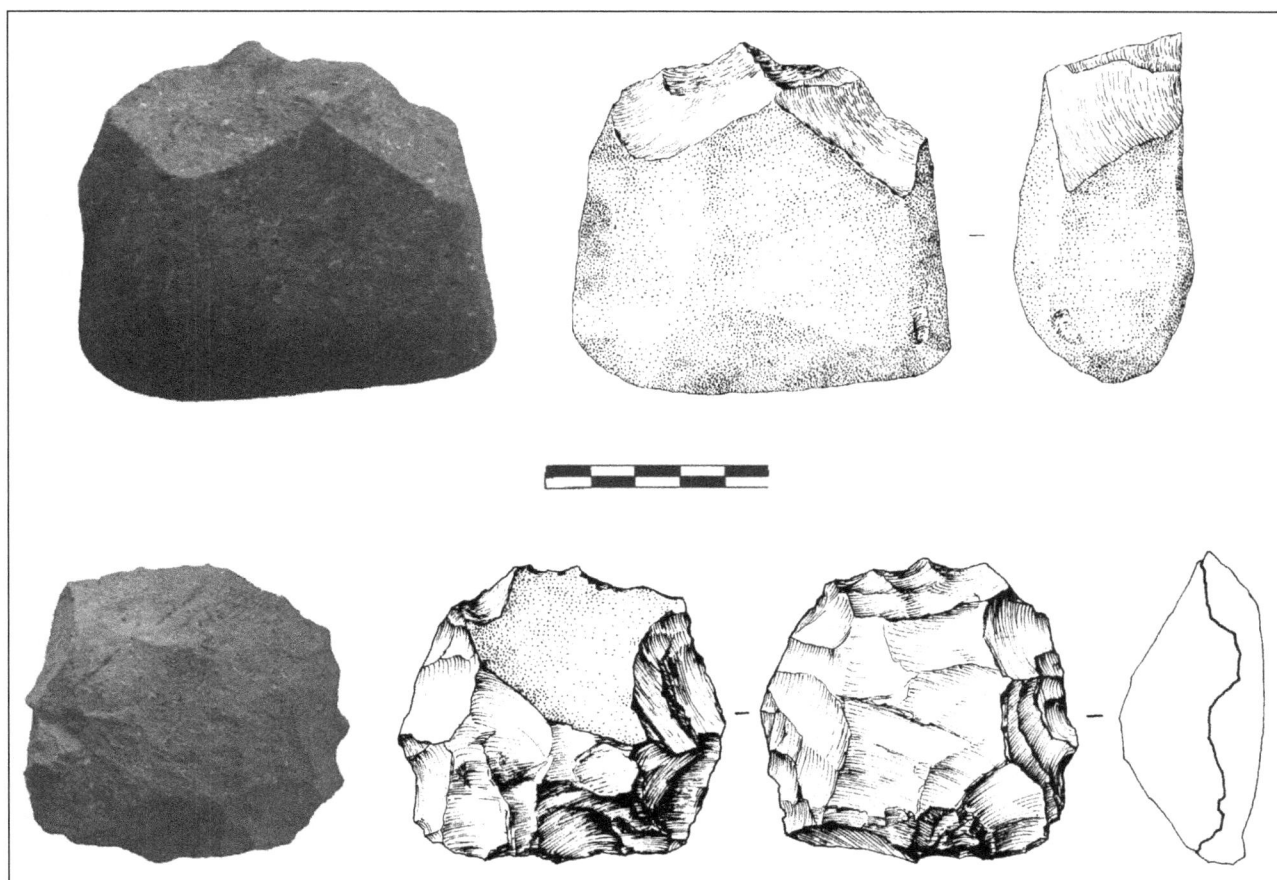

Fig. 2.4. Lithic artifacts from Karpero

cal features again suggest an early age for this assemblage, although no characteristic Lower Paleolithic tool types were found.

FUTURE DIRECTIONS

Given the scarcity of documented Lower Paleolithic sites in Greece, our findings are pivotal in documenting early human presence in the area. Our immediate goals for the coming year and for the final field season include a pilot study of paleomagnetic and Electron Spin Resonance dating analysis of some of the Aliakmon terraces to help resolve the dating of the terrace system. In the field season of 2006 we will survey the normally submerged expanses of the former river bed exposed in the late fall, in order to retrieve additional artifacts and to improve our understanding of the Polemistra site formation processes. More extensive survey will also be conducted on the terrace surfaces at and around the Karpero locality, in order to locate additional possible sites and at the rich fossiliferous sites of Livakos and Kostarazi. Finally, as a long term goal of this project we plan the comparative study of the lithics recovered from this survey in conjunction with previously collected, probably Lower Paleolithic, material from this area.

Acknowledgments

We thank the organizers of the UISPP 2006 symposium "The Paleolithic of the Balkans", Drs. Andreas Darlas and Dusan Mihailovic. This research was funded by grants to K. Harvati from the National Geographic Society, the L.S.B. Leakey Foundation, the Niarchos Foundation, and the Institute for Aegean Prehistory. Additional support was provided by the Greek Ministry of Culture, the Max Planck Institute for Evolutionary Anthropology, New York University and the University of Oregon.

References

ANASTOPOULOS, J.; KOUKOUZA, K.; FAUGERES, L. (1980). Geological Map of Greece 1:50000, Kozani Sheet: Institute of Geology and Mineral Exploration, Athens.

BAR-YOSEF, O. (1998). The nature of Transitions: the Middle to Upper Paleolithic and the Neolithic Revolution, *Cambridge Archaeological Journal* 8(2):141-63.

BERMÚDEZ DE CASTRO, J.M.; ARSUAGA, J.L.; CARBONELL, E.; ROSAS, A.; MARTÍNEZ, I.; MOSQUERA, M. (1997). A hominid from the Lower Pleistocene of Atapuerca, Spain: Possible ancestor to

Neandertals and modern humans. *Science* 276: 1392-1395.

BRUNN, J. (1956). Contribution à l'étude géologique du Pinde septentrional et d'une partie de la Macédoine occidentale. *Annales Géologiques des Pays Helléniques*, 7: 1-358.

CALVO, J.P.; STAMATAKIS, M.G.; MAGGANAS, A. (1995). Clastic huntite in Upper Neogene formations of the Kozani basin, Macedonia, Northern Greece. *Journal of Sedimentary Research*, A65: 627-632.

DAKARIS S.I.; HIGGS E.S.; HEY R.W. (1964). The climate, environment and industries of Stone Age Greece: Part I. *Proceedings of the Prehistoric Society*, 30: 199-244.

DARLAS, A. (1995). The earliest occupation of Europe: The Balkans. In ROEBROEKS, W.; VAN KOLFSCHOTEN, T. (eds.): *The Earliest Occupation of Europe, Proceedings of the European Science Foundation Workshop at Tautavel (France), 1993*. Leiden: University of Leiden, pp. 51-57.

ELTGEN, H. (1986). Feinstratigraphisch-fazielle Untersuchungen an Altpliozän-Sedimenten im Tertiärbecken südlich Neapolis/Kozani, Nordgriechenland. *Geological and Geophysical Research*, Special Issue: 107-115.

GABUNIA, L.; VEKUA, A.; LORDKIPANIDZE, D.; SWISHER, C.C.; III, FERRING, R.; JUSTUS, A.; NIORADZE, M.; TVALCHRELIDZE, M.; ANTÓN, S.C.; BOSINSKI, G.; JÖRIS, O.; DE LUMLEY, M.-A.; MAJSURADZE, G.; MOUSKHELISHVILI, A. (2000). Earliest Pleistocene cranial remains from Dmanisi, Republic of Georgia: taxonomy, geological setting, and age. *Science* 288: 1019-1025.

GABOUNIA, L.; DE LUMLEY M.A.; VEKUA, A.; LORDKIPANIDZE, D.; DE LUMLEY. H. (2002). Découverte d'un nouvel hominidé à Dmanissi (Transcaucasie, Géorgie). *Comptes Rendus Palevol*, 1: 243-253.

HIGGS E.S. (1964). A Hand Axe from Greece. *Antiquity* 38:54-55.

KOUFOS, G.D. (1977). New findings of Mastodonts from Macedonia. *Scientific Annals, Faculty of Physics and Mathematics, University of Thessaloniki*, 17: 97-115.

KOUFOS, G.D.; KOSTOPOULOS, D.S.; KOLIADI-MOU, K.K. (1991). Un nouveau gisement de mammifères dans le Villafranchien de Macédoine occidentale (Grèce). *Comptes Rendus de l'Académie des Sciences*, 313 (7): 831-836.

KOUFOS, G.D.; KOSTOPOULOS, D.S. (1993). A stenonoid horse (Equidae, Mammalia) from the Villafranchian of Western Macedonia (Greece). *Bulletin of the Geological Society of Greece*, XXVIII (3): 131-143.

MANZI, G.; MALLEGNI, F.; ASCENZI, A. (2001). A cranium for the earliest Europeans: Phylogenetic position of the hominid from Ceprano, Italy. *Proceedings of the National Academy of Sciences of the United States of America*, 98: 10011-10016.

MALLEGNI, F.; CARNIERI, E.; BISCONTI, M.; TARTARELLI, G.; RICCI, S.; BIDDITTU, I.; SEGRE, A. (2003). *Homo cepranensis* sp. nov. and the evolution of African-European Middle Pleistocene hominids. *Comptes Rendus Palevol*, 2: 153-159.

MELENTIS J. (1966). Die Pleistozäne Säugeherfauna des Beckens von Haliakmon (Griechenland). *Annales Géologiques des Pays Helléniques*, XVII, 247-266.

PANAGOPOULOU, E.; HARVATI, K.; KARKANAS, P.; ATHANASSIOU, A.; ELEFANTI, P.; FROST, S.R. (2006). The West Macedonia Palaeolithic Survey. *The Archaeological Research in Macedonia and Thrace*, 18: 631-640. [*in Greek*]

RASSIOS A.E. (2004). *A geologist's guide to West Macedonia, Greece*. Grevena: Anaptyxiaki Nomou Grevenon.

ROEBROEKS W. (2001). Hominid behaviour and the earliest occupation of Europe: an exploration. *Journal of Human Evolution*, 41: 437-461.

ROEBROEKS, W.; VAN KOLFSCHOTEN, T. (1994). The earliest occupation of Europe: a short chronology. *Antiquity*, 68: 489-503.

RUNNELS, C. (1995). Review of Aegean Prehistory IV: The Stone Age of Greece from the Palaeolithic to the advent of the Neolithic. *American Journal of Archaeology*, 99: 699-728.

RUNNELS, C. (2001). Review of Aegean Prehistory IV: The Stone Age of Greece from the Palaeolithic to the advent of the Neolithic with an Addendum. In: T. Cullen (ed.) *Aegean Prehistory: A Review*. Archaeological Institute of America, pp. 225-258.

STEENSMA, K.J. (1988). Plio-/Pleistozäne Großsäugetiere (Mammalia) aus dem Becken von Kastoria / Grevena, südlich von Neapolis – NW Griechenland. Clausthal, Technische Universität Clausthal: 315 p.

STRAUS, L.G. (2001). Africa and Iberia in the Pleistocene. *Quaternary International*, 75: 91-102.

TSOUKALA, E. (2000). Remains of a Pliocene *Mammut borsoni* (Hays, 1834) (Proboscidea, Mammalia), from Milia (Grevena, W. Macedonia, Greece). *Annales de Paléontologie*, 86 (3): 165-191.

TSOUKALA, E.; LISTER, A. (1998). Remains of straight-tusked elephant, *Elephas (Palaeoloxodon) antiquus* Falc. & Caut., 1847 ESR-dated to oxygen isotope Stage 6 from Grevena (W. Macedonia, Greece). *Bollettino della Società Paleontologica Italiana*, 37 (1): 117-139.

VEKUA, A.; LORDKIPANIDZE, D.; RIGHTMIRE, P.; AGUSTÍ, J.; FERRING, R.; MAISURADZE, G.; MOUSKHELISHVILI, A.; NIORADZE, M.; PONCE DE LEÓN, M.; TAPPEN, M.; TVALCHRELIDZE, M.; ZOLLIKOFER, C. (2002). A new skull of early *Homo* from Dmanisi, Georgia. *Science*, 297: 85-89.

THE MOUNTAINSCAPES OF UPPER PALAEOLITHIC EPIRUS IN NW GREECE: A VIEW FROM THE BONES

Eleni KOTJABOPOULOU

Archaeological Institute of Epirotic Studies, Papazoglou 16 & Kaningos, 454 44 Ioannina, Greece,
e-mail: eleniktz@otenet.gr

Abstract: This paper compares aspects of the extensive faunal evidence from three upper palaeolithic rockshelter sites situated in the mountainous interior of the Epirus region in NW Greece. The aim is to explore patterns of land use and mobility within a profoundly dissected, varied, largely unstable yet resourceful landscape. In spite of some differences in taphonomic histories and site-specific particularities it is argued that several features of the animal bone remains are effectively commensurate from a regional perspective. It is proposed that high mobility and various levels of resource selectivity have shaped the archaeological record at hand. Furthermore, it is argued that production goals were not simply conditioned by palaeoeconomic, cost-benefit, variables, but were enmeshed in and even oriented towards the (re)production of mountainscapes with a tendency for sustained cultural traditions.
Keywords: fauna, rockshelter, mountainscape, upper palaeolithic, Greece

Résumé: Le présent article compare différents aspects de l'étude faunique détaillée de trois abris sous-roche, situés en arrière-pays montagneux de l'Épire, au Nord-Ouest de la Grèce, datant du Paléolithique Supérieur. Le but de cette étude est la recherche des modes d'aménagement de l'espace et de mobilité dans un paysage profondément disséqué, varié, très instable et, encore, riche en ressources. Malgré l'histoire taphonomique et certaines particularités de chaque site, l'étude propose que plusieurs caractères des restes osseux reflètent des paramètres régionaux. Il est soutenu que la mobilité intense, ainsi que différents niveaux de sélection de ressources, ont formé le bilan archéologique disponible. De plus, il est proposé que les objectifs de la production n'étaient pas simplement conditionnés par des variables paléoéconomiques et de rentabilité, mais qu'ils étaient aussi impliqués, et même orientés vers la reproduction de paysages montagnards, avec une tendance à respecter les traditions culturelles.
Mots-clés: faune, abris sous-roche, paysage montagneux, Paléolithique supérieur, Grèce

INTRODUCTION

A long-standing tradition in archaeological and historical thinking has tended to approach mountainous bio-spaces as marginal to human history (but see Otte 1992, Braudel 1993). Certain physical characteristics, such as broken terrain, dispersed or restricted biomass, have been used in a normative way to support the notion that mountainous bio-spaces are *a priori* unstable and thus "difficult to deal with" in cultural terms. Much like deserts, mountain environments have been archaeologically conceptualized as stage-boards of restricted plasticity and variability not only in economic but by implication in social and historical terms. Palaeolithic research, in particular, has adopted a profoundly deterministic attitude whereby exploitation of mountains has been viewed as an adaptive, often 'short-lived' economic addendum, interlocked with the response of people to the waxing and waning of climatic conditions (e.g. Straus 1987). This ecologically reductionist point of view has masked important aspects of cultural variability that is recently surfacing across the European and especially the circum-Mediterranean Upper Palaeolithic record (eg. Mussi 2001). Although still hindered by various research biases the Upper Palaeolithic record of the Balkan Peninsula, which is dominated by a plethora of extensive mountain ranges, offers ample ground for modern research to scrutinize the ways hunter-gatherer societies of the Late Pleistocene shaped and/or changed their socio-economic landscapes and to further approach regional variability. In this context, it is the principal aim of this paper to compare aspects of the extensive faunal evidence recovered from three Upper Palaeolithic rockshelter sites, namely Kastritsa, Klithi and Boila, situated in the mountainous interior of the Epirus region in NW Greece, in an attempt to trace patterns of land use and mobility within a markedly dissected, varied, largely unstable yet, as we shall see, resourceful landscape, and to use the evidence in hand to understand hunters *in* their mountainscapes (cf. Ingold 1993, Gamble & Gaudzinski 2005).

SITE CHARACTERISTICS AND GENERAL ARCHAEOLOGY

The three sites under consideration are located in the hinterland of Epirus in NW Greece in proximity to the high peaks of the Pindus massif (Fig. 3.1), which forms the backbone of the Greek Peninsula. A distance of 40km, as the crow flies, separates the Voidomatis sites (Klithi and Boila) from Kastritsa.

Kastritsa cave is located in the largest inland basin of the region and lies on the southeastern shore of a large permanent body of water, namely Pamvotis lake. Excavations were effectuated in the 1960s and revealed a 9m deep sequence of discrete geological and/or anthropogenic lithostratigraphic packages (e.g. Higgs *et al.* 1967, Bailey *et al.* 1983a). Intra-site topography underwent changes owing to several episodes of roof collapse.

Klithi is a rockshelter situated deep within the Voidomatis river valley immediately below the glaciated high terrain (c. 2650m a.s.l.) of western Pindus (see papers in Bailey 1997). Systematic field research in the 1980s exposed a large part of the occupation surface of the site; above

Fig. 3.1. Perspective map of the Epirus hinterland with upper palaeolithic sites mentioned in the text

some meters of archaeologically sterile screes, indicative of massive erosion, the stratigraphic record does not exhibit neatly demarcated geological or cultural facies. This site is also of low spatial integrity.

Boila is a shallow and elongated rockshelter positioned right on the western narrow mouth of the Voidomatis valley just before the river gives into a large flat basin flanked by rolling hills. It was excavated in the 1990s and produced a condensed archaeological sequence of distinct depositional histories (Kotjabopoulou et al. 1997, 1999). During full glacial times the site was unavailable for occupation as the river flowed right against the southern limestone walls of the gorge; when deglaciation was well under way on the sandy substratum of a major flooding episode, coincident with a global climatic setback, hunters soon came in and kindled their campfires.

As can be seen in Table 3.1, wherein some basic features of the sites and their archaeology, besides faunal remains, have been assembled, there exists no significant altitudinal difference between the sites, which, as mentioned above, are all closely associated with an aquatic resource. Effectively, also, their distance from the Last Glacial Maximum (LGM) coast is comparable if this is measured from a nearest approximate point. Kastritsa and Boila share a similar size and aspect that leaves them exposed to the north-blowing winds. Klithi, on the other hand, is a spacious south facing abris that would have provided, in comparison, better living conditions. Furthermore, what needs to be noted is that the sites themselves are not found on that high a ground,

considering the altitudinal gradient in Epirus, but it is in fact the sharp geometry of the surrounding terrain which emerges as a significant factor in terms of land use organization.

In terms of chronology the total timespan covered by the cultural horizons identified at all three sites amounts to c.15 millennia, i.e. from before the onset of the LGM up to the Pleistocene/Holocene transition. In a broad sense, some overlap in site use is documented around the early Late Glacial, but if the main phase(s) of occupation at each site are considered, a scenario of successive occupations of the particular locations can be put forward. However, caution should be raised as regards the extent to which occupation of these rockshelters is to be equated with a pattern of hominid use of the physiographic units they are located in, as other sites (naturally protected or not) may lie undetected. For instance, evidence from an open-air findspot in the plain, just around the corner from Boila, that has yielded some red deer remains and a few flint artifacts, gave a date around 24 kyr BP, making it contemporaneous with the lower horizons of Kastritsa (for discussion see Kotjabopoulou 2001). In addition, based on evidence from a minimally excavated small cavity, namely Megalakkos (Sinclair 1997), deep within a side-stream of the Voidomatis, the indication is strengthened that mobile hunters repeatedly traveled through and stopped overnight in the sinuous ravine over the Late Glacial/Early Holocene.

All three sites are minimally furnished usually with open-hearth complexes, fueled with locally available woods, to

Tab. 3.1. Selected features of the Epirus hinterland rockshelter sites and their archaeological records. Two values are given for the distance from the LGM coastline: one at right angle and another (in italics) from a nearest approximate point. The Kastritsa living surface ignores the possible greater extent of the inner cavity

	KASTRITSA	KLITHI	BOILA
Site type	cave	rockshelter	rockshelter
Aspect	N-NW	S	N
Potential living surface (m²)	c. 80	c. 300	c. 80
Location	lakeshore	riverbank	riverbank
Altitude	c.460m	c.430m	c.410m
Surrounding Topography* (20km circle)	0-200m: 0% 200-600m: 38% 600-1000m: 45% >1000m: 17%	0-200m: 0% 200-600m: 37% 600-1000m: 34% >1000m: 29%	similar to Klithi
Distance from LGM coast (c.-100m)	c.115km *c. 70km*	c. 75km *c. 75km*	c. 75km *c. 75km*
Chronological range of use (Kyr BP, uncalibrated)	24? - 13?	17 - 10	14,5 - 9,5
Main occupation (Kyr BP, uncalibrated)	22? - 16?	16 - 13	13,5 - 9,5
Site furniture	several open and some stonelined hearths, stakeholes (subsistence related structures?)	a large repeatedly used open hearth area	several short-lived open hearths
Lithic Toolkit	emphasis on hunting gear, transformation tools well represented	emphasis on hunting gear, transformation tools well represented	hunting gear predominant, transformation tools limited
Organic Toolkit (bone/antler)	large sample locally produced: mainly points, some awls & spatulae, few needles	moderate sample mostly locally produced (highly expedient): mainly needles & awls, some spatulae, few points	small sample of points and awls mostly locally produced (highly expedient)
Ornaments (from habitation fills)	mostly perforated sea shells (cyclope and dentalium), pierced deer canines, few engraved (notched) bone frags, a couple of stone beads	mostly perforated sea shells (cyclope, homalopoma and other varieties), few pierced deer canines, few engraved (notched) bone frags	mostly perforated sea shells (cyclope, homalopoma and other varieties), one pierced deer canine, one stone bead

* after Bailey *et al.* (1983b): Tab. 7.2

judged from the charcoal evidence produced at Boila (see Ntinou & Kotjabopoulou 2002). For Kastritsa, at times perhaps, a greater investment and or variability/integrity in the organization of domestic space are inferred (Galanidou 1997).

Provisioning of lithic raw materials for the manufacture of toolkits was essentially from local (usually secondary) sources, but invariably the production line was complemented with allogenic varieties of flint, if only on a limited scale (e.g. Adam 1997, Kotjabopoulou *et al.* 1999, Elefanti 2003). In situ manufacture, repair and maintenance of hunting gear mark a blueprint at all three sites. However, the evidence is compelling, for Klithi and Kastritsa, that an array of domestic activities (e.g. treatment of game, hide processing, clothing or other every day gear manufacture) was undertaken under the roofed shelters, including the production of organic (bone and where available antler) implements (e.g. Adam & Kotjabopoulou 1997).

Finally, and on the basis of the symbolic items recovered from the habitation fills, it appears that the users of the shelters habitually wore ornaments and/or carried other personal equipment (e.g. garments, containers) adorned with a restricted and eclectic, perhaps even monotonous, variety of Mediterranean sea shells and herbivore (deer) teeth. As things stand at present, the lack of any significant diachronic disruption, at least from the LGM onwards, in the ways of marking objects and building up social identities underlines the existence of sustained trends and traditions at the regional scale (Kotjabopoulou & Adam 2004).

THE FAUNAL ASSEMBLAGES

The sites under consideration have produced large faunal collections, which have been studied in detail (Gamble 1997, Kotjabopoulou 2001, 2003). The reconstruction of faunal remains geometric densities (N/m³) presented in

Tab. 3.2. Bone geometric density at the hinterland Epirus sites. For Kastritsa and Boila raw data and further discussion in Kotjabopoulou (2001). Data for Klithi based on Gamble (1997): Tab. 12.1, 12.2. Small rodents and homo remains are excluded

Geometric density	KASTRITSA					KLITHI	BOILA
	S 1	S 3	S 5	S 7	S 9	All strata	All strata
Identified bones & teeth (N/m^3)	214	85	34	37	29	1142	194
Unidentified bones & teeth (N/m^3)	2589	1027	409	319	315	11923	2048
Total (N/m^3)	**2803**	**1112**	**443**	**356**	**344**	**13065**	**2242**

Table 3.2 gives a preliminary, if minimal in interpretative terms taste of the taphonomic histories, which are not identical. For instance: the low values for the lowest strata from Kastritsa (S9 & S7) is testimony effectively to post depositional biases related to the inundation of the cavity by fluctuating lake levels. Deposition of bones at Kastritsa stratum 5 remains low, even though no post depositional winnowing can be invoked. This (along with other evidence) implies either short-lived/transient (perhaps by small or of restricted social identity groups) or infrequent (widely spaced in time) use of the shelter (see Kotjabopoulou 2001 for further discussion). Thereafter, apparently more intensive use is depicted, with the Kastritsa stratum 3 and 1 and the Boila records being comparable (though not necessarily in qualitative terms). Klithi exhibits by far the highest geometric density of bone. Given that at least Klithi and Boila have been investigated with identical standards of recovery methods and that their faunas are largely similar, the disparity is striking: differences in the mode of occupation, e.g. frequent/repeated use and/or by a larger or of mixed social composition group at Klithi as opposed to Boila, in conjunction with the pattern/rate of sedimentation and the consequent effects on diagenetic processes, provides the most plausible explanation (see below). As regards Kastritsa, we can venture that, in spite of some degree of excavation/curation bias and not withstanding winnowing owing to post depositional loss of structurally vulnerable skeletal elements, the reconstructed geometric density, in terms of order of magnitude, entails aspects relevant to the mode of occupation. In other words, the geometric density figures, if taken at face value, can be read as indicating progressively more intense use; a point that appears to hold when strata 3 and 1 are compared to stratum 5. However, the apparent higher density of stratum 1 may comply with activity concentrated within a more restricted available space inside the recessed cave shell (see Kotjabopoulou 2001). It is of importance to remark that the lithic component of the sites exhibits a similar geometric density pattern in broad terms (*ibid*, Bailey & Woodward 1997).

Hence, although we are dealing with variability in taphonomic histories, the assemblages to hand share some common analytical denominators.

It has been established by several lines of evidence (e.g. butchery, fragmentation, burning, species composition) that diachronically humans were the primary agents of accumulation and modification of the animal bone remains. Carnivore skeletal elements (of small and medium sized species) and gnawing attrition are remarkably low-key, clearly pointing to a restricted and/or infrequent (or in the case of Kastritsa with strands of spatial configuration) use of these shelters as lairs/dens, while palaeolithic occupation lasted. Particularly interesting is that at Kastritsa evidence of dismembering cut marks on badger and fox bones shows that these fur animals were purposefully targeted at least in the Late Glacial.

Identifiability (excluding microfauna and homo remains) is quite low at all sites alike (Kastritsa: stratum 9= 8,4, stratum 7=10,3, stratum 5=7,6, stratum 3=7,7, stratum 1=7,6, Klithi: all strata=8,7, Boila all strata=8,7). This feature directly signals the most pertinent character of the assemblages that is their *high* fragmentation. To give only an idea of the fragmentation regime in Table 3.3 the unidentified component of the three sites is arranged according to a size survivability scheme set at three centimeters intervals. The stark dominance of fragments measuring less than three centimeters in any direction is lucid, allowing for the confounding effect related to the original size of the most common ungulate in the respective collections, i.e. deer in the former and caprines in the latter (see below). Significantly, these battered assemblages have been produced by intensive subsistence and consumption strategies in the first instance. As a

Tab. 3.3. Fragmentation pattern of the bone Unidentified component at the hinterland Epirus sites. Size classes (maximum length in any direction) are set at 3 cm intervals. For Kastritsa and Boila data from Kotjabopoulou (2001) Tab. 3.8 and 4.5 respectively, and for Klithi from Gamble (1997) Tab. 12.3.

	KASTRITSA	KLITHI	BOILA
Size class	All strata	All strata	All strata
≤3cm	70,5	93,0	93,2
3,1-6cm	26,2	5,5	5,5
6,1-9cm	2,9	0,5	0,9
9,1-12cm	0,4	0,04	0,4
>12,1cm	0,06	0,04	0

Tab. 3.4. Incidense of butchered bone (cutmarked + split + chopped) at the hinterland Epirus sites. For Kastritsa and Boila data from Kotjabopoulou (2001) and for Klithi from Gamble (1997) Tab. 12.28.

	KASTRITSA (all taxa)					KLITHI (caprines)	BOILA (all taxa)
	S1	S3	S5	S7	S9	All strata	All strata
Identified butchered bones (N)	349	403	368	24	21	1632	145
% (of NISP)	**39,2**	**33,7**	**41,8**	**41,4**	**42,0**	**13,4**	**15,1**

Tab. 3.5. Relative frequency of species at the hinterland Epirus sites (based on NISP). For Kastritsa and Boila data from Kotjabopoulou (2001) Tab. 3.13 and 4.6 respectively, and for Klithi from Gamble (1997) Tab. 12.2 (excluding small rodent and homo remains)

TAXON	KASTRITSA						KLITHI	BOILA
	S9	S7	S5	S3	S1	All strata	All strata	All strata
	NISP %						NISP %	NISP %
Large Bovid	11,6	3,0	4,6	5,2	2,4	4,3	0,0	0,1
Red Deer	**62,3**	**62,1**	**72,1**	**58,0**	**64,7**	**64,4**	**0,1**	**18,7**
Gracile horse	2,9	0,0	3,4	19,9	5,6	10,5	0,0	0,0
Wild boar	0,0	1,5	0,6	1,1	1,2	1,0	0,0	0,5
Caprines	**2,9**	**12,1**	**3,3**	**1,5**	**7,3**	**3,7**	**97,6**	**60,3**
Roe deer	2,9	0,0	0,9	0,7	1,2	0,9	0,0	0,0
Deer/Capra	0,0	0,0	0,0	0,0	0,0	0,0	0,0	5,1
Carnivores	**5,8**	**4,6**	**1,5**	**1,1**	**4,4**	**2,2**	**0,1**	**1,7**
Castor	0,0	0,0	0,0	0,0	0,0	0,0	0,3	0,2
Lagomorphs	0,0	0,0	0,3	0,4	0,5	0,4	0,2	3,0
Bird	10,2	16,7	12,4	11,0	11,5	11,6	1,6	5,3
Fish	0,0	0,0	0,0	0,0	0,0	0,0	0,1	3,3
Mammal	0,0	0,0	0,0	0,0	0,0	0,8	0,0	1,2
Other	1,4	0,0	0,9	1,1	1,2	0,2	0,0	0,6

result, they are dominated by long-bone shaft splinters. The extent of intentionally modified bones -cutmarked, split and chopped- is depicted in Table 3.4. At Kastritsa nearly four in every ten identified bones, across the stratigraphic sequence, bear some sort of butchery impact marks related to transport decisions and sharing/consumption of game and/or fracturing for the provisioning of fat macronutrients (e.g. splitting of hollow bones, even phalanges, for marrow extraction). The values are lower at Klithi and Boila but comparable between nevertheless. For the latter site the poor preservation of bone has most certainly obscured the evidence. At Klithi, where bone surface and matrix is very well preserved, further post depositional mechanical stresses (e.g. trampling within a highly stony matrix) could have winnowed the observational units.

As is depicted in Table 3.5 ungulates dominate the collections. In contrast, small-sized prey, like water birds (Anatidae) at Kastritsa (see also above discussion on carnivores) and a combination of lagomorphs, freshwater fish and large rodents (castor) at the riverside shelters

made up a minor addition to the menus, but perhaps not a negligible element in terms of wider subsistence objectives (e.g. provisioning of pelts, feathers for use in composite utensils and/or for symbolic decoration). The negative evidence of fish procurement at Kastritsa, even though fish-eating birds such as the grebes were quarried and locally butchered, offers a clear window into the qualitative aspect of resource acquisition structure, i.e. the ranking of resources not simply in accordance to quantitative availability.

Invariably at all habitation horizons considered and irespective of diachronically distinct ecoclimatic conditions, emphasis of exploitation goals revolved around a single resource. Throughout Kastritsas' use, the ubiquitous red deer was procured with intensity, consistently though complemented by other ungulates. Notably during the formation of the stratum 3 record a greater interest (or opportunity to do so) in obtaining hydruntine equids, at the expense of deer, is registered. If not a reflection of palaeoecological fluctuations, echoing perhaps a relatively warmer and/or more humid regime, this profile may imply differences in the regional organization of production and the grain of social landscapes, e.g. greater availability of hands and/or variety of social residents or less constraints on available cropping/processing time. At the Voidomatis sites caprines formed the hunting focus, remarkably so at Klithi, but with evidence at Boila suggestive of a more mixed-bag of prey; seemingly red deer lingering on the fringes of the nearby flatland, or attempting to cross the watershed, was not a target to be missed within a catch-as-can exploitation strategy.

Body-part frequency expressed in a tripartite carcass unit scheme and viewed also within the frame of food utility ranking, of the major ungulate resource at each site/phase is comparable, as shown in Figure 3.2 and 3.3. Clearly upper limbs account for c. 60% of the samples and combined high and medium utility parts for c. 80% of the economic anatomy. It is of importance to note that the data are constructed on counts, namely Corrected NISP, that compensate for the differential frequency of skeletal elements in the relevant mammalian skeletons and in which diaphysis (instead of just epiphysis) fragments, where relevant, are included in order to minimize density-mediated biases. Thus, it is fair to assume that, since equifinality problems are not at issue, the patterning obtained, albeit irrespective of particular modes of occupation, entrains aspects of selective behaviour in terms of local transport decisions made by the hunters who inhabited the three sites and further strongly supports the proposal of *in situ* consumption as a dominant theme. By extension, little, if any, amount of food obtained locally was forwarded to other locations at least during the Late Glacial[1]. As a rule, preliminary butchery of prey, resulting in abandonment of heads and feet, was effectuated in the field, at kill locations presumably situated at some distance from the shelters themselves, if the rationale of the food utility models is to be followed. From a regional perspective this tallies with earlier hypotheses, based on off-site data, that the excavated site locations are strategically placed along but actually off-set from the main long-distance seasonal migration routes of red deer (and other medium and large sized ungulates) or the locally vertical, altitudinal, shifts of caprines (see Sturdy *et al.* 1997). At Klithi, Gamble (1997) has additionally demonstrated that when of lesser nutritious quality, e.g. as a condition of age or simply when weight was not perceived as a constraint, whole carcasses where transported back to the camp; this two-tiered tactic could have been also pursued by the Boila occupants, although owing to preservation biases this option is undermined. The possibility cannot be ruled out that at this sporadically and/or ephemerally occupied site hunters could not afford to be selective, or alternatively hunting grounds were in close proximity. A combination of limited on-site faunal evidence and off-site palaeogeographic reconstruc-

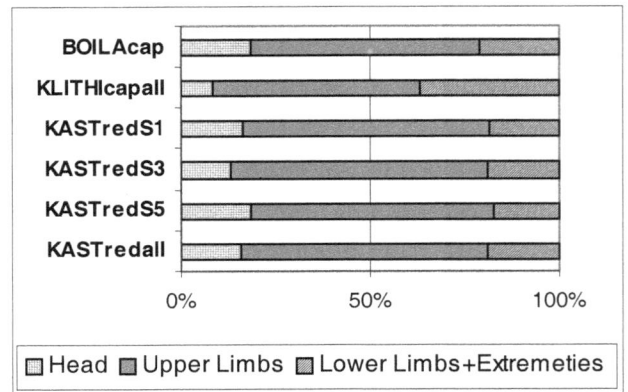

Fig. 3.2. Epirus Upper Palaeolithic faunal assemblages: comparison according to a tripartite body-part division. Only the main ungulate at each site/phase is treated. Raw data and method used to generate the schemes for Kastritsa and Boila from Kotjabopoulou (2001) and for Klithi from Gamble (1997). Abbreviations: KAST=Kastritsa, red=red deer, all=all strata, S=stratum, cap=caprines

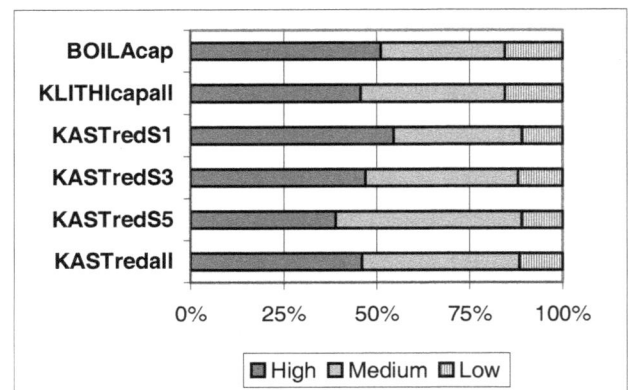

Fig. 3.3. Epirus Upper Palaeolithic faunal assemblages: comparison according to Utility groups. Only the main ungulate at each site/phase is treated. Raw data and method used to generate the schemes for Kastritsa and Boila from Kotjabopoulou (2001) and for Klithi from Gamble (1997). Abbreviations: KAST=Kastritsa, red=red deer, all=all strata, S=stratum, cap=caprines

tions suggests a summer use of the Voidomatis sites, with data from Klithi (i.e. neonatal bones) pointing to forays in the late spring/early summer. At Kastritsa the general rule of ranked segments of the anatomy applies to the red deer samples of strata 5, 3 and 1, with further contingency related to carrying back male red deer heads for using antler and pearl teeth as raw materials. Notwithstanding the intensity of fragmentation, reconstruction on the basis of dental data of the red deer mortality profile falls in the range of a living structure model (*sensu* Stiner 1990). At this site a further insight into production goals and the texture of social life has emerged with relation to the equid fraction, the second most common ungulate. The horse body part relative abundance (Fig. 3.4) is dominated by heads and hoofs, whereas the remaining appendicular

---

[1] Subtle differences in the structure of the statum 5 faunal record, in comparison to the superimposed strata, hint to possibilities of some abandonment of still usable meal leftovers and/or forwarding of selected anatomical parcels to other consumption locations (see Kotjabopoulou 2001 for further discussion).

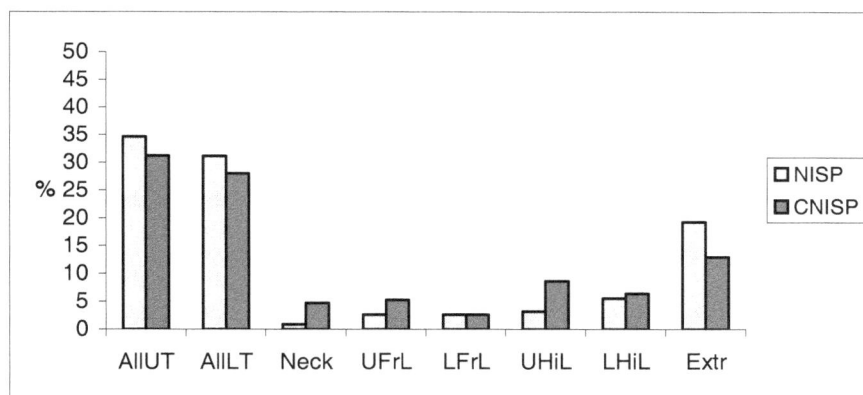

Fig. 3.4. Hydruntine horse body-part relative abundance from Kastritsa (all strata combined) using NISP and Corrected NISP values. Raw data and method used from Kotjabopoulou (2001). Abbreviations: AllUT= All Upper (cheek) Teeth, AllLT= All Lower (cheek) Teeth, UfrL= Upper Front Limb, LfrL= Lower Front Limb, UHiL= Upper Hind Limb, LHiL= Lower Hind Limb, Extr= Extremeties

elements are clearly depressed. This has been shown, by the comprehensive taphonomic, food utility and age structure analysis undertaken, to be largely a function of susceptibility to destruction of bony structures belonging to juvenile horse, the most abundant age cohort in the dental assemblage. As I have argued in detail elsewhere there are no grounds for interpreting horse acquisition as the outcome of delayed access to this resource or of subsequent selective removal for delayed consumption in the context of intra or inter-group obligations (Kotjabopoulou 2001, 2003). Hence, it appears that these animals, along perhaps with the large bovids – herbivores highly dependent on water availability/distribution, were encountered not far from the cave. In this sense the lake environment was upgraded into a real tool, rather than simply being treated as a physiographic unit of extraction. Determining seasonality, i.e. duration of occupation and whether prey was seasonally targeted, is gravely hampered by the quality of the Kastritsa excavated assemblages, and not least by analytical shortcomings. It can, though, tentatively be argued that seasonal coincidence of procurement strategies exerted on the three main ungulates (deer, gracile horse and cattle) over the warm part of the annual cycle in broad terms is a possibility (see also Kotjabopoulou & Kaftantzis in press).

A LAND OF CONTRASTS OVER SHORT DISTANCES

Any discussion that aims to go beyond approaching mobile land use management as an ecological institution and whereby social life is not reduced to struggles against nature, needs to evaluate the confounding features and structure of past bio-spaces *in* which cultural landscapes unfolded and attained their specific characters and history.

Our current appreciation of the Upper Palaeolithic physical space of Epirus draws from a vast and varied corpus of research objectives and respective results,

assembled under distinct epistemological frameworks over the past 40 years. Consensus is not always reached, but some principal parameters and processes can be compiled. One such concise epitome is offered below.

Tectonic activity and its specific regional regime, which operates at time scales not easily reconciled – at first glance – with those of human presence and settlement, emerges as the principal parameter behind the dissected and undulating Epirotic terrain (e.g. King & Bailey 1985). No doubt, the structural geometry of Epirus, by way of its position at the junction of three tectonic plates, is the underlying force that, in tandem with palaeoenvironmental conditions, has shaped a most complex, often profoundly unstable, patchwork of *local* micro-habitats even at short distances (horizontal and or vertical) *within* specific geomorphic features.

The mountain ranges form the most dominant feature *across* the landscape in question. As a rule, limestone ridges stand at higher altitude than flysch ones owing to the pronounced instability of this rock type to erosion, which results in the creation -allowing for ecoclimatic variables- of extensive badland zones. Most Upper Palaeolithic sites are associated with areas of limestone bedrock, whereas the flysch badlands have produced thin evidence (e.g. Bailey *et al.* 1997). However, and setting, for the moment, aside problems of archaeological visibility, the presumed flysch "non-story" needs to be reconsidered in particular with respect to time-slices recording expansion of woodland cover and/or restricted erosion (see Kotjabopoulou 2001 for further discussion). The geological matrix of Epirus abides with lenses of flint, of various textures and colours, the rock that overwhelmingly dominates the palaeolithic toolkits. The mountains are not only confined to the high altitude Pindus massif, which is heuristically taken as the eastern margin of the region. Several tall and steep, but of lesser extent, ridges run basically along the same direction and are to be found even at close distances (< 25km) from, or even rise abruptly immediately above, the present shores. On the Pindus, research has documented extensive tracks of glaciated terrain and periglacial zones (e.g. Woodward *et al.* 1995), indicating lowered permanent snow contours in the past, e.g. at around 1700m over the LGM (Sturdy *et al.* 1997: 592). Effectively adjacent to these are found the Voidomatis valley sites and several more unexcavated rockshelters – spanning perhaps use into the early Holocene- in the Upper Vikos (which comprises the headwaters of the Voidomatis) (Bailey *et al.* 1997).

The specific orographic regime of NW Greece holds crucial insights into the peculiarities of regional Pleistocene vegetation evolution and temperature regimes (e.g. Bennett *et al.* 1991, Tzedakis 1993, Turner & Sanchez-Goni 1997). During the last full glacial (c. 25-16 kyr BP) conditions were generally cool and arid, with open vegetation of steppe-grassland being dominant. However, locally variable regimes did exist, as suggested by the persistence of tree-patches (refugia) in favourable locations across Epirus. Thereafter, over the Late Glacial, a sustained and earlier, in comparison to even neighbouring areas of Europe or the Greek mainland east of the Pindus, expansion of moisture-demanding woodland is firmly traced. The mute vegetation response to climatic regretssions, like the Younger Dryas chronozone, as Lawson *et al.* argue, can be attributed to "the preservation of high moisture availability through orographic precipitation and proximity to the western coast" (2004: 1621). Dense tree cover right on the Pindus high ground plateaux (>1800m) at least by 9,5 Kyr BP is well documented (Willis 1997). In this context I propose, that the attractiveness and not least improved accessibility of such truly upland territories especially for the very late Pleistocene and Early Holocene communities undermines the presumed low archaeological visibility– which in the past has been taken at face value as equaling virtual depopulation. Increasing evidence from both sides of the Pindus suggests restructuring of territories involving high mobility patterns within wooded environments and regular traversing of high mountain ridges.

The hydrological regime of Epirus is extremely complex and variable but undoubtedly of pivotal significance for hominid lifeways and mobility scheduling in many respects. A vast network of subparallel major and lesser rivers along with their tributaries literally gouges a country with extremely limited flatlands, except for the coastal strip -especially under low sea level stands. It has been established that the valleys floors were particularly sensitive to climate change experiencing alternating phases of aggradation and entrenchment (e.g. Woodward *et al.* 1994, see also Vita Finzi 1978). During glacial conditions these were high-energy delivery systems, marking perhaps important (at least seasonal, e.g. during spring/early summer ice melting) barriers to animal and hominid circulation or dispersal. It remains to be seen whether some of these physical features could have potentially qualified as territorial markers to certain animal communities (e.g. ibex) as much as to humans. At the same time it is conceivable to assume that the lower reaches of these river systems (parts of which are now submerged under the Ionian Sea) would have been especially productive, though not without limiting factors, in biomass terms and consequently potentially luring to mobile lifeways. Over interstadial times and when ice retreat was well advanced the upper reaches of rivers became more amenable to exploitation, as evidenced by the Voidomatis valley sites (see below). Still research has shown that deglaciation was not a linear process, but a most unpredictable one, thus constantly imposing challenges to be met by and/or providing decisive windows of subsistence opportunities to mobile hunters with repercussions as regards the modalities of social landscapes. In all, the alluvial systems and formations of Epirus were also decisively important to palaeolithic groups in one more sense: they were an incessant medium of lithic raw material dispersal and hence a reliable source of ready-to-hand acquisition.

An eye-catching and prolific array of physiographic units *across*, I would like to emphasize, the landscape of Epirus comprises the enclosed and elongated, small to medium sized, basins (mostly tectonically controlled) that are formed on the runoff-collecting karstic substratum. Often these are infilled with primary or more often redeposited terra rossa, preserving extremely fragmentary sedimentary histories. As Runnels and van Andel point out "Epirus west of the Pindos front contains poljes in every stage of evolution from recent birth, to old age, to stream incision and removal' (2003: 59). Irrespective of the lack of research convergence and not least the inherent caveats involved in determining the origin, formation, modifycation and dating of the redbeds and their archaeology, it remains a fact that, for the general time fraction under discussion, human exploitation is persistently attested at these often seasonally favourable locations, supporting the view of high mobility patterns. One serious drawback for evaluating land use organization is the hostile depositional environment of redbeds to the survivability of bioarchaeological remains.

The effects of global climate changes during the Last Glacial had had a profound impact on the overall regional topography of NW Greece. Notably, at times of low sea level positions the continental shelf between the present Ionian islands and the mainland was exposed, adding a continuous, even though narrow at intermediate stands, increment of lowlands but more importantly, as at the glacial maxima, opening up roots of dispersal and communication to the north, towards the Adriatic plain and the fringes of the Dinaric plateaux, and to the south, towards the western Peloponnese. The land bridge that connected the present island of Corfu with the mainland and which stood there for the best part of the period from 90 to 10kyr BP (see *ibid.*) must have been decisive for animal and human movements. This is well supported by the as yet not fully studied faunal record from the Upper Palaeolithic Grava rockshelter on Corfu (Sordinas 1969) wherein the full array of ungulates we encounter on the mainland is recorded (see Kotjabopoulou 2001 for further discussion).

In sum, what needs to be highlighted is the *stochastic* aspect of the landscape configuration of NW Greece. Unstable and unpredictable as this may have been it nevertheless raises the curtain, when approached from a regional perspective, to a diachronically resourceful mosaic of closely packed habitats and niches. Furthermore, it undermines the simplistic, though acute and insightful for its time, bi-annual seasonality exploitation model advanced by Higgs, in the pioneering days of palaeolithic research in the 1960s, and the great emphasis he ultimately placed on the differences between the coastal areas and the hinterland (e.g. Higgs & Webley 1971).

MOBILE LIFEWAYS IN UNPREDICTABLE ENVIRONMENTS

Contrary to models that favour the nature-culture dichotomy as a means to explain subsistence and land use strategies emphasizing adaptation in direct response to environmental limitations, the faunal evidence from the inland rockshelters of Epirus leads me to argue that hunting (and gathering) was not merely an extractive technique, governed by cost-benefit rules, but a component of a mode of production and thus a historically contingent social institution. In this sense, as Gamble & Gaudzinski (2005) contend we ought to keep the options open for tracing patterns in the data that are not only rational but relational as well.

Even though the faunal records at hand have been produced over several millennia and under different environmental conditions and taphonomic regimes it becomes clear that an element of apparent continuity is traced, albeit not devoid of variability.

It thus becomes evident that although we are most probably dealing with at least three distinct regional social landscape regimes – over the full glacial (c. 25-18/17 kyr BP), during the early Late Glacial (17/16-13 kyr BP) and the late Late Glacial up into the early centuries of the Holocene (13-9 kyr BP) at least, these shared, as it were, a common denominator: locally *multi-selective* goals of production.

From a regional perspective, however, it needs to be emphasized that it was the *integration* of local management strategies, which in various combinations and interconnections, contributed to the shaping of probably distinct social landscapes. In Epirus, the faunal evidence is conclusive in that these were structured on various forms of *high* mobility, whereby as a rule people were moved to resources. The ever-present risks and possibilities of failure to fill up the stomach at any particular local could be compensated at a stone's throw, allowing for flexibility in social organization and structure. This reading fits well the evidence from

Kastritsa stratum 3 and 1(?) and Klithi, which can be interpreted as repeatedly used sheltered locations in a territory within which families often shifted their camp arrangements and whereat they engaged in a variety of labour intensive activities associated with the respective catchment resources. Earlier, at times of full glacial conditions marked by pronounced ecological assymetry, forays deep in the interior, as the Kastritsa stratum 5 record hints, appear to have been less regular or intensive, exploratory in a sense, or at any rate reflecting a more linear mobility fashion, undertaken, for example, by hasty and/or fragmented groups otherwise exploiting rather large and risky territories. Whether these human communities originated or were displaced in the first instance from far flanked and more sensitive to the glacial impact areas -in the Balkan peninsula or central-eastern Europe- (cf. Housley *et al.* 1997) remains to be seen. Undoubtedly, the progressive loss of coastal plains to the rising seas and the increasing fragility of late Pleistocene biomass did not result in the abandonment of the region. Perhaps aided by the enhanced accessibility of high mountain ridges that also opened up corridors into adjacent but hitherto effectively disconnected geographic regions (e.g. over the Pindus and to the east) we can tentatively imagine human settlement as re-organized, in terms of degree rather than emphasis. Although the evidence over the Pleistocene/Holocene transition is sparse overall, it does though point to *familiar* routes *through* the mountains and along the littoral contours. High mobility was here again at issue but under different modes of subsistence and cultural reproduction.

The mountainous interior -if indeed we can maintain further such a partitioning- was consequently not simply an economic (seasonal) addendum of restricted plasticity, but an integral and sustained constituent, admittedly with diachronically variable status, of regionally complex socioeconomic relations, which appear to have emphasized modes, means and expressions of maintaining group cohesion/identity over large (though fluctuating in extent and/or content), dissected and variously unstable territories.

Acknowledgments

I extent my deep thanks to Dimitris Kalpakis for compiling the perspective map of Figure 3.1, even though he was swamped, as usual, with loads of work.

References

ADAM, E. (1997). To know and to have: raw material availability and Upper Palaeolithic stone assemblage structure in Epirus. In. BAILEY, G.N (ed.), *Klithi: Archaeology of a Late Glacial Landscape in Epirus (Northwest Greece), Volume 2*. Cambridge: McDonald Institute of Archaeological Research, p. 481-96.

ADAM, E. & E. KOTJABOPOULOU (1997). The organic artefacts from Klithi. In BAILEY, G.N (ed.), *Klithi: Archaeology of a Late Glacial Landscape in Epirus (Northwest Greece), Volume 1*. Cambridge: McDonald Institute of Archaeological Research, p. 245-99.

BAILEY, G.N. ed. (1997). *Klithi: Archaeology of a Late Glacial Landscape in Epirus (Northwest Greece), Volumes 1, 2*. Cambridge: McDonald Institute of Archaeological Research.

BAILEY, G.N. & J. WOODWARD (1997). The Klithi deposits: sedimentology, stratigraphy and chronology. In BAILEY, G.N (ed.), *Klithi: Archaeology of a Late Glacial Landscape in Epirus (Northwest Greece), Volume 1*. Cambridge: McDonald Institute of Archaeological Research, p. 61-94.

BAILEY, G.N.; CARTER, P.L.; GAMBLE, C.S. & H.P. HIGGS (1983a). Asprochaliko and Kastritsa: further investigations of Palaeolithic settlement and economy in Epirus (North-west Greece). *Proceedings of the Prehistoric Society* 49: 15-42.

BAILEY, G.N.; CARTER, P.L.; GAMBLE, C.S. & H.P. HIGGS (1983b). Epirus revisited: seasonality and inter-site variation in the Upper Palaeolithic of north-west Greece. In BAILEY, G.N (ed.), *Hunter-Gatherer Economy in Prehistory: a European Perspective*: 64-78. Cambridge: Cambridge University Press.

BAILEY, G.N.; CADBURY, T.; GALANIDOU, N. & E. KOTJABOPOULOU (1997). Rockshelters and open-air sites: survey strategies and regional site distributions. In BAILEY, G.N (ed.), *Klithi: Archaeology of a Late Glacial Landscape in Epirus (Northwest Greece), Volume 2*. Cambridge: McDonald Institute of Archaeological Research, p. 521-36.

BENNETT, K.D.; TZEDAKIS, P.C. & K.J. WILLIS (1991). Quaternary refugia of north European trees. *Journal of Biogeography* 18: 103-15.

BRAUDEL, F. (1993). The Mediterranean and the Mediterranean World in the Age of Philip II. Volume A. Athens: The National Bank Education Institute (trans. in Greek).

ELEFANTI, P. (2003). Hunter-Gatherer Specialised Subsistence Strategies in Greece during the Upper Palaeolithic from the Perspective of Lithic Technology. Oxford: British Archaeological Reports, International Series 1130.

GALANIDOU, N. (1997). *Home is Where the Hearth is. The Spatial Organisation of the Upper Palaeolithic Rockshelter Occupations at Klithi and Kastritsa in Northwest Greece*. Oxford: British Archaeological Reports, International Series 687.

GAMBLE, C.S. (1997). The animal bones from Klithi. In BAILEY, G.N (ed.), *Klithi: Archaeology of a Late Glacial Landscape in Epirus (Northwest Greece), Volume 1*. Cambridge: McDonald Institute of Archaeological Research, p. 207-44.

GAMBLE, C.S. & S. GAUDZINSKI (2003). Bones and powerful individuals. Faunal case studies from the Arctic and the European Middle Palaeolithic. In. GAMBLE, C.S & PORR, M. (eds), *The Hominid Individual in Context*. London and New York: Routledge, p. 154-75.

HIGGS, E.S. & D.P. WEBLEY (1971). Further information concerning the environment of Palaeolithic man in Epirus. *Proceedings of the Prehistoric Society* 37: 367-80.

HIGGS, E.S.; VITA-FINZI, C.; HARRIS, D.R. & A.E. FAGG (1967). The climate, environment and industries of Stone Age Greece, part III. *Proceedings of the Prehistoric Society* 33: 1-29.

HOUSLEY, R.A.; GAMBLE, C.S.; STREET, M. & P. PETTITT (1997). Radiocarbon evidence for the Lateglacial human recolonisation of Northern Europe. *Proceedings of the Prehistoric Society* 63: 25-54.

INGOLD, T. (1993). The temporality of the landscape. *World Archaeology* 25: 152-174.

KING, G. & G. BAILEY (1985). The palaeoenvironment of some archaeological sites in Greece: the influence of accumulated uplift in a seismically active region. *Proceedings of the Prehistoric Society* 51: 273-82.

KOTJABOPOULOU, E. (2001). Patterned Fragments and Fragments of Patterns: Upper Palaeolithic Rockshelter Faunas from Epirus Northwestern Greece. Unpublished Ph.D. Thesis, University of Cambridge (UK).

KOTJABOPOULOU, E. (2003). Food utility indices as a tool for pattern recognition in faunal assemblages: examples from the Upper Palaeolithic of Epirus, NW Greece. In *The Prehistoric Research and its Perspectives: Theoretical and Methodological Considerations. Proceedings of the International Symposium in the memory of D.R. Theocharis* (Thessaloniki-Kastoria 1998. Thessaloniki: University Studio Press (in Greek), p. 117-25.

KOTJABOPOULOU, E. & E. ADAM (2004). People, mobility and ornaments in Upper Palaeolithic Epirus, NW Greece. In OTTE, M. (ed.), *La Spiritualité (Actes du Colloque International de Liège 10-12 décembre 2003)*. Liège: ERAUL 106, p. 37-53.

KOTJABOPOULOU, E., & C.N. KAFTANTZIS (in press). Seasonality and Radiology: a pilot application on red deer (*Cervus Elaphus*) dentaries from the Upper Palaeolithic cave of Kastritsa, NW Greece. *In Proceedings of the 4th Symposium on Archaeometry* (Athens 2003). British Archaeological Reports.

KOTJABOPOULOU, E.; PANAGOPOULOU, E. & E. ADAM (1997). The Boila rockshelter: a preliminary report. In BAILEY, G.N (ed.), *Klithi: Archaeology of a Late Glacial Landscape in Epirus (Northwest Greece), Volume 2*. Cambridge: McDonald Institute of Archaeological Research, p. 427-37.

KOTJABOPOULOU, E.; PANAGOPOULOU, E. & E. ADAM (1999). The Boila rockshelter: further evidence of human activity in the Voidomatis gorge. In. BAILEY, G.N., ADAM, E., PANAGOPOULOU, E., PERLÈS, C. & ZACHOS, K. (eds.), *The Palaeolithic Archaeology of Greece and Adjacent Areas. Proceedings of the ICOPAG Conference, Ioannina.* London: British School at Athens, Studies No 3, p. 197-210.

LAWSON, I.; FROGLEY, M.; BRYANT, C.; PREECE, R. & P. TZEDAKIS (2004). The Lateglacial and Holocene environmental history of the Ioannina basin, north-west Greece. *Quaternary Science Reviews* 23: 1599-1625.

MUSSI, M (2001). *Earliest Italy. An Overview of the Italian Palaeolithic and Mesolithic.* New York: Kluwer Academic-Plenum Publishers.

NTINOU, M. & E. KOTJABOPOULOU (2002). Charcoal analysis at Boila rockshelter: woodland expansion during the Late Glacial in Epirus, north-west Greece. In S. Thiebault (ed.), *Charcoal Analysis. Methodologcial Approaches, Palaeoecological Results and Wood Uses.* Oxford: British Archaeological Reports, International Series 1063, p. 79-86.

OTTE, M. (1992). L' homme paléolithique et la montagne: art et chasse. *Preistoria Alpina* 28: 29-36.

RUNNELS, C. & T.H. VAN ANDEL (2003). The Early Stone Age of the Nomos of Preveza: landscape and settlement. In WISEMAN, J.& ZACHOS, K. (eds), *Landscape Archaeology in Southern Epirus, Greece I.* Hesperia (Supplement 32), p. 47-134.

SINCLAIR, A. (1997). Lithic and faunal assemblages from Megalakkos: some problems in the interpretation of small sites. In BAILEY, G.N (ed.), *Klithi: Archaeology of a Late Glacial Landscape in Epirus (Northwest Greece), Volume 2.* Cambridge: McDonald Institute of Archaeological Research, p. 415-26.

SORDINAS, A. (1969). Investigations of the prehistory of Corfu during 1964-1966. *Balkan Studies* 10: 393-424.

STINER, M.C. (1990). The use of mortality patterns in archaeological studies of hominid predatory adaptati-ons. *Journal of Anthropological Archaeology* 9: 305-51.

STRAUS, L.G. (1987). Upper Palaeolithic ibex hunting in Southwest Europe. *Journal of Archaeological Science* 14: 163-78.

STURDY, D.; WEBLEY, D. & G. BAILEY (1997). The Palaeolithic geography of Epirus. In BAILEY, G.N (ed.), *Klithi: Archaeology of a Late Glacial Landscape in Epirus (Northwest Greece), Volume 2.* Cambridge: McDonald Institute of Archaeological Research, p. 587-614.

TZEDAKIS, P.C. (1993). Long-term tree populations in northwest Greece through multiple Quaternary climatic cycles. *Nature* 364: 437-40.

TURNER, C. & M.-F. SÁNCHEZ GOÑI (1997). The Late Glacial landscape and vegetation in Epirus. In BAILEY, G.N (ed.), *Klithi: Archaeology of a Late Glacial Landscape in Epirus (Northwest Greece), Volume 2.* Cambridge: McDonald Institute of Archaeological Research, p. 559-85.

VITA-FINZI, C. (1978). *Archaeological Sites in their Setting.* London: Thames and Hudson.

WILLIS, K.J. (1997). Vegetational history of the Klithi environment: a palaeoecological viewpoint. In BAILEY, G.N. (ed.), *Klithi: Archaeology of a Late Glacial Landscape in Epirus (Northwest Greece), Volume 2.* Cambridge: McDonald Institute of Archaeological Research, p. 395-413.

WOODWARD, J.C.; LEWIN, J. & M.G. MACKLIN (1995). Glaciation, river behaviour and the palaeolithic settlement of upland northwest Greece. In LEWIN, J.,. MACKLIN, M.G & WOODWARD, J. (eds.), *Mediterranean Quaternary River Environments.* Rotterdam: Balkema, p. 115-29.

WOODWARD, J.C.; MACKLIN, M.G. & J. LEWIN (1994). Pedogenic weathering and relative-age dating of Quaternary alluvial sediments in the Pindus Mountains of northwest Greece. In ROBINSON, D.A. & WILLIAMS, R.B.G. (eds.), *Rock weathering and landform evolution.* Chichester: Wiley, p. 259-83.

MIDDLE PALAEOLITHIC EXPLOITATION OF THE LAKE PLASTIRAS PLATEAU, WESTERN THESSALY – GREECE

Orestis APOSTOLIKAS and Nina KYPARISSI-APOSTOLIKA

Ephoreia of Speleology and Palaeoanthropology, Athens, Greece

Abstract: A series of field surveys during the last three years has produced a substantial number of Middle Palaeolithic artefacts from the high plateau of Lake Plastiras in western Thessaly, Greece. The recently discovered Middle Palaeolithic open-air site is the westernmost known in Thessaly and one of the very few in Greece to be found at an altitude of 800 m above sea level or more. The climatic conditions in the area during the summer provide a great shelter for herds moving from the very hot Thessalian plains to the uplands where grazing lands are abundant and the temperatures rarely exceed 30° C. However during winter months the area becomes hostile as snowfall and very low temperatures create a very difficult environment to survive. Our aim is to explore the functionality of the site in terms of seasonal mobility, raw material procurement, and population movements.
Keywords: Middle Palaeolithic, Thessaly, Greece, high plateau, open-air site

Résumé: Une série de prospections pendant les derniers trois ans a donné un nombre considérable d'artefacts du Paléolithique moyen provenant du haut plateau du lac Plastiras (Thessalie occidentale, Grèce). Le site du Paléolithique moyen récemment découvert est le site le plus occidental connu en Thessalie et un des rares sites de Grèce localisés à une altitude de 800 mètres voire plus. Les conditions climatiques estivales de cette aire offrent un grand abri pour les troupeaux qui transhument des plains thessaliens très chaudes vers les contrées élevées où le pâturage est abondant et les températures dépassent rarement les 30° C. Néanmoins, pendant l'hiver cette aire devient hostile puisque la neige et les températures très basses constituent un environnement difficile à survivre. Notre but est d'explorer le fonctionnement du site en termes de mobilité saisonnière, approvisionnement des matières premières et mouvement de populations.
Mots-clés: Paléolithique moyen, Thessalie, Grèce, haut plateau, site de plein air

INTRODUCTION

The artificial Lake Plastiras was created at the end of the 1950s with the construction of a dam for the production of hydroelectric power. Since then, the fluctuations in the lake's water levels have brought to light a large quantity of archaeological material, mainly prehistoric. The systematic field surveys of 2006 revealed a number of Palaeolithic artifacts over a large area covering most of the lake's west coast. The fluctuations in the water levels as well as the intensive rainfalls throughout the year constantly move the archaeological material, thus making it extremely insecure to speak of in situ finds. Although there are specific areas that produce more artefacts than others, the lack of a stratified record makes it almost impossible to distinguish specific assemblages as belonging to certain sites. The quality as well as the quantity of the artefacts collected, points out to a nearby raw material source that was quite intensively exploited, although waste products have not been well represented in the assemblages so far. In our effort to understand the functionality of the site as well as the mobility patterns of its Middle Palaeolithic inhabitants we will investigate any possible affinities of Lake Plastiras site with the nearby Theopetra Cave, since it is probable that the same hominids exploited both sites following seasonal mobility patterns.

ENVIRONMENTAL SETTINGS AND GEOLOGY

The plateau of Lake Plastiras lies at an altitude of about 800m above sea level at the westernmost part of the Thessalian plain and to the foot of Pindus Mountain range at about 40 km from the city of Kardhitsa. The access to the uplands from the plains has been naturally provided by the formation of two gorges that lie at the vicinity of the plateau. In fact, the only way to reach the uplands is via these gorges at least as far as the NW parts of Thessaly are concerned. This route is also being used every summer by pastoralists who lead their flocks from the plains to the mountains where grazing land is abundant and the climate is milder for the herds. Temperatures on the plateau vary considerably from season to season with the mean highest being reported during July and August (about 28° C) and the mean lowest during January (about 3° C). The area around the lake is covered by deciduous woodland and thick vegetation that hosts a wide range of species from spring up to the end of fall. During winter however, the climate becomes harsh and snow covers the area forcing most of the wild species to migrate further down towards the lowlands.

The melting water from the ice that has been formed throughout the winter as well as a series of springs and creeks that run down from the mountains to the plateau accumulate into the lake causing the water levels to rise. During the Middle Palaeolithic however, this water would have created marshes and minor rivers that would run through the plateau and towards the gorge where the modern dam is built.

The geology of the site is characterised by an extended formation of flysch that underlies the entire artificial lake and spreads in the area around it. In certain cases the flysch formation has reached the surface and gradually becomes decomposed by weathering and trampling. The mountains that surround the plateau are rich in limestone and flysch while cherts and flints are also present especially inside limestone formations. The latter appear frequently in old and new river channel deposits in the form of pebbles, although they are characterised by their poor quality. The geomorphology of the area immediately around the lake is characterized by the deposition of alluvial fans (P. Karkanas, personal communication). The drainage system of the surrounding mountains has carried towards the plateau a huge bulk of flysch material that gradually deposited very thick layers of alluvial debris consisting of very coarse clastics in the proximal parts and sand and small to medium sized gravels in the distal parts of the fans. Most Middle Palaeolithic artifacts are found in the distal parts of the older and cemented formations of the alluvial fans. However, deposition continued throughout the Holocene forming mainly loose dark brown fine-grained sediment which in one case encloses a Neolithic settlement.

FIELD SURVEY METHODOLOGY

The field surveys that were conducted around the lake since 2004 revealed that the vast majority of the artefacts were collected at the west shore of the lake. Taking this into account along with the shortage of time that we were faced with, we decided that the survey should be restricted on areas that were rich in finds during past surveys. Moreover, the fieldwork was conducted only on areas were ground visibility exceeded 90%, since surveying on grassed areas would cost in time and effort.

With the help of the topographer Theodoros Hatzitheodorou we established 167 ground marks, which were later used to form the rectangles of the field survey. The marks were placed in a distance of about 30 m from one another and they basically made up the top side of the rectangles, while the lower side was formed by the coastline. The width of the rectangles varied according to the shoreline with the widest being established on areas where ground inclination was small. The greater the ground inclination is, the shorter the distance from the top of the rectangles to the shore. This happens because a given change in the water levels can affect different areas in different ways. For example, if we measure the highest and the lowest ground levels of a square and we find that they differ less than a meter, then we know that a change in the water levels by one meter would definitely cover the whole square independently of its area. In this sense, the higher the altitude difference of a square with the levels of the lake, the more the possibilities that the square hasn't been disturbed by the lake's water.

The survey team consisted of three people, all experienced field walkers. During artefact collection, all finds were placed in separate bags given a find number, a square number, and a collection date. After the comple-

tion of the first phase of the survey on all squares, a table was made with the nature and the number of finds in each square. The second phase of the project aimed at the intensification of the survey with a complementary survey at the squares that produced many finds during the first phase.

RESULTS

A total of 188 Middle Palaeolithic stone implements were collected during the two phases of the 2006 field survey. The typological and technological information that derived from the evidence is substantial, although it must be noted here that this is not an attempt to interpret the lithic assemblages from the existing evidence since the lack of a stratigraphical context would make such an effort pointless. However, the predominance of certain artefact types instead of others gives us a hint of what might be the case in an in situ site as well. The following table (Table 4.1) provides an analytical account of the types of stone tools that were collected.

Tab. 4.1. Stone tool types, numbers, and percentage representation

	No	% in assemblage
1. Levallois Flakes	50	36,0
2. Blades	14	10,0
3. Scrapers	50	36,0
4. Points	9	6,5
5. Notches	3	2,1
6. Burins	13	9,4
Total	139	

The lithic assemblage is completed with another 29 cores – a comparatively large number – and 20 pieces of waste products. Most of the blanks were produced on excellent quality brown radiolarite and the rest were made on grey and green flints. According to the Bordes' type list (Bordes 1961) this assemblage would most properly be characterised as a Ferrassie Mousterian assemblage, with Levallois flakes and scrapers being the dominant tool types, although without a solid stratigraphical context this is no more than a simple speculation as far as the original deposited material is concerned. From the existing evidence it is apparent that the Middle Palaeolithic hominids intended to produce large and elongated blanks. Almost half of the artefacts have not been retouched, and where retouch is present it has been applied mostly for shaping and not for resharpening purposes. The cores exhibit traces of centripetal, unipolar, and bipolar reduction techniques, with the first being used mainly for the production of flakes and the other two for the production of blades. The large number of cores as well as the fact that most of the artefacts are made on excellent

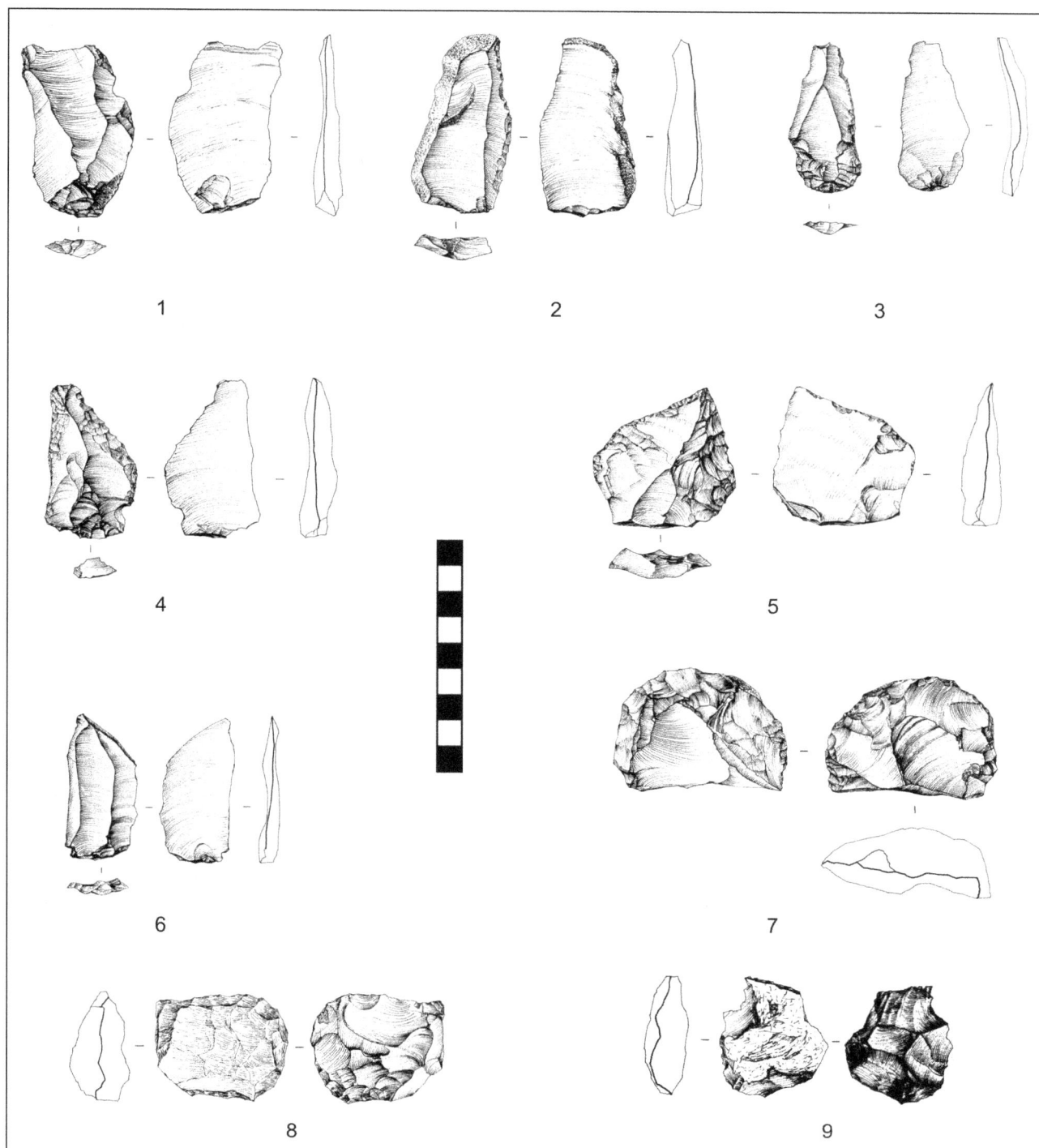

Fig. 4.1. Middle Palaeolithic artifacts from Lake Plastiras: 1- Levallois flake blade, 2- naturally backed knife, 3- side scraper, 4- point, 5- pseudo-Levallois point, 6- blade, 7,8,9- Levallois cores

quality material, implies that a nearby raw material source was probably available. However, extended surveys in the region for the tracing of such a source produced only medium quality grey flint and very poor quality reddish-brown radiolarite. From the evidence so far collected, it seems that the hominids transported raw material to the site in its raw state and probably in the form of unmodified blocks. A number of artefacts with cortex and the presence of primary flakes on the site strengthen such a hypothesis. On the other hand, the small number of waste products indicates that the cores were probably introduced as performs on the site for the production of blanks, while the initial forming of the cores probably took place at the quarry sites. This is another question that can only be answered through detailed excavation and recording processes.

COMPARING LAKE PLASTIRAS WITH THEOPETRA CAVE

Theopetra Cave lies about 60 km north-east of Lake Plastiras plateau and is the closest known Middle Palaeolithic site. In order to explore the functionality of the new site we hypothesised that the hominids that occupied Theopetra Cave throughout the Middle Palaeolithic could have exploited Lake Plastiras plateau on a seasonal basis as part of their subsistence strategies. This scenario seems ideal since the plateau is close enough for the hominids to walk there within a day or two independently of their group size and composition. Furthermore, the milder climate and the abundance in wild plants and game would definitely tempt the hominids to exploit it on a steady seasonal basis rather than during short-term opportunistic hunting trips.

A preliminary comparison of the 2006 finds from Lake Plastiras with those from the Middle Palaeolithic deposits of Theopetra produced interesting points. The Middle Paleolithic material from Theopetra is attributed to three different lithic phases (Panagopoulou 2000). Lithic Phase 1 is the oldest and dates at about 100 kya (after recent TL dating). The assemblage consists mainly of flakes and scrapers (about 87% of the assemblage) and it is attributed to the Mousterian Quina industries. Lithic Phase 2 has been radiometrically dated at about 46-40 kya and has been characterised as a Levallois-Mousterian industry. The prevalence of flakes and scrapers is also apparent in this phase, although certain tool types like burins have not appeared yet in the assemblages. Lithic Phase 3 is dated at about 40-33 kya and marks the transitional periods from the Middle to the Upper Palaeolithic. This phase is also characterised by the dominance of flakes and scrapers in the assemblages and certain Upper Palaeolithic types like retouched blades and burins start to make their appearance. The Middle Palaeolithic assemblages of Theopetra as a whole are characterised by the scarcity of raw material. The cores are represented by a very small proportion in any Lithic Phase and as a result the hominids were forced to follow raw-material-efficient strategies. The cores were reduced as much as possible and the technological modes were shifting from the production of elongated blanks to the production of broad and short flakes. This restriction literally forced the hominids to follow certain reduction sequences and most probably alienated their initial intentions in terms of stone tool production. In this sense, it is very difficult to compare Lake Plastiras assemblages with those from Theopetra, since it is possible that the lack of adequate raw material could have resulted in the same groups of hominids to produce two different types of assemblages. However, the presence of elongated blanks on both sites indicates that when the Theopetra hominids had enough raw material in their hands they produced similar tool types to those found on the plateau of Lake Plastiras. If indeed the two sites were exploited by the same groups then it is possible that raw material from the same source exists on both sites. A series of petrographical analyses could prove this to be the case.

Another prominent difference in the assemblages of the two sites is the use of retouch for tool rejuvenation purposes. But this one too, is an immediate result of raw material scarcity. The hominids of Theopetra had to utilise the same tools over and over again, and when they blunted they didn't produce new ones but they retouched them in order to re-sharpen them. This procedure is absent in the Lake Plastiras assemblages but this is no surprise since it seems that it was easier for them to flake a new blank from a prepared core than to rejuvenate the edges of an old one by retouching it. However, we must note once more that the recovered material from the new site is probably a small fragment of what was originally deposited and any observations that we currently make do not necessarily constitute future interpretations.

DISCUSSION

The geographical position of the new site must have made it a crossroad at an intermediate level for several Middle Palaeolithic populations. It is situated at about a day's walk from the plains of Thessaly and constitutes the last barrier before the high mountains of Pindus. Whether the site was used as a permanent camp, a seasonal base camp or as a temporary hunting camp, it provided its inhabitants with a variety of choices in terms of environmental cache exploitation. From the evidence that has been examined so far it seems that the site was exploited for quite a long period, repeatedly, and by many different groups. The primal source for raw material procurement must be somewhere in the vicinity of the site, although certain artefacts are made on excellent quality material which is probably imported from areas outside the region. Exchange networks and population movements on a year-round basis are of great importance in this project and future work will move towards this direction.

The discovery of an in situ site in the area would aid in the understanding of Palaeolithic societies and would also give us an insight about the hominid species that wandered on the Middle Palaeolithic landscape.

Acknowledgments

We would like to thank the Institute for Aegean Prehistory (INSTAP) for funding this project and the director of the LD' Ephorate of Prehistoric and Classical Antiquities in Kardhitsa Mr Leonidas Hatziagelakis for his cooperation.

References

BAILEY, G.N.; ADAM, E.; PANAGOPOULOU, E.; PERLES, C.; ZACHOS, K. (eds) (1999). The Palaeolithic Archaeology of Greece and adjacent areas. Proceedings of the ICOPAG conference, Ioannina., British School at Athens, London.

BORDES, F. (1961). "Typologie du Paléolithique ancien et moyen". 2 Vols. Mémoires de l'Institut Préhistoriques de l'Université de Bordeaux 1. Bordeaux : Delmas.

DEBENATH, A.; DIBBLE, L. H. (1994). Handbook of Paleolithic Typology, Vol. 1, University of Pennsylvania, Philadelphia.

INIZAN, L.M.; ROCHE, H.; TIXIER, J. (1992). Technology of Knapped Stone, CREP, Meudon.

KYPARISSI-APOSTOLIKA, N. (2000). Theopetra Cave: twelve years of excavation and research. The Ministry of Culture, Athens.

PANAGOPOULOU, E. (2000). The Middle Palaeolithic assemblages of Theopetra Cave: Technological Evolution in the Upper Pleistocene. In KYPARISSI-APOSTOLIKA N. (ed), Theopetra Cave: twelve years of excavation and research, The Ministry of Culture, Athens.

MIDDLE PALAEOLITHIC INDUSTRIES OF KLISSOURA CAVE, GREECE

Valéry SITLIVY

Royal Museums of Art and History, Parc du Cinquantenaire 10, B-1000, Brussels, BELGIUM
e-mail: valery.sitlivy@teledisnet.be

Krzysztof SOBCZYK

Jagiellonian University of Cracow, Institute of Archaeology, ul. Gołębia 11, 31-007 Cracow, POLAND

Panagiotis KARKANAS, Margarita KOUMOUZELIS

Ephoreia of Palaeoanthropology-Speleology, Ardittou 34b, 11636 Athens, GREECE

Abstract: The long Middle Palaeolithic sequence in Cave # 1 in the Klissoura gorge (Eastern Peloponese), shows a microlithic character and a toolkit rich in side-scrapers, with some convergent tools, and poor in Quina elements and in Levallois debitage. During the excavations in 2001-2006, the Middle Palaeolithic levels yielded big opened fireplaces and abundant lithic industries, rich in retouched tools (various scrapers, points), as well as reduced cores and debitage products. Levallois items (e.g., for the first time in this cave a burnt Levallois point), elongated Mousterian points and convergent scrapers surprisingly appear in the upper part of the Middle Palaeolithic sequence. The thickness of the Mousterian layers is more than 6,5 meters.
Keywords: Mousterian, Greece, Lithic assemblages

Résumé: La longue séquence du Paléolithique moyen dans la grotte 1 de la gorge de Klissoura (Péloponnèse oriental), présente un outillage riche en racloirs, accompagnés de quelques outils convergents, et pauvre en éléments Quina et en débitage Levallois. Au cours des fouilles de 2001-2006, le Paléolithique moyen a livré de grands foyers ouverts et d'abondantes industries lithiques, riches en outils retouchés (racloirs variés, pointes), ainsi que des nucléus réduits et des produits de débitage. Eléments Levallois (par exemple, et pour la première fois dans cette grotte, a été mise au jour une pointe Levallois brûlée); des pointes moustériennes allongées et des racloirs convergents apparaissent de façon surprenante dans la partie supérieure de la séquence du Paléolithique moyen. L'épaisseur des couches moustériennes dépasse 6,5 mètres.
Mots-clefs: Moustérien, Grèce, assemblages lithiques

INTRODUCTION

Although the Middle Palaeolithic of Greece is known at cave and open-air sites (Darlas 1994, 1999; Kyparissi-Apostolika 1999; Panagopoulou 2002-2004; Papaconstantinou 1988; Papagianni 2000), until recently not a single location with long and rich *in situ* sequence was documented.

The excavations of the Middle-Upper Palaeolithic stratified site of Klissoura, Cave 1 (eastern Peloponnesus) have yielded important data dealing with origins, sediment stratigraphy, typological-technological patterns and human activities. To date only the uppermost Mousterian layers VII, VIIa, VIII and X, from the limited test pit excavated in 1997, have been analysed (Koumouzelis *et al.* 2001b); these reveal a microlithic character and a toolkit rich in scrapers, with some convergent tools, and poor in Quina elements and Levallois debitage. The extension of the excavated area during the 2001-2006 field seasons resulted in numerous MP occupations with open hearths, abundant faunal remains and lithic industries, rich in retouched tools (various scrapers, points), as well as reduced cores and debitage products. Levallois items, elongated points and convergent scrapers surprisingly appear in the upper part of the MP sequence. This preliminary paper presents the Mousterian industries with results from inter-assemblage technological and typological analyses. The observed patterns are based on a sample of 37411 artefacts coming from 14 layers (Table 5.1). Additionally, part of upper unit XX was included in some analyses.

The Middle Palaeolithic sequence (up to 6.5 m thick) is represented by numerous high density occupations (from the top to bedrock throughout layers VI–XX a-g) and is as yet undated (a TL dating program directed by N. Mercier and H. Valladas is in progress). The Early Upper Palaeolithic industry with arched backed blades (Uluzzian) in layer V, which caps the MP, was radiocarbon dated to 40.010 ± 740 BP (GifA-99168) (Koumouzelis *et al.* 2001b). Layer VI was mixed with overlying Uluzzian in the initial test pit (Koumouzelis *et al.* 2001b); however, in another part of the trench a pure Mousterian assemblage was found.

KLISSOURA CAVE SEDIMENTS. MIDDLE PALAEOLITHIC SEQUENCE

The Middle Palaeolithic sequence of the Klissoura cave markedly contrasts with that of the Upper Palaeolithic. The layers of the latter are richer in anthropogenic components, and are looser and very stony. They have a gray to whitish coloration due to high amounts of dispersed calcitic ash and other burnt remains. They are also characterized by well defined clay-hearth structures and superimposed ashy layers (Karkanas *et al.*, 2004;

Tab. 5.1. Klissoura. Sample of middle palaeolithic artefacts

	VI	VII	VIIa	VIII	X	XIb	XII	XIII	XIV	XV	XVI	XVII	XVIII	XIX	Total
chips	1711	1189	1334	1270	820	101	29	82	649	698	1542	1543	4141	493	15602
chunks/fragments	607	0	244	425	297	15	2	13	40	34	64	75	259	19	2094
preforms	0	0	0	0	2	1	1	0	1	0	3	0	2	0	10
cores	36	23	29	43	49	12	17	10	35	19	40	56	148	70	587
flakes	571	705	742	945	1044	287	263	241	638	547	862	1288	4791	1489	14413
blades	41	22	22	20	33	9	17	14	18	14	20	41	439	265	975
tools	103	95	108	240	340	106	89	61	212	150	254	202	1028	677	3665
hammerstones	1	0	0	5	2	0	0	0	2	3	2	1	12	0	28
resharpening flakes	1	0	0	0	7	2	6	2	4	6	6	3	8	4	49
choppers	0	0	0	0	2	0	0	0	1	0	0	0	1	0	4
tested blocks	2	0	0	0	0	0	0	0	0	0	0	5	5	2	14
Total	3073	2034	2479	2948	2596	533	424	423	1600	1471	2793	3214	10834	3019	37441

Koumouzelis *et al.* 2001a, b). In contrast, the upper part of the MPL sequence (layers VII-XV, top to bottom) changes gradually but distinctly to more compacted, brownish or reddish fine-grained sediment with some stony layers towards the back of the cave. These features are the result of the incorporation of higher amounts of clay and other fine-grained clastic materials in the sediment, indicating the dominance of natural processes during the formation of the upper part of the MPL sequence. In addition, the anthropogenic component often appears in the form of discreet sub-layers of multicolored burnt remains in a predominately natural matrix.

Several episodes of natural and anthropogenic sedimenttation are defined in this upper part of the MPL sequence, separated by clear erosional contacts. Layers XI to XIV consist of alternating reddish clay-rich layers and thin, multicolored burnt layers. Most likely, the formation of the clay-rich layers was the result of surface rainwash that deposited clastic material transported from the hills above the cave. Layers XI to XIV also preserve well-developed carbonate crusts due to cementation of the underlying surface, and thus define small gaps in the depositional process. Layer XI is also a multicolored burnt layer that delineates the end of deposition of layers XVI-XI. Part of this sequence was eroded away forming a depression towards the exterior of the rockshelter. The formed discontinuity truncates layers XI and XII. Layers X and IX are locally strongly lithified and have a whitish color with some dark gray to black intercalation, apparently formed when burnt remains were cemented by the action of surface water. Another erosional event formed a trough that truncated all of the previously deposited layers of the upper MPL sequence. The trough runs from the northern profile in the back of the rockshelter to the western profile. The trough is filled with layers XIa and XIb, which are a mixture of burnt remains and natural

sediments showing some stratification. At this point, it is unclear whether this sediment filling represents natural filling, or if the trough was used as a dump. Near the back of the cave the trench filling and the sequence below XI are directly beneath layers VIII to VI, which are the result of a combination of natural and anthropogenic processes. They are mostly clay-rich, with a brownish tint, but are occasionally enriched with burnt remains that give a darker colour to the sediment. It is clear that natural process in the form of rainwash material, catastrophic erosional events, or even secondary alterations by water action are characteristic features of the upper MPL sequence.

The contact between the upper and the lower MPL sequence is locally sharp, bringing in contact totally different sediment types: stone-rich reddish clayey sediment of the upper sequence, and fine-grained gray, silty and ashy sediment of the lower sequence. This difference is probably related to the change of the karstic configuration of the cave. At about the time that layer XV was forming, the back chamber of the cave probably collapsed and became the open chimney present today. Thus, surges of rain water, terra-rossa and roofspall entered the cave and produced the depositional and erosional features of the upper part of the MPL sequence.

The lower MPL sequence (XVI to XX) is highly coherent and fine-grained with signs of post-depositional chemical alteration that become dominant in the lowermost layer, XX. The alteration is in the form of phosphate nodules, and phosphate reaction rims around limestone boulders. There is also a gradual increase in the inclination of the layers towards the entrance from the top to the bottom of the lower MPL sequence.

Layers XVI and XVII consist of alternating gray and whitish ashy sub-layers with considerable lateral continuity. Layer XVIII is brownish-gray, silty, and very rich in bone and lithics. The large amount of artefacts gives almost a stony appearance to the layer. Layer XIX is dark gray, silty and homogeneous. Layers XXa, XXc, and XXf have a considerable amount of burnt remains in the form of whitish and black lenses. In contrast, layers XXa, and XXb are light brownish, silty and less anthropogenic. The lateral variation of XXa is layer XXa1, which is reddish and defined by a considerable terra-rossa component. Layers XXe and XXf are moderately cemented by large amounts of phosphate veins and nodules, which also have a major sand component. Layer XXg is a loose, gray, sandy layer probably forming a cut-and-fill structure inside layers XXe and XXf. Layer XXI is found only towards the eastern wall of the cave, forming a small dark red fan that rests directly on the limestone bedrock of the cave. It consists of terra-rossa with large amount of limestone boulders and gravel with signs of intense phosphate alteration. The contact between layer XXI and the rest of the overlying sequence is a discontinuity, likely reflecting a major environmental change.

Although it is premature to make definite conclusions, it seems that the majority of the MPL sequence was deposited under a more humid climate in relation to the UPL. In particular, the lowermost sand-rich layers seem to have been deposited by running water, probably by the river that is flowing along the gorge of Klissoura and at the time the sediments were deposited was flooding the area close to the cave. This has probably resulted in a rise of the water table that facilitated the observed chemical alteration of the sediments. Phosphate in the alteration features was most likely released by decayed guano present at that time in large amounts in the cave.

GENERAL ARTEFACTS COMPOSITION

The general structure of all Middle Palaeolithic assemblages exhibits the dominance of small debitage/retouching products: chips (<1.5 cm) (usually 30-55% after preliminary count) and small fragments (up to 20%; they are numerous in uppermost layers from X to VII) as well as small flakes. However, chips become less frequent (less than 20%) in industries from the middle part of the MP sequence (XIb, XII, XIII). There is a mostly moderate to rather high presence of tools (from 3.7% to 20%) and some retouching products (re-sharpening flakes) in contrast with the low quantity of cores was documented. In essential counts (without chips, chunks and fragments), flakes dominate (70-83%) over the other categories of lithic artefacts, where tools occupied second position (11-25%; the lowest rate is in upper layers VII and VIIa). The percentages of cores (from 2.3% to 4,4 %) and blades (1.5%-4.4%) are the lowest. While the percentage of cores remains low throughout the entire sequence, blades become more frequent in lowermost layers XVIII and XIX (6.8-10.5%). Tested blocks, chunks (as raw material reserve) as well as hammerstones, knapped pebbles are absent or occurred in very small quantity in several, also

mostly lowermost, layers. The tool to core ratio is high throughout all MP assemblages: from 3.6:1 up to 9.6:1. The blank to core ratio displays also a high level: usually from 20:1 to 35:1; the highest ratios were recorded at the top as well as at the bottom of MP section. Thus, the lithic artefact composition of MP assemblages suggests on-site core reduction, tool production and use. A few differences in artefact composition were documented throughout MP sequence. The most considerable is an increase in blades/bladelets in the oldest MP assemblages.

The radiolarite group dominates in all Palaeolithic layers in Cave 1 (fig. 5.1) and comprises from 60-80% of Middle Palaeolithic assemblages. Flint is always in the second place (15-32%). Other rocks play a minor role in knapping activity (never more than 4%, usually 1-2%). However, in the middle and lowermost layers, limestone and especially quartz were used more often. On the other hand, some rare materials (such as chalcedony) become scarce and occurred in small quantities in the lowermost layers. Nothing changed with respect to quality and quantity of the used materials: small sizes of initial chunks, *plaquettes* and fragments; average quality of most of modified stones which produces many examples of false burin fractures (Siret accident), hinging and breakage. The raw material characteristics (and especially of some types of radiolarite) show a rather high level of diffused bulbs on flakes, which probably gives a wrong impression about the use of soft hammers.

CORES

Three main types of cores are dominant: unidirectional, centripetal and discoidal (Table 5.2) (fig. 5.2:14). Unidirectional flake and blade/bladelet cores (fig. 5.2:12-13) are more numerous (up to 50%) in the uppermost two layers (VII and VIIa) and in the lowermost layers (XV, XVIII and XIX). Often they are transversal with a final invasive broad flake scar present. Rare cores bear traces of preliminary preparation (crest) and a partially turned flaking surface. Platforms normally are plain. Bidirectional cores are scarce, but, however, occurred more frequently in both the upper and lower parts of the sequence (layers VII and XIX).

Blade/bladelet cores are mostly narrow-faced, made on the thin part of a flake or on *plaquettes*. Orthogonal cores appeared in moderate quantity, with some polyhedral items. Centripetal and discoidal cores (in the same proportions or c>d) prevail in the middle part (layer VIII or XIV). Levallois cores occur, as well as intentional flakes, in restricted quantity without a clear tendency of increase throughout the MP sequence. Levallois cores in the uppermost layers are as frequent as in the lowermost, but are more numerous in the middle part. Flake Levallois cores are often lineal (fig. 5.2:1-2) and recurrent. Point and blade cores are rare (fig.5.2:3, 6). Fragmented and non-identifiable exhausted cores are common and abundant in the lowermost layers. The majority of chunks

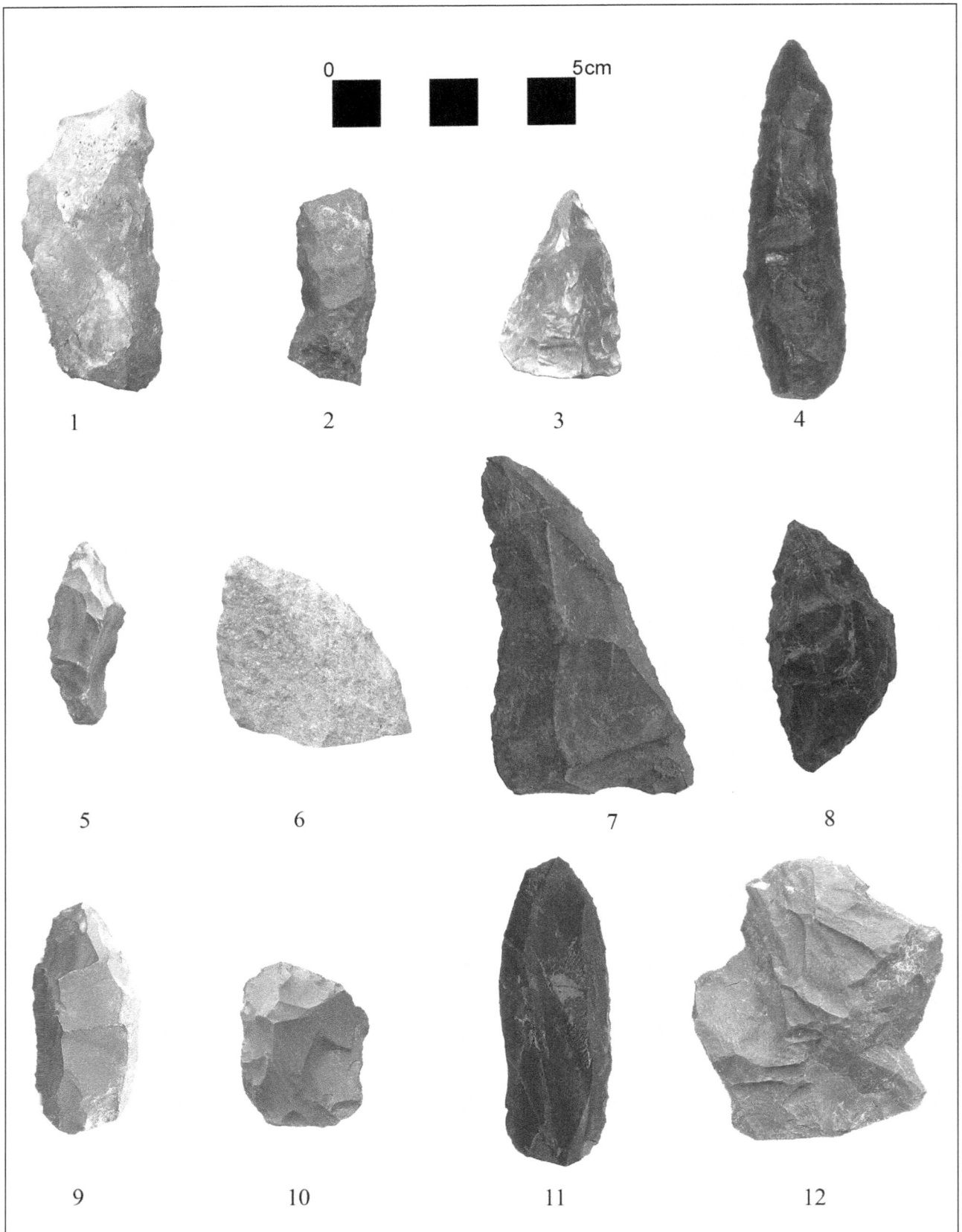

Fig. 5.1. Klissoura. Middle Palaeolithic: *limace* (1, 5), scraper: trapezoidal (2), canted (6, 7), crescent (8), double (9), with distal and back thinning (10), lateral on blade (11), point (3), point on blade (4), Levallois flake (12). Layer X (5), XI (2, 6, 11), XII (7), XIV (1, 3, 8, 9, 10, 12), XIX (4). Chalcedony (1), radiolarite (2, 3, 5, 7-12), flint (4), volcanic rock (6)

Tab. 5.2. Cores

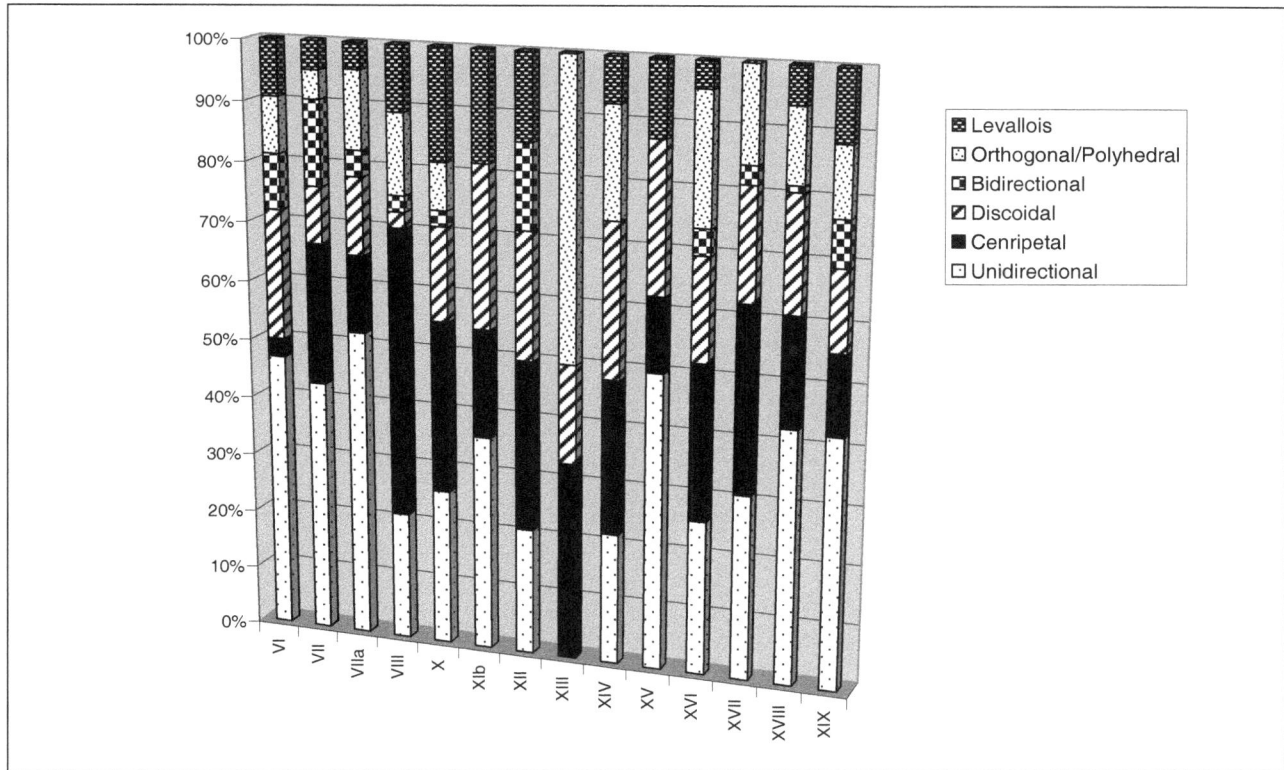

Legend:
- ⊠ Levallois
- ⊡ Orthogonal/Polyhedral
- ◧ Bidirectional
- ▨ Discoidal
- ■ Cenripetal
- □ Unidirectional

FLAKES AND BLADES

are represented by small pieces of raw material. Tested larger items were found only in layers XVII-XIX. Pre-cores are rare and occurred in small numbers in layers X, XV, XVII and XIX.

Blades occurred in a small quantity in most MP layers (VII throughout XVII). The blade index is below 5 (except for layer XII). A considerable increase in the blade/bladelet component was recorded in the three lowermost layers: from 9.7 to 16. For the first time, crested blades (fig. 5.2:11) and flakes appear. An increase in unidirectional cores (mostly exhausted) in these layers corresponds to the high blade composition. On the other hand, dominance of these cores in uppermost layers VII and VIIa (even with the presence of some bladelet cores, 1 and 5 respectively) resulted mostly in flake production.

The majority of flakes are 'non-Levallois' with prevailing of unidirectional and centripetal dorsal pattern. The Levallois Index is low (between 1 and 7) throughout all MP industries. Levallois blanks occurred in all layers in varying but low proportions without a clear quantitative tendency for change. Blades normally have unidirectional scars (fig. 5.2:10); a centripetal pattern is rare, including Levallois blades (fig. 5.2:5). Blank dorsal patterns show, with rare exceptions (VIII), the same tendency as cores.

Parallel (uni-/bi-directional) cores and corresponding flakes are dominant over the centripetal core/flake group (which also includes discoidal and Levallois flake items) in the upper units and vice versa for the middle part (X-IX). Then, after a relative parity in flake dorsal pattern (although centripetal and discoidal cores remain more numerous), parallel flaking became again common. In layer XVIII, the unidirectional pattern (48.7%) clearly dominated over centripetal (10.8%) in comparison with the uppermost layers. The rarity of primary and partially cortical flakes and blades in all assemblages attests to off-site initialisation of debitage. With respect to platform preparation, plain butts dominate in all Mousterian layers (40-60%), with no clear tendency to decrease. Crudely prepared butts (dihedral and polyhedral) remain stable with a slight increase in polyhedral butts in the assemblages in the middle part of a sequence. Fine faceting shows a sudden increase in layer VIII and especially in X, which does not result in a significant rise in IL in layer VIII (what contrasted with X). Afterwards, a gradual decrease of faceted butts via the oldest layers was documented. The assemblage in layer X (and probably the underlying industry in layer XI) appears to be the most 'Levallois' across the Klissoura sequence in terms of platform preparation, Levallois indices, core presence and blank selection. Generally, faceting indices are rather low or medium with the highest value in layer X (IFl=43.1; IFs=28.4). Large faceting, in comparison with strict, displays little change and more stability throughout all layers. The blade and flake butt pattern is usually quite similar. A significant difference was recorded in the oldest MP assemblages. In layer XVIII, for example, faceting was much higher for flakes (IFss=8.4; IFs=16.5; IFl=32.1) than for blades (IFss=3; IFs=7.5; IFl=20.4), whereas plain (58.3% versus 51.8%), linear (10.6% against 3%) and punctiform (17.5% against 1.9%) butts are more common for blades than for flakes. Blades with parallel scars have mostly plain butts (67.9%) and together with linear and punctiforme reach 83.4%, when faceted buts are very rare (4.1%). On the other hand, Levallois blanks are well faceted (IFss=45.6; IFl=86.8), although some plain butts are present (10.8%). The technique of blank production is no surprise: well developed bulbs (> 70%) and obtuse angles (70-90%) attests to use of a hard hammerstone (whose use slightly increased in comparison with the lower units). Blade production in the lowermost industries was also based on the hard hammer technique: lipping is low (2.9%) and diffuse bulbs are less frequent than in any other layer (5% against 11-24.4%).

Most local varieties of stones are responsible for the "microlithic" aspect of the industries and probably for the presence of small blades (together with the application and adoption of various reduction strategies). Artefacts more than 70 mm in size are rare throughout the Middle Palaeolithic sequence (they are often made from quartz, limestone and sandstone). However, e.g., in layer XVIII, artefacts >50-70 mm are more frequent (n=67) than in layer XVII (4). Cores are usually in the smaller category (max. length 68 mm; average less than 35 mm, mostly in between 25 and 32 mm) and they are heavily reduced or were 'naturally' small from the beginning of their reduction. In some cases, unmodified blanks reach 60-70 mm (which is longer than core sizes) but, on average, they are 'microlithic" (20-27 mm long) and smaller than retouched tools (average length: 30-35 mm). A few tested blocks, which were found during excavations, also show small sizes. It appears that 'bigger' unmodified blades and flakes as well as tools, occurred at the bottom of the sequence (XVIII, XIX).

Numerous assemblages of retouched tools, unmodified blanks and debitage waste were found at this cave site. Primary flaking played an important role in the excavated area. Nevertheless, testing and decortication stages took place unquestionably outside this area as is suggested by the low number of cortical items and pre-cores. Debitage products (i.e., mostly flakes) bearing no cortex become even more common in the middle units (from 60-64% to 70-80%).

Thus, according to the general composition, debitage products and metric data, we can conclude that the reduction sequences are not complete. Initial stages are missing as they took place outside the cave. On the other hand we can easily identify the full debitage stages of different methods and especially the final phases of core reduction, exhaustion, abandon and transformation of some cores into tools. Also, pre-forming, retouching, re-

preparation, accidents (fragmentation) and abandon of tools were recorded.

DEBITAGE METHODS

Several co-existing debitage systems were identified in upper layers VII, VIIa, VIII and X (Koumouzelis *et al.* 2001b). They were also used for recurrent flake production during the time-span of the rest of the MP industries: 1) unidirectional recurrent method with no preliminary preparation of flaking surface (direct 'flat' exploitation) and platform (naturally plain or single-blow); accompanying bi-directional and orthogonal mode; 2) discoidal method or conical/bi-conical centripetal method (Sitlivy 1996) uni- and bifacial with secant exploitation; 3) centripetal non-Levallois method with 'flat' non-secant (in a parallel direction with the working surface) exploitation; 4) centripetal recurrent and linear Levallois flake method. The resulting products of the different debitage methods remain the same: broad and some elongated, massive, flakes derived from the unidi-rectional method; short, rather thick flakes, often debor-dant (fig. 5.2:9) with extended prepared butt (discoidal, centripetal non-Levallois methods); preferential flakes with centripetal preparation (fig. 5.1:12; 5.2:4) as well as secondary flakes (fig. 5.2:8) obtained from Levallois lineal or recurrent cores. Platforms were faceted, some-times prepared by single blow. These are the principal methods used throughout the MP sequence of Klissoura cave. The Levallois stra-tegy, however, was less common than unidirectional or discoidal and centripetal. Several additional technologies were recognised: 5) Levallois unidirectional convergent for broad points: sporadically appearing across the entire sequence e.g. in layers VII, XIV and XIX; 6) Levallois recurrent unidirectional for elongated blanks, e.g., in layer VIII and more frequent in the lowermost layers; 7) non-Levallois blade methods: a) direct (with no preliminary shaping) exploitation of flat and partly turned cores with plain non-faceted platforms (mostly reduced uni- rarely bi-directional, narrow-faced or polyhedral cores); b) prepared flaking surface (lateral or central crests) with plain platform formation (rare volumetric cores with crest remnants, however, there is a series of crested blades: two-sloped and lateral). Both modes of core reduction yielded several final blanks: long blades with straight profile, narrow thin or thick with high triangular and trapezoidal section as well as small blades, including bladelets. Blades occurred in restricted numbers in all MP assemblages, however, the prepared volumetric Upper Palaeolithic method was attested only in the lowermost layers (XVIII, XIX, XX), resulting in their productivity.

The MP industries from layer XVII to the Initial Upper Palaeolithic do not exhibit major change in priorities for core reduction (combination of unidirectional and centripetal/discoidal flake methods with some Levallois debitage). Blade production became isolated, occasional with low statistical background presence after a stronger presence at the beginning of the MP sequence in the cave.

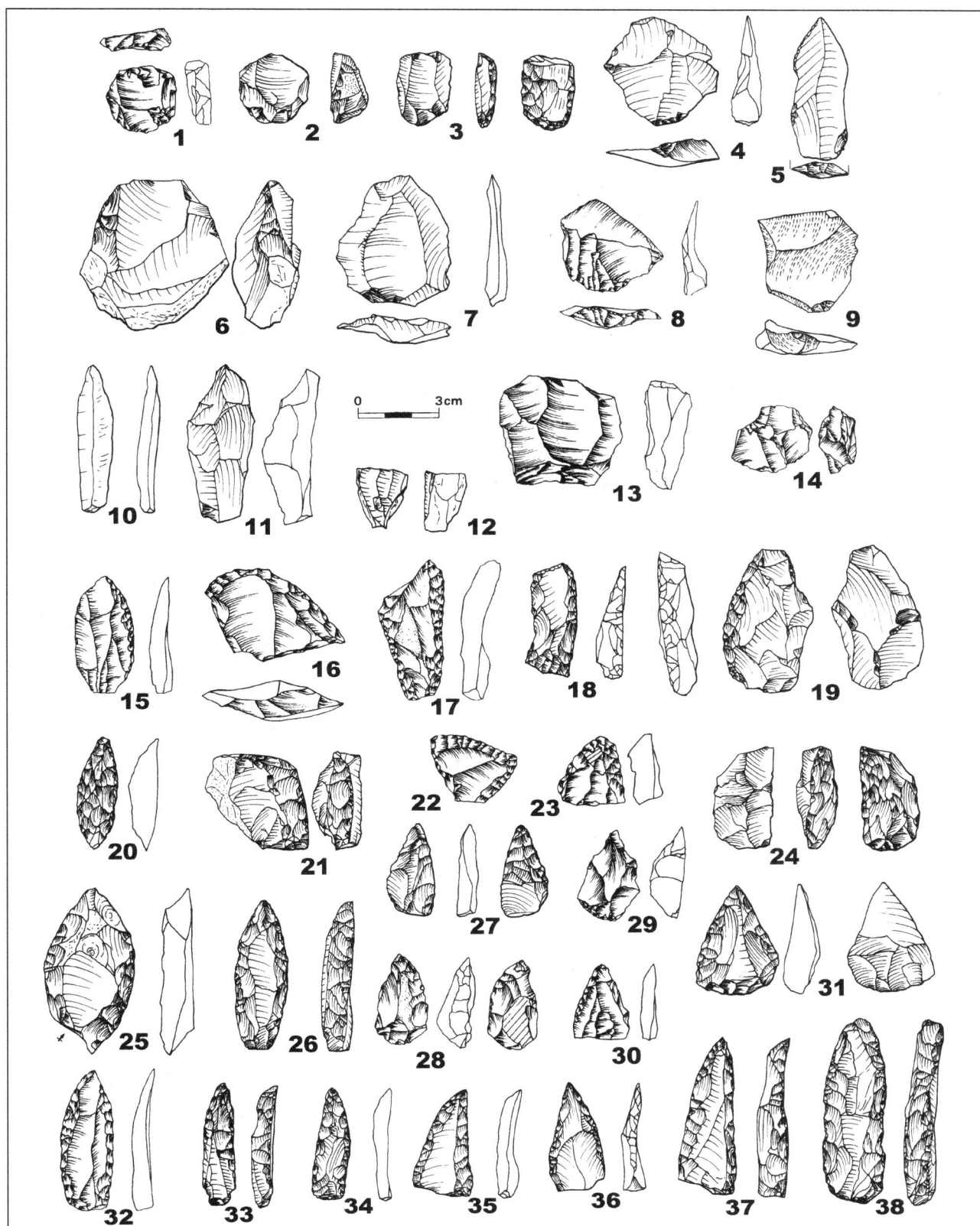

Fig. 5.2. Klissoura. Levallois cores (1-3, 6), flakes (4, 8), blade (5) and point (7), debordant flake (9), blade (10), crested blade (11). Cores: blade/bladelet (12), unidirectional (13), discoidal (14). Scrapers: lateral (15), transverse, Quina (16), double (17), trapezoidal (18), crescent, bifacial (19), *limace* (20), angled, Quina (21), canted (22), convergent (23, 38), crescent, resembling a Pradnik knife (24). Points: leaf-shaped (25), elongated (26, 32-34, 37), Tayac (29), bifacial (27-28), proximally thinned (30-31), asymmetric (35). Layer VII (7, 35), VIII (2-3, 5, 34, 36), X (19, 21, 37-38), XI (5, 9, 28, 30), XII (1), XIII (26, 29), XIV (15-16, 22, 30, 33), XV (24, 32), XVI (18), XVII (12), XVIII (10, 20), XIX (27), XX (25), XXc (11, 31), XXg (6)

TOOLS

As for the raw material structure in tool manufacturing, the first role is played by radiolarite in all layers: not less than 50% and up to 82%. Flint was used in proportions from 11-30%. Other stone (quartzite, chalcedony, limestone, volcanic rock) was episodically modified; however, quartz tools occur in all rich layers. The raw material scale for retouched tool production was normally restricted for these three types i.e., not less variable than in Upper Palaeolithic assemblages (Koumouzelis *et al.* 2001a). Tools of all classes were often produced on small and rather thick flakes. In the case of non-invasive retouch, it is possible to identify the type of blanks selected for tool production. It was usual to choose debordant (e.g. 10-17% in layers XIII-XVI) and asymmetrical (off-axis) short flakes as well as natural backed blanks (fig. 5.2:21) for side-scrapers and backed knives. Primary blanks were used episodically or in restricted quantity (e.g. 2.4% in XI or 7% in XIV and XV). *Plaquettes* of radiolarite were more rarely selected. Reduced cores were also transformed as scrapers (fig.5.2: 3). Modified Levallois blanks occur in small quantities, except in layer X. Blades were selected much more often; the highest level of blade tools (18-23%) was recorded in layers XVIII, XIX and XX as well as gradual decreasing of them via the top. Nevertheless non-Levallois flakes were mostly used for tool production (>77%).

MP layers are still characterised by a small sized tool-kit (average length 30.5-35.5 mm) with a tendency for bigger blanks, especially blades and tools on blades, in the lowermost unit. Tool production was achieved mainly by semi-steep and steep scalar retouch; other kinds of retouch were less often used, e.g., sub-parallel, flat, Quina, bifacial, sometimes plano-convex (fig. 5.2:19) and irregular. However Quina and semi-Quina retouch occurred sporadically, sculpting massive side-scrapers (fig. 5.2:16, 21), *limaces* (fig. 5.1:1, 5; 2:20) and other convergent tools, but especially in the lowermost layers (e.g., 5.3% of all complete tools and 7.6% of scrapers/points in layer XIX). Retouch is typically neither invasive nor heavy. Many tools show insignificant marginal blank modification. Nevertheless, new rich tool samples display examples of covering, unifacial and heavy retouch as well as bifacial pieces (scrapers, points). Heavy modifications often occurred in the lowermost layers. Direct retouching is dominant (e.g. 89.9% in XVI) in Klissoura inventories. Ventral retouch occurs rarely in all layers (e.g. 5.7% in layer XVI and 8.2% in XV as maximum values). Bifacial retouch reaches about 3% (e.g., layers XV and XVI); alternating mode is not common. Various kinds of truncation and thinning (basal, distal back) of side-scrapers (fig. 5.1:10; 5.2:23), knives and especially points (fig. 5.1:3; 5.2:30-31) were observed; however, such tool modifications appeared additional in comparison with a big mass of ordinary scrapers. It seems that tool production, their future reduction and re-use varied according to the initial blank. Ordinary flakes and some blades were used directly or

were partly modified (retouched, thinned, truncated pieces). The majority of such blanks were transformed by means of scaled and marginal retouch into single scrapers, denticulates, etc. Reduction of these tools via multiple items was not significant and resulted in the dominance of simple lateral scrapers. Also, when it is the case, scrapers (even multiple) have light retouch, which slightly modified the initial blank. On the other hand, large and thick flakes and blades (with high section) were intensively reduced by abrupt, steep and Quina, invasive, covering and bifacial retouch into various scrapers (single and multiple), *limaces*, points and some retouched blades. Thus, other kind of modification reduced the mass of the initial artefact, changing or not the initial tool type. In cases of heavy reduction, tools are characterised by off-axis symmetry and disproportional pattern: high sections (*limaces*), extremely wide and short (some canted and transverse scrapers and even points, narrow, elongated with false blade appearance (some double, convergent tools) (fig. 5.2: 18, 38).

Side-scrapers are dominant among the retouched tool types; their ratio is very high (from 63% to 84.7% in essential count without fragments). An increase of the side-scraper percentage and the maximum can be seen in the middle part (layer XIII) when the lowest ratio occurred in the top (VII, VIIa) as well as in the bottom (XVIII, XIX) (Table 5.3). This fact is due to the rather high level of Upper Palaeolithic types (18-16.8%) in the uppermost layers and points, retouched flakes and blades in the lowermost layers. Thus, gradual disappearance of Upper Palaeolithic types of tools in layers VII, VIIa and VIII (end-scrapers, burins, perforators and particularly numerous splintered pieces) and their replacement by an exclusively Mousterian tool-kit from Layer XI (by side-scrapers, points) is well documented. UP tools are absent or occurred only as single pieces in lower layers (XIV-XIX) even when retouched blades appeared in large proportions (XVIII, XIX). Mousterian points were found in all layers (except layer VIIa) after extension of a test pit. They remain in low proportions (1.4-3.7%) and become more representative in layers XVIII (4.7%) and XIX (7.5%). Other types, such as denticulates and retouched flakes, occur in moderate and low amounts (2.6-11.9% and 7-17% respectively). Notches and natural-backed knives are less common. The latter reached 4.4-6.5% in some cases (layers XV-XIX with isolated examples of retouched backed knives). Other types are represented by single items and were found in separate layers: *raclette*, truncated and thinned flakes, *bec*, composite tools, 'chopper'. Unidentifiable tool fragments are common (about 10%) and sometimes reach 25% (layer XVI). Together with other broken tools (especially scrapers and tips from convergent pieces), they are very abundant.

Points

Two main classes of points occurred: Mousterian elongated and short, often massive (fig.5.1:3). Other types

Tab. 5.3. Tools

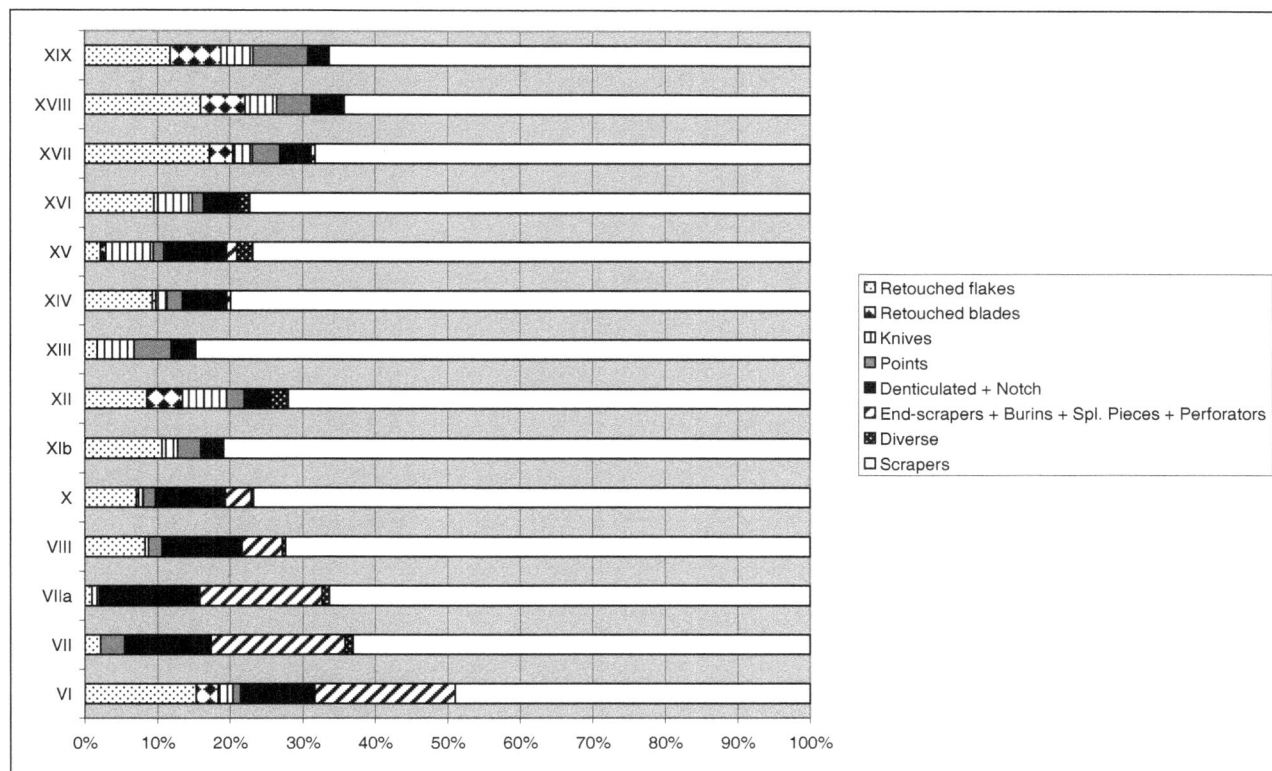

Legend:
- Retouched flakes
- Retouched blades
- Knives
- Points
- Denticulated + Notch
- End-scrapers + Burins + Spl. Pieces + Perforators
- Diverse
- Scrapers

are very rare (Tayac, Quinson). Tayac points occurred as single pieces, e.g., in layers XIII and XIV (fig. 5.2:29). Both Mousterian point categories are subdivided into symmetrical and asymmetrical, even with long retouched convergent edges (lateral and distal points are rare or do not exist) forming different shapes: triangular (fig. 5.2: 36), scalene, *déjeté* (fig. 5.2:35), perforator-like, beak-like, crescent, leaf-shaped (fig. 5.2:25), including bi-pointed. They also vary according to the selected blanks with respective elongation and mass (blades, flakes and even *plaquettes*), as well as to type of retouching: marginal, scalar and steep invasive, Quina, rarely bifacial (fig. 5.2:27, 28) and flat. Some points show distal or basal thinning, ventral or dorsal. Numerous tips were found; however, their precise identification, as well as for some convergent pieces, is not always clear. Different kinds of points were recognised throughout the MP sequence, but all of this variability could be found only in lowermost layers XVIII, XIX and XX.

Scrapers

Single scrapers prevailed over multiple (60-78%) with one low rate in layer VII (52.2%). The ratio of lateral scrapers is high (normally about 40-50% and about 60% in XIV and XVIII and up to 63% in layer X and XIX) (Table 5.4). Their quantity increases progressively throughout the "Upper" units to layer X, showing after several 'ups' and 'downs' to the base. Transverse scrapers are less numerous, but are still frequent (usually about

10% to a maximum of 15-16% in VIIa and XVII). Oblique scrapers occurred in proportions of about 5% and 13-16%. Double side-scrapers are steadily represented by a ratio of about 10-14% with several exceptions: min. 4% (XX) and 6% (XVI) and max. 23% in layer VII. Convergent scrapers are represented by proportions between 2-5% and 10% with the highest rate of 22% in layer XX. Canted (*déjeté*) scrapers have a similar tendency: the first rate is ± 5%, the second is between 9-14%. *Limaces* were not present in all layers, but are very characteristic in the middle and especially in the lower-most layers (1%-2%). The highest rate of convergent and canted scrapers is documented in VIII, XI-XIII layers (± 20%) and in XX (36%, incomplete count). Generally, all together, convergent tools (including points) are rather representative in the Klissoura MP sequence comprising 10-25%. Other scrapers, such as angular (fig. 5.2:21), alternate, truncated-faceted, as well as with continuous, peripheral working edge and sometimes with bifacial retouch, e.g., trapezoidal, rectangular, oval and crescent, are scarce and do not occur in all layers (fig. 5.1:2, 8; 5.2:19, 24). Nevertheless, the latter categories, e.g., crescent scrapers are more frequent in the lower part: from layer XIV to XX. Here some scraper and tool pre-forms appeared, especially in layer XIX. Many layers yielded a high quantity of fragmented scrapers (12-27%) and characteristic re-sharpening flakes. Scraper fragments are absent only in layer XIII (two other tool fragments are, however, present); low proportions (1-5%) are attested in layers VIII, XI, XV and XIX which are

Tab. 5.4. Scrapers

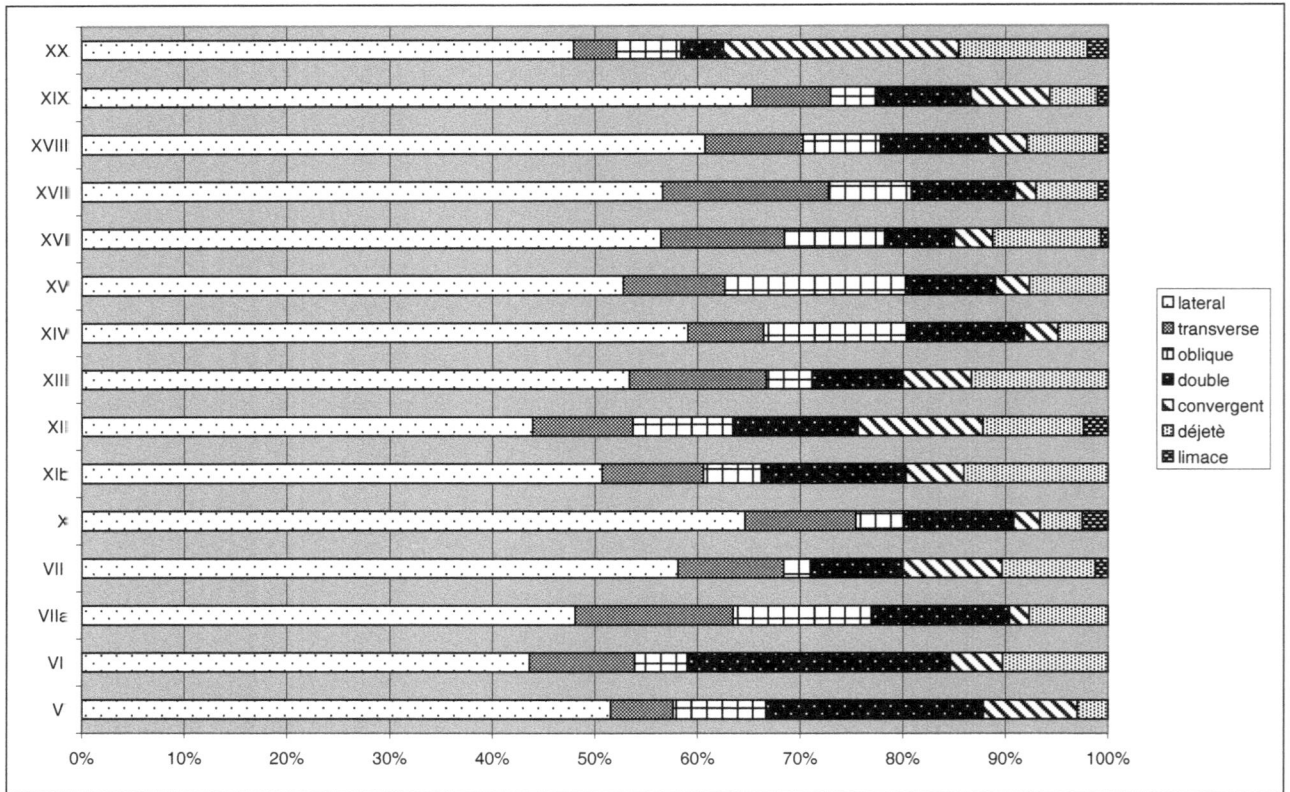

Legend: lateral, transverse, oblique, double, convergent, déjetè, limace

compensated by other abundant tool fragments. The tool fragmentation, which is rather common, can express the high intensity of their use, reduction, re-sharpening and, in some cases, some post-depositional effects, which should be verified.

CONCLUSIONS

The overall impression, which relies on statistics, technology and tool morphology, is the homogeneity and many common features between the MP industries: selection and raw material procurement, "microlithic" sizes incomplete reduction sequences (off-site testing and decortication stage), heavy core and some tool reduction, flat parallel/discoidal/centripetal debitage strategies accompanied by Levallois technologies (preferential flake and recurrent, sometimes point and blade methods), medium/low faceting rates in favour of single-blow platforms, dominance of the Mousterian tool-kit (simple lateral scrapers with a rather important frequency of multiple scrapers and convergent tools, including points), direct scalar semi-steep and steep retouch complemented by some Quina, invasive, bifacial modifications on one hand and thin marginal retouch on the other. Significant differences and change can be observed in: 1) the presence in considerable quantity of Upper Palaeolithic tools, mostly splintered pieces, in the uppermost layers (VI – VIIa and their

disappearance after layer X); 2) the additional parallel use of UP blade/bladelet volumetric prepared (by crest) methods in the lowermost layers (XVIII – XX) together with several flake core reduction strategies, including Levallois. Blade debitage did not result in a real UP tool-kit, except for retouched blades/MP tools on blades. Other techno-typological patterns vary slightly from layer to layer, and are less visible or pronounced. Thus, the uppermost fully MP layers differ from the rest mostly typologically (by a high UP component: splintered pieces), and the lowermost technologically (by UP blade production). Levallois debitage persists throughout the sequence, being statistically more significant in some industries in the middle part of the Mousterian sequence. These facts, apart from many similarities, and taking into consideration recent studies (e.g., Papagianni 2000), do not fit well with the Aspro-chaliko schema, where "micro-Mousterian" covers Levallois-Mousterian. Also, the absence of bifacial pieces at the top of the Klissoura MP sequence and their evidence (even rare) in the lower units contradict the general line of local evolution. In sum, new data recorded from Klissoura Cave 1 and preliminary inter-assemblage comparisons demonstrate significant technological variability, the homogeneity of many industries, some common features with regional in situ MP occupations as well as unique technological and typological features, specific tendencies and changes throughout the long Klissoura sequence.

References

DARLAS, A. (1994) – Le Paléolithique inférieur et moyen de Grèce. *L'Anthropologie*. Paris. 98: 2-3, p. 305-328.

DARLAS, A., LUMLEY de (1999) – Palaeolithic research in Kalamakia Cave, Areopolis, Peloponnese. In BAILEY G.N., ADAM E., PANAGOPOULOU E., PERLÉS C. & ZACHOS K., eds. – *The Palaeolithic Archaeology of Greece and Adjacent Areas. ICOPAG Conference*, Ioannina. 1944, p. 293-302. (London: British School at Athens Studies 3).

KARKANAS, P. *et al.* (2004) – The earliest evidence for clay hearths: Aurignacian features in Klissoura Cave 1, southern Greece. *Antiquity*. 78: 301, p.513-525.

KOUMOUZELIS, M. *et al.* (2001a) – The Early Upper Palaeolithic in Greece: The Excavations in Klissoura Cave. *Journal of Archaeological Science*, 28, p. 515-539.

KOUMOUZELIS, M., *et al.* (2001b) – La fin du Paléolithique moyen et le début du Paléolithique supérieur en Grèce: la séquence de la grotte 1 de Klissoura. *L'Anthropologie*. Paris. 105, p. 469-504.

KYPARISSI-APOSTOLIKA, N. (1999) – The Palaeolithic deposits of Theopetra Cave in Thessaly (Greece). In BAILEY G.N., ADAM E., PANAGOPOULOU E., PERLÉS C. & ZACHOS K., eds. *The Palaeolithic Archaeology of Greece and Adjacent Areas. ICOPAG Conference, Ioannina 1944*. p. 232-239. (London: British School at Athens Studies 3).

PANAGOPOULOU, E., *et al.* (2002-2004) – Late Pleistocene Archaeological and Fossil Human Evidence from Lakonis Cave, Southern Greece. *Journal of Field Archaeology*. 29: 3 and 4, p. 323-349.

PAPACONSTANTINOU, V.S. (1988) – *Micromousté-rien: les idées et les pierres. Le Micromoustérien d'Asprochaliko (Grèce) et le problème des industries microlithiques du Moustérien*. Nanterre. Thèse de Doctorat de l'Université Paris X, 2 t.

PAPAGIANNI, D. (2000) – *Middle Palaeolithic Occupation and Technology in Northwestern Greece. The Evidence from Open-Air Sites*. Oxford. BAR International Series. 882.

SITLIVY, V. (1996) – Le Paléolithique moyen ancien: variabilité technologique, typologique et fonctionnelle en Europe. *Préhistoire européenne*. Liège. 9, p. 117-155.

LE PALÉOLITHIQUE SUPÉRIEUR DANS LA PÉNINSULE DU MANI (PÉLOPONNÈSE, GRÈCE)

Andréas DARLAS

Ephorie de Paléoanthropologie-Spéléologie de la Grèce du Nord, Navarinou 28, 55131 THESSALONIKI, GRÈCE,
andreas.darlas@eps.culture.gr

Eleni PSATHI

Ephorie de Paléoanthropologie-Spéléologie de la Grèce du Sud, Ardittou 34B, 11636 ATHÈNES, GRÈCE

Abstract: *Very numerous caves are opened on the western coast of Mani peninsula (Peloponnese, Southern Greece), containing Upper Pleistocene fillings rich in archaeological material. In this paper, six of them (Kolominitsa, Kastanis, Skoini 4, Skoini 3, Tripsana, and Melitzia) are presented, in which test pits have been carried out and brought to light remains dated to the Upper Palaeolithic. Kolominitsa cave contains aurignacian levels, while in all the other caves the excavated levels have yielded gravettian–epigravettian material. The faunal study shows the progressive replacement of fallow deer (Dama dama) by red deer (Cervus elaphus) and, more generally, subsistence changes from Middle to Upper Palaeolithic.*
Keywords: *Greece, Mani, Upper Palaeolithic, lithic industries, fauna*

Résumé: *Sur la côte occidentale de la péninsule du Mani (Péloponnèse, Grèce méridionale) s'ouvrent des très nombreuses grottes contenant des remplissages du Pléistocène supérieur, riches en matériel archéologique. Dans cette note sont présentées 6 grottes (Kolominitsa, Kastanis, Skoini 4, Skoini 3, Tripsana, et Melitzia), dans lesquelles des sondages effectués ont mis au jour des vestiges du Paléolithique supérieur. La grotte de Kolominitsa contient des couches de l'Aurignacien, alors que dans toutes les autres grottes, les couches fouillées ont livré du matériel appartenant au Gravettien-Epigravettien. L'étude faunique a mis en évidence le remplacement progressif du bouquetin (Dama dama) par le cerf élaphe (Cervus elaphus) et, de façon plus générale, des changements de subsistance par rapport au Paléolithique moyen.*
Mots-clés: *Grèce, Mani, Paléolithique supérieur, industries lithiques, faune*

INTRODUCTION

Le Paléolithique supérieur de Grèce reste encore très peu connu (cependant mieux connu que le Paléolithique inférieur et moyen). Les premiers gisements du Paléolithique supérieur furent fouillés en Epire (NO de la Grèce) dans les années 1960 par E. Higgs: la grotte de Kastritsa et l'abri d'Asprochaliko (Higgs & Vita-Finzi 1966; Bailey *et al.* 1983). La première a livré une séquence importante du Gravettien-Epigravettien, alors que le deuxième a livré deux ensembles du Paléolithique moyen surmontés par un ensemble du Paléolithique supérieur (Gravettien-Epigravettien). Plus tard, dans les années 1990 et toujours en Epire, ont été fouillés les abris de Klithi (Bailey 1997) et de Boïla (Kotjabopoulou *et al.* 1997), qui ont livré de nombreux vestiges du Paléolithique final. En Thessalie, des couches du Paléolithique supérieur ont été mises au jour dans la grotte de Théopetra (Adam 2000). Il s'agit apparemment d'un Epigravettien, bien qu'une distinction précise des couches n'ait pas été faite.

Des couches du Paléolithique supérieur ont été également fouillées dans la grotte de Seïdi, en Grèce centrale (Schmidt 1965). En Péloponnèse, la grotte de Franchthi a livré la séquence la plus complète du Paléolithique supérieur, allant de l'Aurignacien au Mésolithique (et au Néolithique), avec un important hiatus du XXème au XIIIème millénaire (Perlès 1987). Non loin de Franchthi, la grotte de Kephalari a livré des couches du Paléolithique supérieur (Reisch 1980). Dans la même région, la Grotte 1 de Klissoura, fouillée récemment, a donné une séquence très importante, allant du Paléolithique moyen au Mésolithique (Koumouzelis *et al.* 1996; 2001). Le Paléolithique supérieur y débute avec une phase de transition (Paléolithique supérieur archaïque), qui précède l'Aurignacien (trois phases), l'Epigravettien et le Mésolithique.

Dans ce contexte, la localisation d'un grand nombre de grottes contenant des remplissages avec des vestiges du Paléolithique supérieur dans la péninsule du Mani, à l'extrémité méridionale de la Grèce continentale, s'avère très importante.

LA PÉNINSULE DU MANI

Le Mani occupe l'une des trois péninsules du Sud du Péloponnèse (Grèce du Sud), celle du milieu, qui constitue le prolongement de la chaîne montagneuse de Taÿghetos. Cette dernière prend naissance au centre du Péloponnèse et se termine au cap Tainaron, le point le plus méridional de l'Europe continentale. Toute la péninsule est constituée essentiellement par des calcaires marmoréens d'âge Crétacé supérieur-Eocène inférieur (Thiébault 1982).

De très nombreuses grottes, appartenant à un vaste réseau karstique, s'ouvrent sur les falaises verticales, hautes de plusieurs dizaines de mètres dominant le rivage tout au long de la côte occidentale (Bassiakos 1993). Elles sont pour la plupart de petites cavités, de quelques dizaines de mètres de profondeur. Elles s'ouvrent au niveau de la mer actuelle, voire un peu plus haut.

LA RECHERCHE ARCHÉOLOGIQUE

Des recherches antérieures dans les petites grottes d'Apidima avaient mis au jour deux crânes d'hominidés fossiles, qui pourraient être attribués à des prénéandertaliens, ainsi qu'une sépulture féminine, très probablement du Paléolithique supérieur (Pitsios 2000). La grotte de Kalamakia a livré de nombreux vestiges du Paléolithique moyen, associés à des restes de néandertaliens (Darlas & de Lumley 2004).

Un programme de recherche mis en place ces dernières années a conduit à la localisation de très nombreuses grottes contenant des vestiges paléolithiques. En effet, des remplissages pléistocènes ont été reconnus dans plus de 50 grottes. Dans la plupart de cas il ne s'agit que de lambeaux de remplissages, ces derniers ayant été démantelés par la remontée de la mer holocène. Assez nombreuses sont cependant les grottes qui ont conservé leur remplissage entier ou en grande partie. Des sondages ont été effectués dans certaines de ces dernières, afin de constater si elles contiennent des vestiges archéologiques, ainsi que de donner une première estimation de leur âge. En règle générale, ces sondages ont été très restreints, aussi bien en superficie qu'en profondeur, puisque leur objectif n'était pas de traverser toute la stratigraphie (exception faite d'un seul site), mais d'atteindre uniquement les couches supérieures[1].

Ici sont présentées seulement les grottes qui ont livré des vestiges du Paléolithique supérieur. Les recherches étant très récentes, cette note est préliminaire; son but est simplement de présenter ces nouveaux sites et les premiers éléments qui en proviennent, ainsi que de signaler la grande densité de sites de cette période. Ces gisements constitueront, par la suite, l'objet de recherches systématiques et détaillées, qui permettront une meilleure étude du Paléolithique supérieur de la péninsule du Mani, et plus généralement de la Grèce du Sud.

Du Nord vers le Sud, les grottes dans lesquelles des sondages ont été effectués, sont: Kolominitsa, Kastanis, Skoini 4 (et Skoini 3), Tripsana et Melitzia (fig. 6.1). Elles sont toutes situées dans la baie d'Itylon et plus au nord. Elles s'ouvrent dans les falaises verticales dominant une terrasse Tyrrhénienne (qui longe le bord de la mer) ; des éboulis, accumulés pendant la dernière période glaciaire au pied de la falaise, forment un talus qui conduit à l'entrée de ces grottes.

KOLOMINITSA

La grotte de Kolominitsa s'ouvre vers l'ouest, à 22 mètres de hauteur et à 100 mètres du bord de la mer, au milieu d'une très haute falaise verticale, au sommet de la pente formée par les éboulis. C'est une grande cavité de 10 m de largeur, 12 m de hauteur et environ 40 m de profondeur.

Cette grotte contient un épais remplissage. Les couches supérieures (de plus de 3 m d'épaisseur) ont été démantelées dans la plus grande partie de la grotte. Ce n'est qu'au fond que ces couches sont conservées, riches en vestiges archéologiques. Ainsi, dans la partie médiane et antérieure de la grotte, les couches les plus profondes se sont trouvées en surface et constituent le sol actuel.

Le sondage, effectué sous le porche de la grotte, est arrivé à 94 cm de profondeur (en enlevant 10 couches); il n'a pas atteint la base du remplissage, dont nous ne connaissons pas l'épaisseur totale. Dans toute la hauteur du sondage le remplissage est constitué par des dépôts argilo-sableux, de couleur gris beige, avec de rares cailloux.

Les couches inférieures (10-9) du sondage ont livré des artefacts qui ne sont pas incontestablement caractéristiques du Paléolithique supérieur. Les couches 8 à 5 (ainsi que 3) ont livré une industrie aurignacienne. Il faut noter qu'un charbon de bois de la 6ème couche, daté par [14]C (AMS), a donné un age 33.870±550 BP (Beta – 193416). Les couches supérieures (1-2) ont livré une industrie contenant des lamelles à dos.

Les couches supérieures du sondage avaient été perturbées par une fosse contenant de la céramique de la période classique[2].

Au fond de la grotte, où les couches supérieures (non fouillées) du remplissage sont conservées jusqu'à 3 mètres de hauteur, une lamelle à deux bords abattus fut recueillie sur le front de la coupe naturelle.

Industrie lithique

L'industrie lithique est assez abondante (1183 pièces) dans toutes les couches du sondage (fig. 6.1). Elle est faite sur différentes matières premières, principalement du jaspe rouge, des silex des couleurs diverses et du quartz. Il faut signaler l'absence (quasi totale) de l'andésite à oligoclases ("pierre de Krokeès"), une roche très caractéristique et abondante chez toutes les industries du Paléolithique moyen du Mani. A partir de la troisième couche du sondage, les couches inférieures ne contiennent plus de jaspe rouge, mais du silex marron et noir (en fait il s'agit d'un quartzite à grain extrêmement fin). En règle générale, les matières premières ne sont pas de très bonne

---

[1] Dans tous les cas, les sondages avaient une superficie de 1 m[2] et ont procédé par l'enlèvement de couches arbitraires, épaisses de 5-10 cm. Les terres ont été tamisées dans un tamis avec une maille de 5 mm.

[2] Cette fosse témoigne que la troncature du remplissage est bien antérieure de la période classique, puisque la surface de la troncature était déjà formée à cette époque.

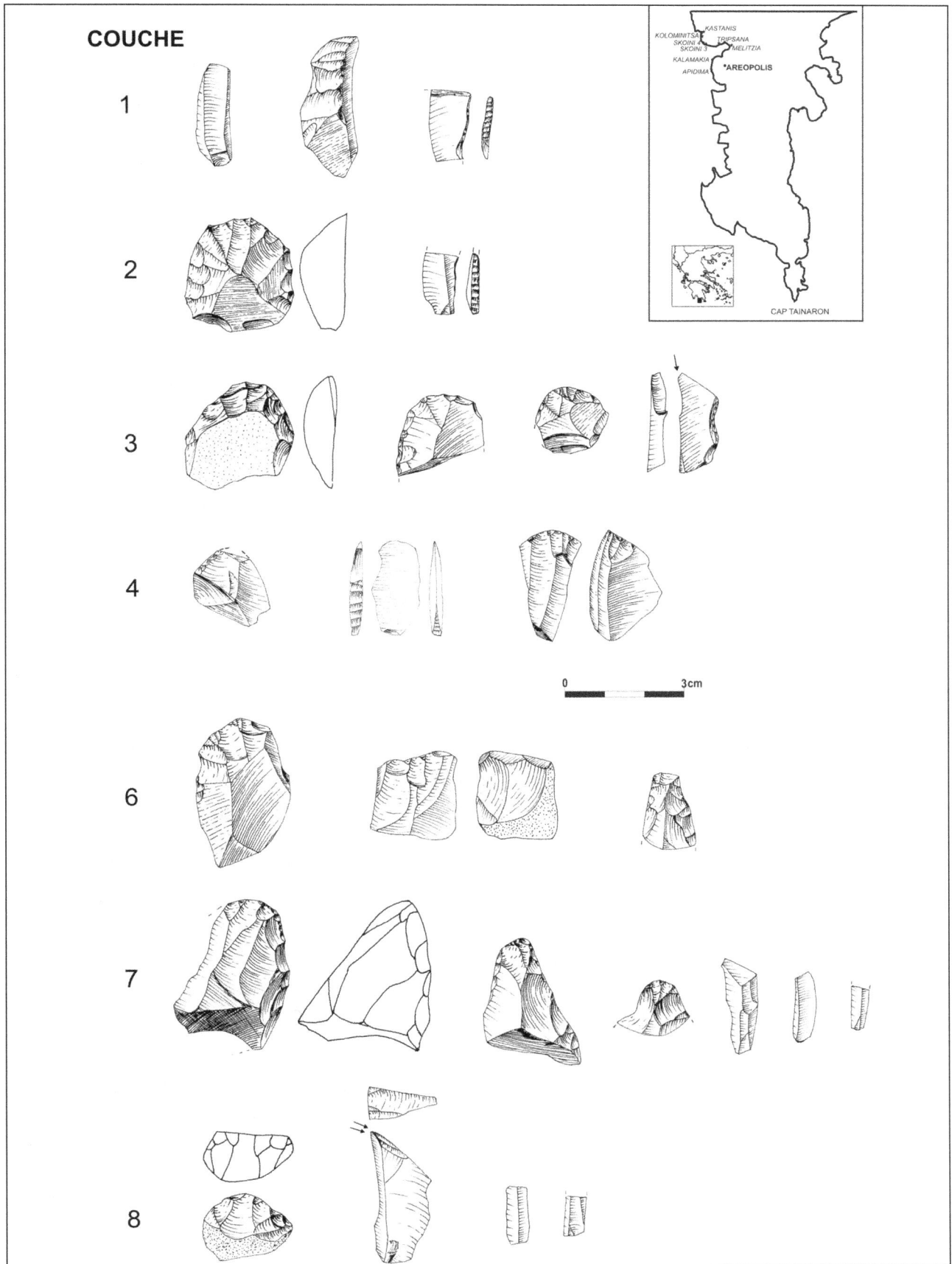

Fig. 6.1. En haut à droit: Sites paléolithiques sur la côte occidentale de la péninsule du Mani.
Reste de la page: outillages lithiques de la grotte de Kolominitsa

qualié. Elles se présentent en morceaux de petites dimensions, alors qu'elles contiennent de nombreux plans de clivage, qui constituent des zones de faiblesse et empêchent leur exploitation régulière. Les artefacts sont, en général, très petits (surtout les outils retouchés). Les produits du débitage sont dominés par les éclats ; les lames sont pratiquement absentes, alors que les lamelles sont peu représentées. Les nucléus à lamelles, néanmoins, sont assez nombreux et de bonne facture. Il faut noter également la présence constante des pièces esquillées dans toutes les couches.

L'industrie des couches supérieures (1-2), caractérisée par les lamelles à dos, se range comme une industrie "gravettoïde", sans pouvoir donner plus de détails, à cause du petit nombre de pièces.

Les couches 3 (et surtout 5) à 8 ont livré une industrie aurignacienne, caractérisée par les grattoirs aurignaciens (carénés et museaux épais), qui sont cependant de petites dimensions. Les lamelles sont présentes, toujours sans bord abattu. Une lamelle à dos découverte dans la couche 4 pourrait s'être infiltrée provenant par des couches supérieures.

Les couches 9 et 10 ont livré des vestiges bien moins nombreux. Il faut noter l'absence des lames, lamelles et d'autres artefacts caractéristiques du Paléolithique supérieur. A l'exception d'une pièce esquillée, les racloirs constituent les seuls outils retouchés. Il faut noter cependant que l'image générale de cet ensemble n'est pas celle d'une industrie du Paléolithique moyen. Une fouille future doit examiner l'éventualité d'être en présence d'une industrie de transition.

Minerai de fer

Toutes les couches ont livré des morceaux (14 pièces au total) de minerai de fer (hématite). La plupart d'entre eux sont en état naturel, alors que quelques rares pièces sont "taillées" et se présentent sous forme d'éclats ou "galets taillés". Cette roche, qui vient du mont Taÿghetos, se retrouve à quelques kilomètres de la grotte, sous forme de "galets" peu arrondis, plus petits que 7-8 cm. Néanmoins, il faut signaler que cette roche est totalement absente des sites du Paléolithique moyen. Par contre, sa présence est constante et systématique dans les couches du Paléolithique supérieur de tous les sites (voir ci-dessous). Il est très probable qu'il a eu servi d'ocre, si l'on tient compte du fait que sa surface donne une couleur rouge, quand deux morceaux sont frottés l'un contre l'autre.

Matériel osseux

Les restes osseux sont abondants (3238 dont 461 déterminés). Ils appartiennent aux taxons suivants: *Ursus* cf. *arctos*, *Canis* cf. *lupus*, *Lepus europaeus*, *Sus scrofa*, *Capra* sp., *Cervus elaphus*, *Dama dama* et *Capreolus capreolus*.

La plupart du matériel appartient aux cervidés et ensuite au bouquetin. Parmi les restes de cervidés, le daim est le mieux représenté. Bien que le matériel ne se prête pas à tirer des conclusions définitives, on remarque que les pourcentages des espèces principales (bouquetin, cerf, daim et chevreuil) oscillent, avec ceux du cerf présentant une tendance inverse de celle des trois autres espèces, de la base vers le sommet du sondage. Cette variation de pourcentages pourrait être attribuée à des facteurs climatiques ou aussi à des changements des stratégies de chasse. Les traces d'origine anthropique sont présentes, mais peu fréquentes, exception faite de traces de feu : entre 25% et 90% des restes de chaque couche sont brûlés. Enfin, quelques traces de carnivores ont été aussi observées. Cependant, l'ensemble du matériel est d'origine anthropique.

Outillage osseux

La fouille a livré quatre spécimens:

– La couche 3 en a livré deux; le premier est un fragment de diaphyse qui porte des stries de façonnage d'une pointe. Le deuxième est l'extrémité d'une pointe façonnée sur un fragment osseux carbonisé; on y observe des stries de façonnage.

– La couche 6 a livré une partie de pointe de bois brûlé de cervidé, fendue et avec les deux bords sciés verticalement.

– La couche 7 a livré une pointe façonnée sur un bois de cervidé.

Mollusques

La fouille a livré de nombreux mollusques, dont la plupart sont terrestres. Il faut signaler la haute fréquence des coquilles de *Helix pomatia* dans la première couche (NMI =33). Elles sont moins fréquentes dans la deuxième (NMI =17), alors que dans les couches inférieures sont beaucoup plus rares.

KASTANIS

Très près de Kolominitsa se trouve la petite et peu profonde grotte de Kastanis, qui contient un remplissage pléistocène. Dans ce cas aussi, la troncature du remplissage a laissé en surface les couches archéologiques, qui constituent le sol actuel. Un très petit sondage fut ouvert: 30x40 cm et à peine 15 cm de profondeur.

Malgré le caractère très restreint du sondage, la grande densité de vestiges archéologiques est apparue. La première couche a livré 63 artefacts lithiques et la deuxième 56; ils sont taillés sur des silex divers et du quartz (mais non sur andésite). Les deux ensembles sont caractérisés par la présence des lamelles à dos. Il faut noter que la première couche a livré de nombreux mollusques terrestres *Helix melanostoma* (NMI=13). Le matériel faunique contient les taxons suivants: *Canis* sp., *Vulpes vulpes, Lepus europaeus, Cervus elaphus, Capra* sp. On souligne l'abondance des restes de lièvres, ainsi que ceux d'oiseaux.

SKOINI 4

Au cap Skoini, environ 500 mètres au Sud de Kolominitsa (en sortant de la baie d'Itylon vers le Nord) s'ouvrent quatre grottes, petites et peu profondes. Les deux d'entre elles, les plus méridionales, ont subi l'action des vagues de la mer, alors que les deux autres conservent plus ou moins la totalité de leur remplissage. C'est dans la dernière de ces grottes, la plus septentrionale et la plus petite, appelée Skoini 4, qu'un sondage fut ouvert.

Skoini 4 est une petite cavité de 6 m de profondeur, 4 m de largeur et 2,5 m de hauteur qui s'ouvre vers l'ouest, à 27 mètres de hauteur et à 60 mètres du bord de la mer. Elle s'ouvre au milieu de la falaise verticale, au sommet de l'éboulis.

Le sondage est arrivé à 85 cm de profondeur. Sur toute sa hauteur, des couches de cendres successives ont été mises au jour, presque sur toute la superficie du sondage. Au fond, une série de pierres (qui se poursuivait en dehors des limites du sondage) a été mise au jour, sans doute partie d'une "construction" anthropique. Un charbon de bois prélevé à cette profondeur a été daté par ^{14}C (AMS) donnant un age 26.240±200 BP (Beta–193419).

Sur la surface du remplissage furent récoltés des vestiges néolithiques et paléolithiques mélangés. En fait, les couches pléistocènes étaient initialement surmontées par des couches holocènes contenant des vestiges du Néolithique récent. Cependant, le remplissage étant exposé aux intempéries (vu la petite profondeur de la grotte), les couches supérieures ont été tronquées, laissant sur la surface de troncature leur contenu: un mélange de vestiges du Paléolithique supérieur et du Néolithique.

Par ailleurs, dans les couches supérieures en place, deux sépultures néolithiques (l'une intacte, l'autre très peu conservée), ainsi qu'une fosse aux parois revêtues de pierres ont été mises au jour. La fosse contenant la sépulture intacte avait été ouverte dans les couches paléolithiques; la sépulture elle-même avait été couverte avec ces mêmes terres, contenant des restes paléolithiques.

Cependant, il faut noter que ni les sépultures ni la fosse n'ont livré d'éléments de datation. Le seul élément disponible reste la céramique récoltée en surface, caractéristique du Néolithique récent.

Industrie lithique

L'industrie lithique est abondante (1389 pièces). Elle est faite sur des roches diverses, plus ou moins les mêmes que celles de Kolominitsa. Il s'agit de différents types de silex et plus rarement de quartz, alors que quelques artefacts en andésite restent anecdotiques. De nombreux artefacts sont taillés en silex de couleur marron, a grain très fin et de texture homogène. En général, l'industrie lithique reste homogène à travers toute l'épaisseur du sondage. Le débitage lamellaire caractérise l'industrie bien qu'il ne soit pas dominant. Il a donné aussi bien des lames que des lamelles. Il faut noter le nombre important des nucléus à lamelles. Le matériel représente toutes les étapes du débitage et de la retouche: lames à crête, plaquettes de ravivage du plan de frappe, lames et lamelles, brutes et retouchées (fig. 6.2A).

Il s'agit d'une industrie gravettienne. Les lamelles à dos sont les outils les plus caractéristiques. Il faut noter encore la présence des pointes à cran, de très bonne facture. En même temps, il faut noter l'absence totale de microlithes géométriques et de la technique du microburin.

Hématite

Toutes les couches du sondage ont livré des pièces d'hématite (34 au total).

Matériel osseux

Les restes osseux sont nombreux (2202 dont 342 déterminés) et appartiennent aux taxons suivants: *Vulpes vulpes*, *Felis silvestris*, *Lepus europaeus*, *Sus scrofa*, *Capra* sp., *Cervus elaphus*, et *Dama dama*. La plupart du matériel appartient aux herbivores et surtout aux cervidés. Il est à signaler que le cerf domine nettement sur le daim. En général, les pourcentages du cerf sont au moins deux fois plus élevés que ceux des autres herbivores. Le bouquetin est présent dans toutes les couches, mais toujours avec peu de restes.

Les restes osseux sont en général très fragmentés (cependant moins fragmentés qu'à Kolominitsa) et brûlés (plus de 30% dans toutes les couches; dans la deuxième couche leur pourcentage atteint 83%). Enfin, la présence de nombreux fragments de bois de cervidés est à noter.

Outillage osseux

Parmi les restes récoltés en surface figure une pointe de bois de cervidé partiellement brûlé. Des stries longitudinales sont observées sur sa surface, sans doute pour le façonnage d'une sagaie ou d'un poinçon.

SKOINI 3

Environ à 20 mètres plus au Sud et à la même hauteur avec la grotte précédente s'ouvre la grotte de Skoini 3, dont le remplissage n'est pas tronqué et conserve son épaisseur d'origine. Pour cette raison un petit sondage fut ouvert ici, afin d'examiner les couches sommitales. Ce sondage a mis au jour une double sépulture néolithique, à

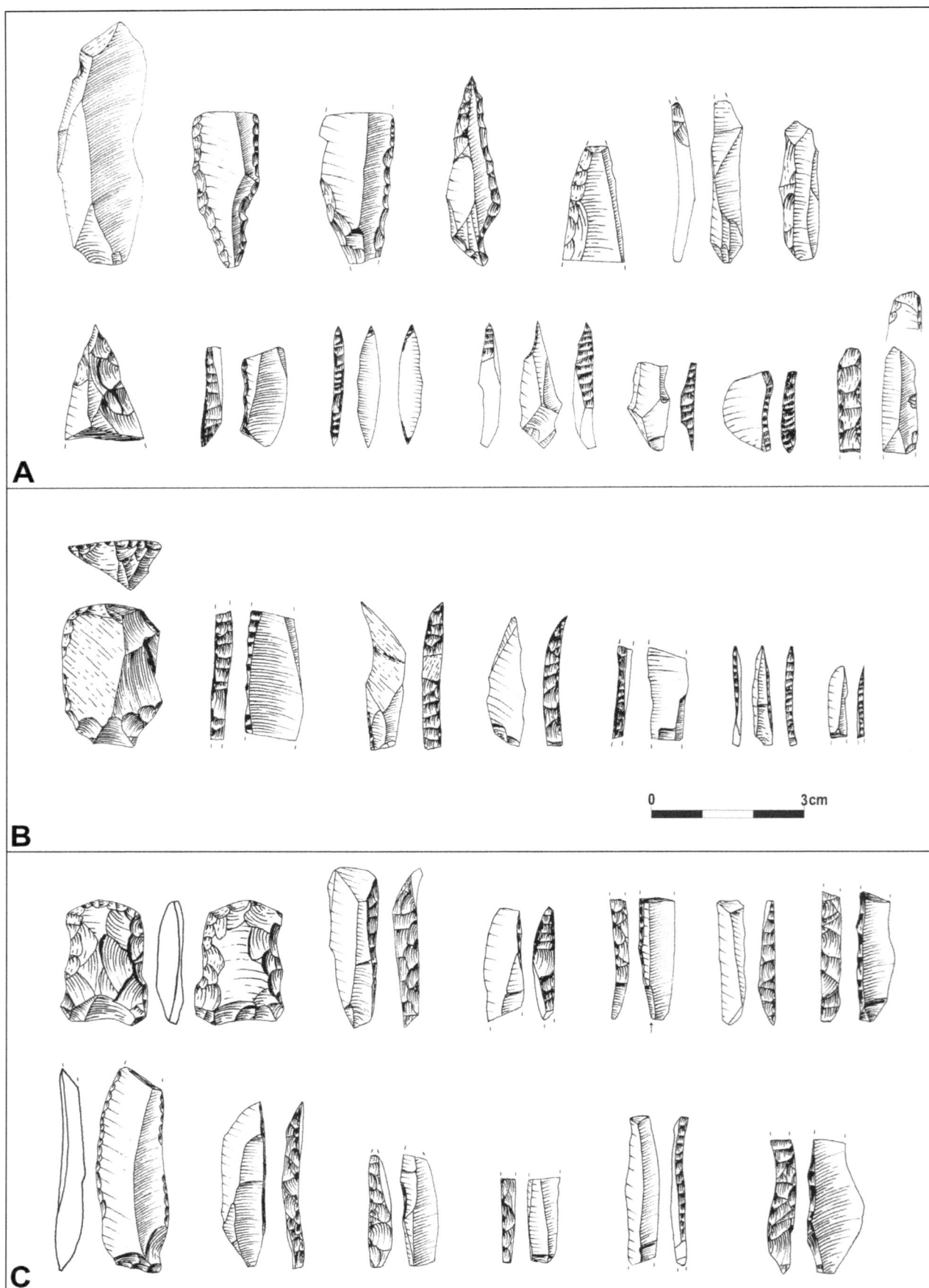

Fig. 6.2. Outillages lithiques des grottes: A. Skoini 4; B. Tripsana; C. Melitzia

peine à 15 centimètres de profondeur. Au dessous de la sépulture, les couches pléistocènes étaient extrêmement pauvres en matériel archéologique, témoignant ainsi que cette grotte n'avait été utilisée que très rarement, à l'inverse de sa voisine. Un charbon de bois, prélevé à 77 cm de profondeur, fut daté par ^{14}C (AMS), donnant un age de 25.560±190 BP (Beta – 193418). Au dessous de cette profondeur quelques rares artefacts furent récoltés, parmi lesquels figurent quelques lamelles à dos et lamelles retouchées.

TRIPSANA

Cette grotte se situe sur la côte septentrionale de la baie d'Itylon. Elle s'ouvre vers le Sud, à 100 mètres du bord de la mer et à 15 mètres environ de hauteur, au milieu d'une falaise verticale, au sommet de l'éboulis accumulé au pied de cette dernière. Il s'agit d'une très petite grotte, de 2,5 m de largeur, 3 m de hauteur et 4 m de profondeur.

Ici, dans le cadre d'une fouille de sauvetage, deux sondages ont été ouverts, qui sont arrivés jusqu'au sol rocheux: le sondage A, vers le fond, est arrivé à 160 cm de profondeur et le sondage B, sous le porche, est arrivé à 130 cm de profondeur.

Le remplissage contenait deux couches archéologiques principales (pas très riches en vestiges); le reste du remplissage contenait des vestiges sporadiques. Des quantités importantes de matériel archéologique ont été récoltées en surface, accumulées par des animaux fouisseurs.

A 1 mètre environ sous le sol actuel, les parois convergent et la grotte devient très étroite. Il est alors évident que cette dernière était à l'origine trop étroite pour être habitable. Plus tard, avec le dépôt des sédiments et la remontée du sol (environ 80 cm plus bas que le sol actuel) sa superficie a atteint ses dimensions actuelles (environ 2,5x4 m) et se prêtait pour accueillir un petit group humain.

Industrie lithique

Le matériel lithique (269 pièces) est nettement moins abondant que le matériel osseux (1826 pièces). Il constitue un ensemble lamellaire attribué à une industrie "gravettoïde" (fig. 6.2B). Les outils les plus caractéristiques sont les lamelles à dos. Par ailleurs, il faut noter que les microlithes géométriques et les microburins sont totalement absents. Il faut noter encore la présence d'artefacts en andésite, avec une fréquence plus élevée que chez les industries précédentes (mais pas très élevée).

Matériel osseux

Les restes osseux (1826 dont 948 déterminés) appartiennent aux taxons suivants: *Vulpes vulpes*, *Felis* sp., *Martes* sp., cf. *Mustela*, *Lepus europaeus*, *Canis* cf. *lupus*, *Canis* sp., *Sus scrofa*, *Capra* sp., *Cervus elaphus* et *Dama dama*. Parmi les mammifères de grande taille, ce sont le cerf et le bouquetin qui dominent, suivis par le daim, alors que le lièvre est présent en quantité non négligeable, mais surtout dans le matériel de surface. Nombreux sont, enfin, des restes d'oiseaux, eux aussi surtout en surface.

Les caractéristiques du matériel (fragmentation à l'état sec, fragments allongés, altérations du cortex) indiquent une exposition prolongée des ossements aux conditions atmosphériques. Ces caractéristiques, associés au très faible pourcentage d'os brûlés, indiquent une utilisation très espacée et restreinte de la grotte par les hommes. Cela est dû, sans doute, aux petites dimensions de la grotte.

Outillage osseux

La fouille a livré 5 fragments d'outils:

- 3 proviennent du matériel de surface: un fragment trièdre diaphysaire, partiellement brûlé, avec des stries de façonnage, une pointe avec des stries de façonnage, et un fragment de diaphyse présentant une série d'enlèvements corticaux ("retouche") sur un bord latéral.

- 2 proviennent du sondage A: un fragment de bois de cervidé (couche 14) fendu et scié verticalement ainsi qu'une pointe (couche 2) portant des stries de façonnage.

Mollusques

Les mollusques, terrestres et marins, sont assez nombreux. On note, en particulier, une grande valve de *Pecten jacobaeus*, dans la 5ème couche du sondage A. Elle était cassée sur place, mais pratiquement tous ses fragments ont été retrouvés et remontés.

MELITZIA

La grotte de Melitzia est située au fond de la baie d'Itylon. Elle s'ouvre vers l'Ouest à 350 mètres du bord de la mer et à 64 mètres au-dessus de son niveau actuel. Elle est constituée d'une grande salle de 20x20 mètres, alors que son entrée est de 2x2 mètres.

Un sondage fut ouvert à l'intérieur de la grotte, à 6 mètres de l'entrée, qui est arrivé à 130 cm de profondeur. La partie supérieure (70 cm), constituée des terres remaniées avec du fumier, contenaient des vestiges des périodes historiques. Ensuite, les dépôts pléistocènes, argiles plastiques rouges avec de rares cailloux, contenaient des vestiges du Paléolithique supérieur. Le sondage avait au sommet une superficie de 1x1 m, mais progressivement fut rétréci par un pilier stalagmitique. Au fond, il n'était plus que 25x40 cm. Il est à noter que nous ne disposons pas encore de datations issues de ce sondage.

Industrie lithique

Le matériel lithique (322 pièces) est de bonne qualité. Il est caractérisé par la haute fréquence des lamelles à dos (fig. 6.2C). Il faut noter encore la fréquence élevée de pièces en andésite. En fait, il s'agit de la seule industrie lithique du Paléolithique supérieur de Mani où l'andésite atteint un pourcentage comparable à celui du silex. A noter dans ce cas aussi, l'absence totale de microlithes géométriques et de microburins.

Hématite

Quelques pièces de minerai de fer sont également présentes.

Matériel osseux

Les restes osseux (1155 dont 440 déterminés) appartiennent aux taxons suivants: *Canis* sp., cf. *Canis*, *Vulpes vulpes*, *Mustelidae*, *Lepus europaeus*, *Sus scrofa*, *Capra* sp., *Cervus elaphus*. On ajoute, aussi, de nombreux restes d'oiseaux. Les restes du cerf dominent, suivis par ceux du bouquetin, alors que les autres espèces sont très peu représentées.

Les restes osseux sont fragmentés, mais pas intensivement. Leur surface corticale présente des traces d'origine climato-édaphique, moins prononcées et moins fréquentes que chez le matériel de Tripsana. Les traces de carnivores sont négligeables, alors que les traces d'origine anthropique sont nombreuses. Enfin, les os brûlés sont peu nombreux.

En général, le matériel est moins fragmenté en comparaison avec celui de Kolominitsa et Skoini 4, et le moins altéré de tous les échantillons présentés ici. Ceci indique éventuellement une utilisation moins intense de ce lieu ou une meilleure protection du matériel vis à vis la dégradation (intérieur de grotte, enfouissement rapide, plus d'humidité). Enfin, en tenant compte de la dominance des restes du cerf, il est possible que ce site avait connu une utilisation saisonnière, peut-être pour la chasse ce cet animal.

Mollusques

Il faut noter la fréquence très élevée des mollusques terrestres (*Helix melanostoma*), surtout dans les trois premières couches de la fouille.

CONCLUSIONS

Les recherches dans la péninsule du Mani ont conduit à la localisation de nombreuses grottes qui contiennent des vestiges archéologiques. Nombreuses sont celles qui ont préservé un remplissage pléistocène. Cependant, beaucoup plus nombreuses, sont celles qui ont été plus ou moins vidées par la remontée de la mer holocène, étant donné qu'elles s'ouvrent près de son niveau actuel. Les sondages effectués ont mis au jour des couches riches en vestiges du Paléolithique supérieur.

Les sites sondés couvrent toutes les phases du Paléolithique supérieur. La plupart d'entre eux appartiennent au Gravetien-Epigravettien, alors qu'un seul site, Kolominitsa, a livré des vestiges de l'Aurignacien. Toutefois, il faut souligner que les sondages sont de faible profondeur et n'ont pas traversé toute l'épaisseur du remplissage (à l'exception de Tripsana).

Malgré les petites quantités de vestiges mis au jour, des caractères généraux des industries lithiques apparaissent. Presque dans tous les cas, les artefacts sont de petites dimensions, le nombre de lames et de lamelles est petit, bien que ces produits soient les plus caractéristiques. Toutes les industries sont caractérisées par la présence des lamelles à dos, à l'exception de l'Aurignacien de Kolominitsa. Dans tous les cas, il faut souligner l'absence totale de microlithes géométriques et de la technique du microburin. En absence d'un nombre suffisant de datations absolues, nous ne pouvons pas encore affirmer si cette absence constitue un caractère local ou si, en fait, les industries sont bien antérieures du Paléolithique final. Un autre trait caractéristique est la présence ou non de l'andésite. Ce dernier est une roche d'origine lointaine, mais qui est constamment présente au sein de toutes les industries du Paléolithique moyen du Mani; or, chez les échantillons du Paléolithique supérieur étudiés ici on constate que cette roche est pratiquement absente des sites en dehors de la baie d'Itylon, mais, à l'inverse, qu'elle est présente dans les cas des sites à l'intérieur de la baie (elle trouve sa fréquence la plus élevée dans la grotte de Melitzia).

Il faut encore noter la présence constante de morceaux d'hématite. Cette roche, très lourde, pourrait être utilisée en tant que percuteur; cependant il semble plus probable que les hommes préhistoriques se servaient de sa propriété de produire de la matière colorante rouge (ocre). Ainsi, s'explique mieux la présence de petits nodules de cette matière (sorte de "crayons").

La faune de grands mammifères se présente appauvrie en espèces chez les grottes présentées ci-dessus, par rapport aux données obtenues pour le Paléolithique moyen de la même région (fouilles systématiques de la grotte Kalamakia; Darlas et de Lumley 2004). Un bon nombre d'espèces carnivores et de pachydermes, identifiées à Kalamakia, ne figurent plus chez les sites du Paléolithique supérieur. Chez ces derniers, on note également deux autres phénomènes intéressants concernant les associations fauniques: d'abord le daim, particulièrement abondant pendant le Paléolithique moyen dans la région, se raréfie progressivement au profit du cerf élaphe. Ensuite, parmi les espèces de petite taille, on note l'augmentation sensible des restes de lièvre, ainsi que d'oiseaux. A l'état actuel de la recherche, on ne peut pas soutenir les causes exactes de ces changements fauniques, lesquels pourraient être recherchés à l'évolution climatique de la dernière partie du Pléistocène supérieur et aux différents modes de subsistance des hommes paléolithiques.

Quand à la question du mode d'occupation des sites présentés ici, les données fauniques distinguent les grottes de Kolominitsa et de Skoini 4 de celles de Tripsana et de Melitzia. L'aspect général du matériel (fragmentation intense, grands pourcentages de restes brûlés) suggère une utilisation plus systématique et intense des deux premières. Chez les deux autres, la fragmentation moins intense, la rareté d'indices de feu, ainsi que l'abondance de restes altérés par une exposition prolongée en surface, indiquent, au contraire, des passages humains moins fréquents et de durée plus courte.

En conclusion, les résultats de ces recherches dans la péninsule du Mani sont très encourageants. L'entreprise des fouilles systématique à l'avenir devrait donner bien plus de renseignements sur le Paléolithique supérieur en Péloponnèse du Sud et, de façon plus générale, enrichir nos connaissances sur le Paléolithique en Grèce.

References

ADAM, E. (2000). The Upper Palaeolithic and Mesolithic Stone Assemblages of Theopetra Cave and their Contribution to an Assessment of Site Use During the Late Pleistocene and Early Holocene. In KYPARISSI-APOSTOLIKA, N. (ed.), *Theopetra Cave. Twelve years of excavation and research 1987-1998*, 163-171, Athens.

BASSIAKOS, E.J. (1993). *Dating of fossils from caves and speleothems: evidence from Electron Spin Resonance (E.S.R.) technique, the study of underground karst morphology and the relevant radiometric and geological conditions in speleoenvironments of Dyros, Mani.* Ph. D, University of Athens (en grec).

BAILEY, G.N., CARTER, P.L., GAMBLE, C.S., HIGGS, H.P. (1983). Asprochaliko and Kastritsa: Further Investigations of Palaeolithic Settlement and Economy in Epirus (North-West Greece). *Proceedings of the Prehistoric Society* 49, 15-42.

BAILEY G.N. (ed.) (1987). *Klithi: Palaeolithic Settlement and Quaternary Landscapes in Northwest Greece*, McDonald Institute for Archaeological Research, Cambridge.

DARLAS, A., DE LUMLEY, H. (2004). La grotte de Kalamakia (Aréopolis, Grèce). Sa contribution à la connaissance du Paléolithique moyen de Grèce. *XIVème Congrès UISPP, Liège, 2-8 Septembre 2001. Actes de la 5ème Section: Le Paléolithique moyen*, 225-233. BAR International Series 1239.

HIGGS, E.S., VITA-FINZI, C. (1966). The Climate, Environment and Industries of Stone Age Greece: Part II. *Proceedings of the Prehistoric Society* 32, 1-29.

KOTJABOPOULOU E., PANAGOPOULOU E., ADAM E. (1997). The Boila Rockshelter: a Preliminary Report. In BAILEY, G.N. (ed.), *Klithi: Palaeolithic Settlement and Quaternary Landscapes in Northwest Greece*, 427-437, McDonald Institute for Archaeological Research, Cambridge.

KOUMOUZELIS, M., KOZLOWSKI, K.J., NOWAK M., SOBCZYK, K., KACZANOWSKA M., PAWLIKOWSKI M., PAZDUR A. (1996). Prehistoric settlement in Klissoura Gorge, Argolid, Greece (excavations 1993, 1994). *Préhistoire Européenne* 8, 143-173.

KOUMOUZELIS, M., GINTER, B., KOZLOWSKI, J.,K., PAWLIKOWSKI M., BAR-YOSEF, O., ALBERT, R.M, LITYNSKA-ZAJAC, M., STZORZEWICZ, E., WOJTAL, P., LIPECKI, G., TOMEK, T., BOCHENSKI, Z.,M., PAZDUR A. (2001). The Early Upper Palaeolithic in Greece: The Excavations in Klissoura Cave. *Journal of Archaeological Science* 28, 515-539.

PERLÈS, C. (1987). *Les industries lithiques taillées de Franchthi (Argolide, Grèce): Tome I, présentation générale et industries paléolithiques*. Indiana University Press, Bloominghton.

PITSIOS, Th. K. (2000). *The Tainarius Man*, Athens (en grec).

REISCH, L. (1980). Pleistozän und Urgeschichte des Peloponnes (non publié). Habilitationschrift, Friedriech-Alexander Universität Erlangen, Nürberg.

SCHMID, E. (1965). Die Seïdi-Höhle eine jungpaläolitische Station in Griechenland. *IVe Colloque International de Spéléologie*, Athènes 1963, 163-174

THIEBAULT, F. (1982). Évolution géodynamique des Hellénides externes en Péloponnèse méridional (Grèce). *Publications de la Société Géologique du Nord 6*.

ENVIRONNEMENT VEGETAL DES NEANDERTALIENS DE LA GROTTE DE KALAMAKIA (AREOPOLIS, GRECE)

Vincent LEBRETON

Département de Préhistoire, Muséum national d'Histoire naturelle, UMR 5198 CNRS
1 rue René Panhard, 75013 Paris, France, lebreton@mnhn.fr

Eleni PSATHI

Ephorie de Paléoanthropologie-Spéléologie de la Grèce du Sud, Ardittou 34B, 11636 Athènes-Grèce, Greece,
epsathi@hotmail.com

Andreas DARLAS

Ephorie de Paléoanthropologie-Spéléologie de la Grèce du Nord, Navarinou 28, 55131 Thessaloniki-Grèce,
andreas.darlas@eps.culture.gr

Abstract: Kalamakia Cave (Areopolis, Greece) has yielded Neanderthal remains associated with numerous archaeological Middle Palaeolithic artefacts. Pollen analyses from speleothems synchronous of the prehistoric occupation provide palaeoenvironment information for the surrounding area. A dry episode is recorded with the mesophilous trees gradually being replaced by the herbaceous and some Mediterranean presteppic forest taxa. Faunal assemblages are consistent with pollen data and define the same landscape features. Archaeozoological study will enable to know whether Fallow Deer and Ibex overrepresentations are natural or related with specific game developed by Neanderthals.
Keywords: palynology, speleothem, palaeoecology, Upper Pleistocene, Neanderthal, Greece

Résumé: La grotte de Kalamakia (Aréopolis, Grèce) a livré des restes humains néandertaliens associés à des vestiges archéologiques du Paléolithique moyen. Les analyses palynologiques de spéléothèmes contemporains de l'occupation préhistorique précisent les paléoenvironnements autour du site. Un épisode d'aridité enregistre le retrait des arbres mésophiles au profit de la strate herbacée et des éléments de la forêt présteppique méditerranéenne. Les assemblages fauniques convergent avec l'étude palynologique pour caractériser le milieu. Les études archéozoologiques permettront de savoir si la surreprésentation du Daim et du Bouquetin est naturelle ou le reflet d'une chasse spécialisée développée par les Néandertaliens.
Mots-clés: palynologie, spéléothème, paléoécologie, Pléistocène supérieur, Néandertal, Grèce

INTRODUCTION

En Grèce continentale, les gisements du Paléolithique moyen documentant l'occupation d'un territoire par les Néandertaliens sont encore limités (Darlas 1994, 1998). Parmi les sites importants, l'abri Asprochaliko en Epire (Bailey *et al.* 1983; Huxtable *et al.* 1992) et la base de la grotte 1 à Klissoura en Argolide (Koumouzelis *et al.* 2001a, 2001b) ont livré une industrie moustérienne où le débitage non-levallois prédomine et où se note une tendance à la microlithisation (Koumouzelis *et al.* 2001b). Dans la péninsule du Mani, au sud du Péloponnèse, une dent de *Homo neanderthalensis* découverte sur le gisement de Lakonis serait associée à des niveaux archéologiques du Paléolithique supérieur initial (Harvati *et al.* 2003). A l'ouest du Mani, le site d'Apidima a livré deux crânes appartenant à des Prénéandertaliens tardifs ou à des Néandertaliens archaïques en association avec des assemblages fauniques du Pléistocène moyen (Harvati & Delson 1999). A quelques kilomètres au nord d'Apidima, les fouilles entreprises dans la grotte de Kalamakia ont mis au jour des restes humains néandertaliens et des vestiges fauniques du Pléistocène supérieur dans des niveaux archéologiques livrant une industrie moustérienne (Darlas & Lumley 1998).

Pour cet article, nous rapportons les premiers résultats des analyses palynologiques entreprises à la grotte de Kalamakia (Lebreton 1997; Lebreton *et al.* 1998), complétés de nouvelles données. L'étude de l'environnement des populations néandertaliennes au Pléistocène supérieur est un champ d'investigation pour comprendre la disparition de cette espèce d'hominidé du continent européen pendant la dernière période glaciaire. Les découvertes de nouveaux sites moustériens sont autant d'opportunité de mettre en œuvre des analyses palynologiques pour reconstituer ces environnements. Malgré la difficulté inhérente aux processus taphonomiques affectant la pluie pollinique en contexte archéologique, il reste parfois possible de caractériser les biotopes occupés par les hommes préhistoriques. Par exemple, l'analyse pollinique d'échantillons prélevés sur des spéléothèmes formés en milieu karstique enregistre un signal local reflétant l'environnement immédiat autour d'un site (Lebreton *et al.* 2007). Quand la formation des spéléothèmes est contemporaine des niveaux archéologiques, les spectres polliniques révèlent alors la composition de la végétation développée au moment de l'occupation préhistorique. Les informations paléoécologiques livrées par la palynologie contribuent ainsi à la discussion sur les modes de subsistance de ces chasseurs cueilleurs néandertaliens.

CADRE DE L'ETUDE

La grotte de Kalamakia (36°40' N, 22°22' E) s'ouvre en bord de mer sur la bordure occidentale de la péninsule du Mani à 2 km au nord-ouest de la ville d'Aréopolis (Fig. 1). La péninsule maniote est marquée par l'influence maritime, seulement atténuée dans l'arrière-pays par des reliefs modérés. Le Makrilakkoma culmine à 892 m, 5 km à l'est du site. Les paramètres climatiques sont caractéristiques du milieu méditerranéen. En basse altitude près du littoral, les conditions climatiques sont clémentes toute l'année. La saison estivale est chaude, avec des températures moyennes autour de 25°C. En hiver les températures oscillent entre 5 et 10°C et les gelées sont rares. Les hivers et les printemps sont pluvieux. Toutefois le couvert végétal est adapté à une longue période de sécheresse estivale. La végétation de la péninsule du Mani, développée sur des sols érodés superficiels, se rattache à l'étage thermoméditerranéen (Quezel & Barbero 1985). Les structures de végétation se rattachent à l'alliance *CERATONIO-RHAMNION OLEOIDIS*, avec des formations préforestières à *Ceratonia siliqua*, *Pistacia lentiscus*, *Myrtus communis*, *Olea europaea* subsp. *sylvestris* et localement *Quercus coccifera*, *Q. calliprinos* ou *Laurus nobilis*. Autour d'Aréopolis, la présence de *Q. coccifera*, au sein d'un couvert dense à *Euphorbia dendroides*, souligne la dégradation de l'alliance *CERATONIO-RHAMNION OLEOIDIS*, en partie liée à l'activité humaine.

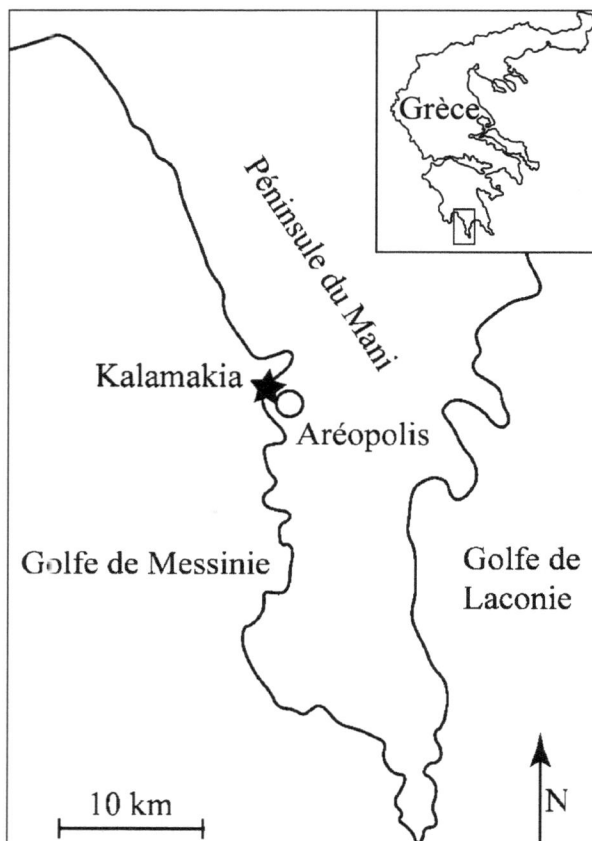

Fig. 7.1. Localisation de la grotte de Kalamakia

La grotte de Kalamakia appartient à un important réseau karstique creusé dans les calcaires marmoréens du Sénonien supérieur (Papavassiliou 1984). Des sédiments détritiques et des spéléothèmes constituent le remplissage quaternaire de la grotte (Lumley & Darlas 1994). Sept unités stratigraphiques furent initialement définies (Fig. 7.2). L'unité I, supposée la plus ancienne, est un imposant pilier stalagmite formée à l'entrée de la grotte. Elle fut définie comme un plancher stalagmitique de base. L'unité II est une plage fossile tyrrhénienne constituée de galets et coquilles marins fixés dans une matrice argileuse concrétionnée. Cette plage est contemporaine de la formation marine de la baie de Dyros, plus au sud, où *Strombus bubonius* est présent (Lumley & Darlas 1994). Ce fossile marqueur est associé à la période de haut niveau marin du stade isotopique 5e en Méditerranée centrale (Ferranti *et al.* 2006). Les unités III, IV, V et VI sont des dépôts continentaux sablo-argileux. Les niveaux archéologiques apparaissent essentiellement dans les unités III et IV. Quelques rares vestiges sont également présents dans l'unité VI. L'étude des vestiges archéologiques révèle que le site était occupé par des Néandertaliens moustériens, chasseurs spécialisés au vu de la prédominance du daim et du bouquetin dans les assemblages fauniques (Darlas & Lumley 1998). Des difficultés méthodologiques ne permettent pas encore une datation précise de ces niveaux archéologiques. Les dates U/Th et ESR ne sont pas cohérentes et reproductibles, même si tous les âges obtenus placent le site dans le Pléistocène supérieur (Voinchet & Darlas 1998). L'unité VII est constituée de petites stalagmites formées localement sur le sommet du remplissage et définie comme plancher stalagmitique supérieur.

Les fouilles archéologiques dans les unités stratigraphiques III et IV ont montré que la position stratigraphique du pilier stalagmitique de base était incorrecte. Comme d'autres petits spéléothèmes trouvés dans les unités III et IV, la base de la stalagmite de l'unité I se place dans l'unité III. Cette découverte implique que ce spéléothème s'est construit pendant le dépôt des sédiments argilo-sableux des unités III et IV. En conséquence, certaines lamines de la stalagmite sont contemporaines des niveaux archéologiques. Elles se sont formées pendant l'occupation du site par les Néandertaliens. Ainsi, l'enregistrement pollinique dans ces spéléothèmes est une source potentielle supplémentaire d'information paléoécologique pour reconstituer l'environnement de ces populations préhistoriques.

MATÉRIEL ET METHODE

Une campagne exhaustive de prélèvements a été mise en œuvre sur l'ensemble des sédiments quaternaires remplissant la cavité. Le traitement chimique des échantillons est standard avec les attaques successives à HCl, HF et KOH (Sittler 1955). Pour les échantillons carbonatés, l'attaque initiale à HCl est plus longue.

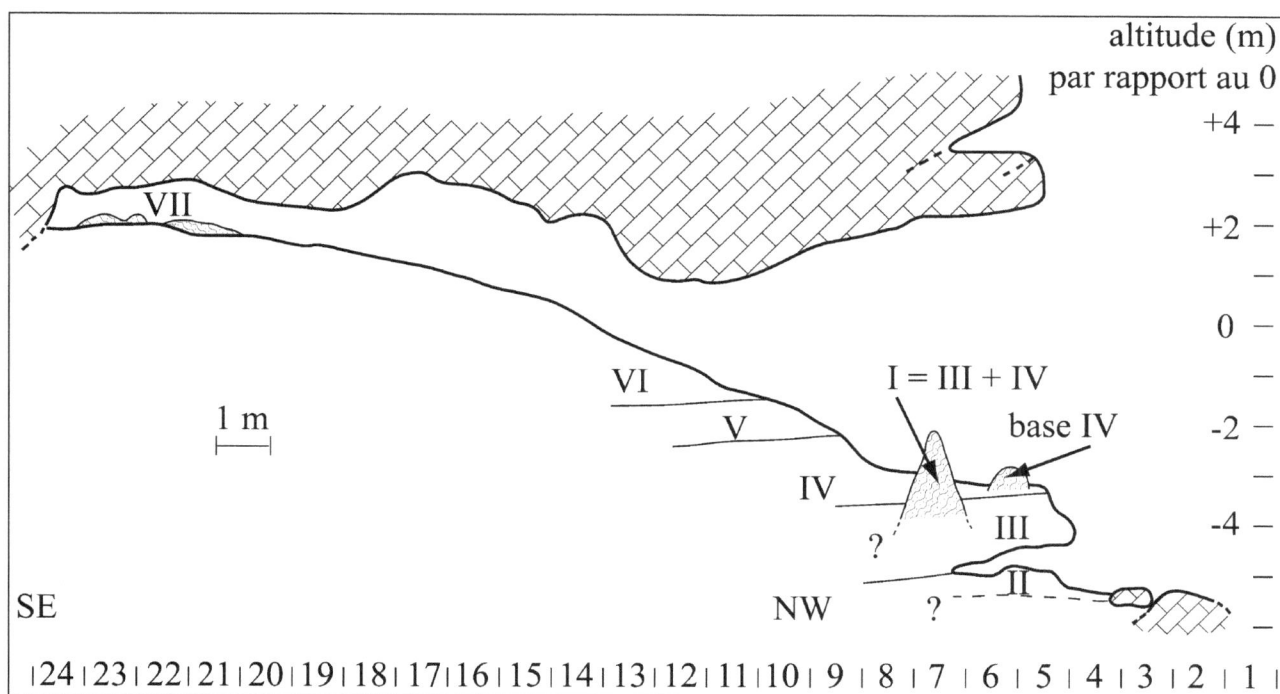

Fig. 7. 2. Unités stratigraphiques de la grotte de Kalamakia

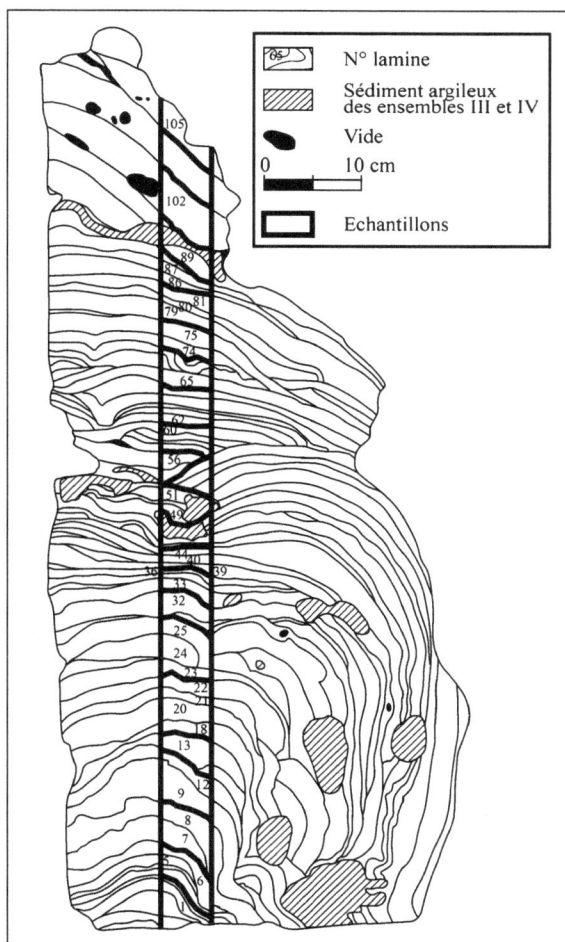

Fig. 7.3. Echantillonnage du pilier stalagmitique de l'unité 1 (modifié d'après Lecervoisier, 2003)

Les échantillons des dépôts continentaux sablo-argileux des unités stratigraphiques III, IV, V et VI sont stériles. La couleur rougeâtre des sédiments est le témoin d'une intense oxydation post-dépositionnelle. Les processus taphonomiques intenses liés à cette oxydation ont détruit l'intégralité du matériel pollinique originel.

Par contre, l'analyse de deux échantillons d'un petit spéléothème de la base de l'unité IV montre la conservation du signal pollinique. Il en est de même pour le pilier stalagmitique (unité I ou désormais III) qui a été échantillonné en suivant les lamines de croissance du spéléothème (Fig. 7.3). Un même échantillon peut regrouper plusieurs lamines quand celles-ci sont trop fines pour être séparées. De plus, les concentrations sporopolliniques étant très faibles, il a parfois été nécessaire de regrouper les comptages d'échantillons contigus et présentant des signaux similaires pour obtenir un spectre pollinique. Une pluie pollinique fossile est aussi enregistrée dans le sédiment concrétionné de la plage tyrrhénienne (unité II). Si pour ces échantillons carbonatés et concrétionnés la concentration est faible, la conservation du matériel pollinique est par contre bonne et la diversité taxonomique est importante, supérieure à 30 taxons par échantillon. Pour le sédiment concrétionné de plage, cela signifie que même sans processus taphonomiques intensifs, le flux pollinique est mal enregistré en terme quantitatif. Pour les échantillons carbonatés, l'enregistrement pollinique est à rapprocher du fonctionnement du karst. L'épikarst peut partiellement retenir le matériel pollinique. Le karst joue alors un rôle de filtre quantitatif expliquant les concentrations faibles. Mais ce filtre n'est pas qualitatif. Il ne semble pas que des taxons soit sélectivement retenus plus que d'autres, au vu de la

Tab. 7.1. Spectre pollinique du sédiment concrétionné de la plage tyrrhénienne (unité 2)

Arboreal Pollen (AP=37%)	Non Arboreal Pollen (NAP=63%)
Ephedra t. fragilis 7%	Amaranthaceae/Chenopodiaceae 3%
Pinus 9%	Apiaceae <1%
Pistacia <1%	Asteraceae type-échinulé 15%
Corylus 1%	Asteraceae type-fenestré 27%
Quercus type-pedunculata/pubescens 4%	Artemisia 6%
Quercus type-ilex/coccifera 7%	Centaurea <1%
Fraxinus 3%	Borraginaceae <1%
Olea 5%	Brassicaceae <1%
	Campanulaceae <1%
	Caryophyllaceae 2%
	Dipsacaceae <1%
	t. Knautia <1%
	Ericaceae <1%
	Euphorbiaceae <1%
	Fabaceae <1%
	Lamiaceae <1%
	Poaceae 2%
	Primulaceae <1%
	Ranunculaceae <1%
	Rosaceae <1%
	Saxifragaceae <1%

diversité importante et homogène dans les spectres polliniques.

RESULTATS

Sédiment concrétionné de la plage tyrrhénienne

Le spectre pollinique de l'unité II montre l'importance de la strate herbacée sur le couvert arboré (Tab. 7.1). Cette végétation semi-ouverte évoque la forêt présteppique méditerranéenne, avec l'importance de *Ephedra*, *Pinus*, *Quercus* t. *ilex-coccifera* et des Asteraceae parmi lesquels *Artemisia*. La forêt mésophile est clairsemée, seulement représentée par *Quercus* et *Fraxinus*. Seul *Olea* est significatif dans la forêt méditerranéenne. La structure de végétation décrite par la palynologie serait à rapprocher des zones semi-arides et reflèterait un important stress hydrique. Cette reconstitution ne s'accorde pas avec l'attribution de la plage au Tyrrhénien, épisode de haut niveau marin du stade isotopique 5e associé à un climat chaud et humide. Le spectre pollinique ne présente pas une image de végétation interglaciaire, ni même interstadiaire, du stade isotopique 5 car la forêt mésophile n'est pas développée. La comparaison du spectre avec les enregistrements de référence du dernier cycle climatique de Kopaïs (Tzedakis 1999; Okuda *et al.* 2001), Ioannina (Tzedakis 1993, 1994, 2003) et Tenaghi Philippon

(Wijmstra 1969; Wijmstra & Smit 1976) ne permettent pas de corrélation avec la végétation développée pendant l'interglaciaire 5e et les deux interstadiaires 5c et 5a. L'hypothèse d'une contamination pollinique provenant de la base de l'unité III lors du concrétionnement, et donc postérieure à la formation de la plage tyrrhénienne, est proposée. En l'absence de cadre chronologique absolu, il est seulement possible de rapporter cette image de la végétation au début du glaciaire weichselien, mais sans pouvoir trancher entre les stades 5d, 5b ou le début du stade isotopique 4.

Pilier stalagmitique de l'unité I et spéléothème de la base de l'unité IV

L'analyse pollinique du pilier stalagmitique (Lebreton 1997; Lebreton *et al.* 1998) a permis de dresser un diagramme pollinique retraçant l'évolution de la végétation pendant la formation des lamines carbonatées (Fig. 7.4). Pour des raisons techniques, il n'était pas possible d'atteindre la base du spéléothème. Au vu des fouilles récentes et des réinterprétations stratigraphiques pour l'unité I, seuls le sommet de l'unité III et la base de l'unité IV sont enregistrés. Aucun élément stratigraphique ne permet de placer précisément la limite entre ces deux unités sur le spéléothème. L'intérêt de l'analyse réside donc essentiellement dans le fait de fournir un enregistrement "indirect" de l'environnement contemporain des

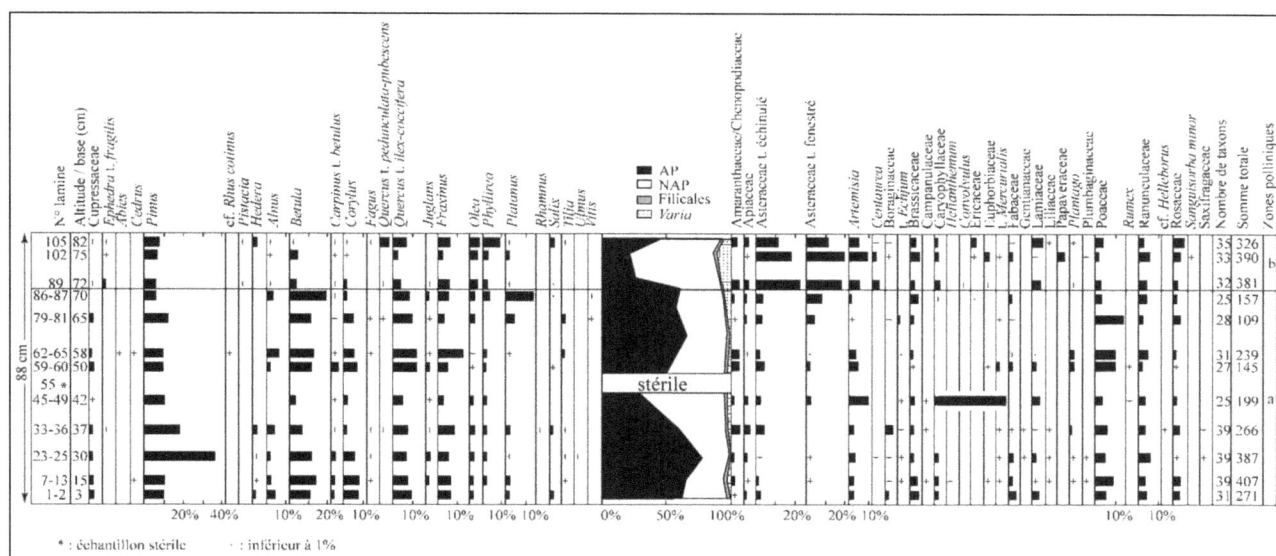

Fig. 7.4. Diagramme pollinique détaillé du pilier stalagmitique de l'unité 1

niveaux archéologiques, là où l'analyse directe des sédiments détritiques est stérile.

Deux zones polliniques sont proposées à partir du diagramme.

La première, la plus longue, montre l'importance des A.P. (Arboreal Pollen), toujours supérieur à 50%. La chute abrupte de la courbe des arbres dans un unique échantillon (Lam 45-49') est un artéfact taphonomique lié au pic du taxon herbacée des Caryophyllaceae atteignant 38%. Cette surreprésentation d'un seul taxon est l'illustration d'une perturbation du signal liée soit au développement d'une plante de cette famille à proximité immédiate du spéléothème en formation, soit à un apport pollinique par les insectes. Pour le reste, *Pinus* et les arbres mésophiles (*Quercus* t. *pedunculat-pubescens*, *Fraxinus*, *Corylus* et *Carpinus* t. *betulus*) dominent les spectres. Dans la végétation méditerranéenne actuelle, ces taxons sont associés à l'étage supra-méditerranéen qui se rencontre en position plus septentrionale des péninsules du Péloponnèse. Les arbres hygrophiles sont également bien développés avec *Betula* et *Alnus*. La forêt méditerranéenne est peu documentée avec les Oleaceae (*Olea*, *Phyllirea*) seulement significatives quand *Quercus* t. *ilex-coccifera* est quasiment absent. L'association des arbres mésophiles caducifoliés indiquerait un climat chaud avec une humidité élevée, favorisant la descente de l'étage supra-méditerranéen vers le littoral. Ces conditions d'humidité se retrouvent notamment pendant des brefs épisodes interstadiaires en milieu méditerranéen. L'interglaciaire éemien (OIS 5e) est exclu pour des raisons stratigraphiques, la formation du spéléothème étant postérieure à la plage tyrrhénienne. Des corrélations avec les zones polliniques du début et du Pléni-Weichselien des séquences de référence (Wijmstra 1969; Wijmstra & Smit 1976; Tzedakis 1993, 1994, 1999, 2003; Okuda *et al.* 2001) sont examinées. Il est possible de

rattacher cette première zone pollinique du pilier stalagmitique de Kalamakia avec les sous-stades 5d ou 5b de l'OIS 5, ou un des interstades connus dans les stades isotopiques 4 ou 3. La principale différence tient dans les taux plus importants de *Betula* et *Alnus* à Kalamakia. La présence de taxons hygrophiles serait alors le reflet d'une humidité locale, pouvant être à connotation édaphique. Ce phénomène serait d'autant plus accentué que l'origine du matériel dans le spéléothème est essentiellement locale, les grains de pollen étant incorporés dans les lamines carbonatées à la suite d'un transport par l'eau depuis le plateau jusqu'à l'intérieur du karst.

Dans la seconde zone pollinique, les arbres caducifoliés régressent fortement, tant les taxons mésophiles qu'hygrophiles. Seuls *Quercus* t. *pedunculata-pubescens* et *Fraxinus* subsistent. L'assemblage de la forêt présteppique méditerranéenne progresse (*Artemisia* et les autres Asteraceae, *Quercus* t. *ilex-coccifera* et *Ephedra*). Les hausses de *Olea* et *Phyllirea* attestent aussi du développement de la forêt arbustive méditerranéenne. La composition de ces spectres polliniques est proche de celle de la base de l'unité III concrétionnée dans la plage tyrrhénienne.

Un environnement végétal semblable est décrit dans les deux spectres provenant d'un petit spéléothème stratigraphiquement connecté avec la base de l'unité IV (Fig. 7.5). La forêt présteppique méditerranéenne et la forêt arbustive méditerranéenne sont mieux représentées. *Olea* et *Quercus* t. *ilex-coccifera* ont des taux élevés.

Ainsi au regard de cette représentation pollinique, il est possible de corréler ces spectres du spéléothème avec la deuxième zone pollinique du sommet du pilier stalagmitique. Faisant suite à un interstadiaire humide, les environnements forestiers présteppiques méditerranéens décrits traduiraient la mise en place d'un épisode climatique

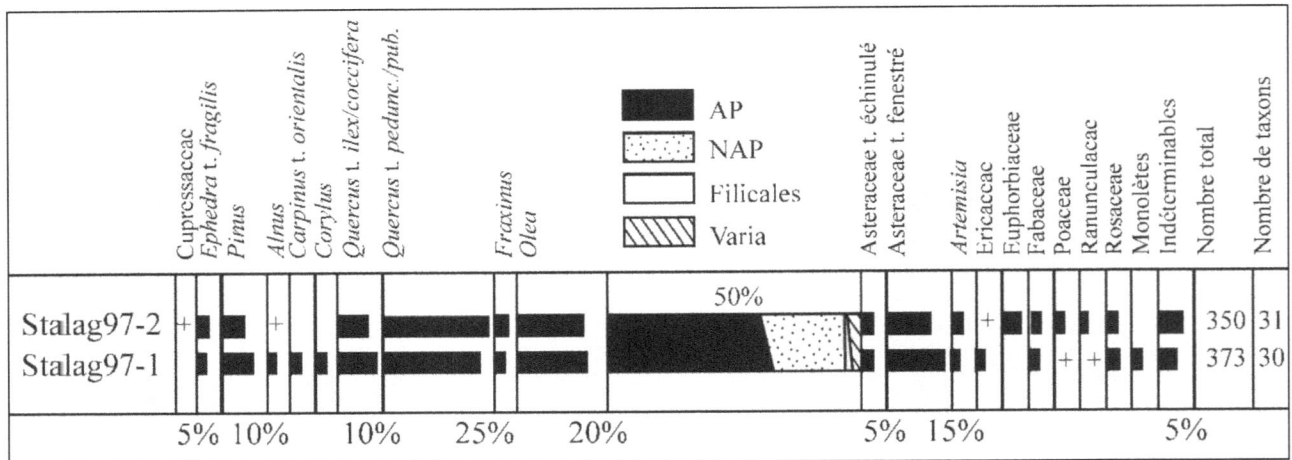

Fig. 7.5. Diagramme pollinique du spéléothème de la base de l'unité 4 figurant les taxons les plus significatifs

sévère avec une aridité estivale probablement longue et accentuée. En l'absence de données radiométriques reproductibles (Voinchet & Darlas, 1998), il est impossible de placer ces données polliniques dans un cadre chronologique précis du Pléistocène supérieur. Cette végétation présteppique méditerranéenne, adaptée à de longues périodes de sécheresse a pu se développer pendant le stade isotopique 4 au Weichselien inférieur ou pendant le stade isotopique 3 du Pléniglaciaire. Le maintien des essences xérophiles souligne que la structuration et l'évolution de la végétation méditerranéenne pendant les périodes glaciaires est plus dépendante de l'aridité que des températures.

DONNEES POLLINIQUES ET FAUNIQUES

L'étude des vestiges fauniques mis au jour lors des fouilles des unités III et IV est une source supplémentaire d'information paléoécologique pour reconstituer les paléoenvironnements régnants aux alentours du gisement. La liste faunique est présentée dans le Tableau 7.2, d'après les données d'E. Psathi. L'étude archéozoologique est en cours.

La grande faune est diversifiée et il faut noter l'absence complète de taxons de faune froide. *Dama dama* et *Capra* sp. dominent considérablement l'assemblage faunique. *Dama dama* est une espèce typiquement méditerranéenne. Sa présence est bien attestée dans le sud de la Grèce continentale au Pléistocène supérieur. Son biotope est un environnement semi-ouvert peu humide, l'animal se nourrissant principalement d'herbacées et de feuilles d'arbustes. *Dama dama* devait facilement trouver sa place dans l'environnement forestier présteppique méditerranéen mis en évidence par l'analyse pollinique. *Capra* sp. évolue dans les milieux ouverts montagneux avec des pentes escarpées, sous des conditions de sécheresse marquée. Il colonisait vraisemblablement les reliefs proches de la grotte, dans l'immédiat arrière-pays. Avec l'élévation de l'altitude, la forêt présteppique s'ouvrait

Tab. 7.2. Liste faunique des grands mammifères mis au jour à Kalamakia

Taxons de grands mamifères
Ursus arctos
Panthera pardus
Lynx lynx
Felis silvestris
Canis lupus
Vulpes vulpes
Dama dama
Capra sp.
Mustelidae
Palaeoloxodon antiquus
Stephanorinus sp.
Sus scrofa
Bos et/ou Bison
Rupicapra rupicapra
Cervus elaphus
Capreolus capreolus
Lepus europaeus

progressivement, en relation avec une baisse des températures quand l'aridité restait constante. Ces caractéristiques géomorphologiques limitaient le développement des arbres méditerranéens.

A la base de l'unité IV, l'association de *Capreolus capreolus*, *Cervus elaphus* et *Sus scrofa* reflète un milieu forestier semi-fermé relativement humide. Ce type d'environnement végétal est décrit par la palynologie dans la première partie du diagramme pollinique du pilier stalagmitique. Malheureusement, il n'y a aucun moyen de préciser avec certitude la corrélation entre cette partie du diagramme et la base de l'unité stratigraphique IV.

Du point de vue paléoécologique, les données de la faune de Kalamakia s'accordent avec les reconstitutions paléo-environnementales fondées sur l'analyse palynologique. Partant de ces données, il est intéressant d'examiner si les Néandertaliens de Kalamakia ont développé des techniques de chasse particulières qui traduiraient une adaptation à cette mosaïque d'environnement. Même si les restes de *Dama dama* et *Capra* sp. sont surreprésentés dans l'assemblage faunique du site, ils peuvent finalement ne refléter que l'abondance naturelle de ces deux espèces dans le milieu proche de la grotte. Le croisement des données polliniques et paléontologiques n'est pas suffisant pour considérer et évaluer d'éventuelles techniques cynégétiques spécifiques. Seuls les résultats de l'étude archéozoologique pourraient apporter des informations validant l'hypothèse d'une chasse sélective.

CONCLUSION

Les analyses polliniques sur les spéléothèmes sont une source d'informations paléoécologiques non négligeables dans le cadre des investigations multidisciplinaires à entreprendre sur des gisements paléolithiques. Il est toutefois nécessaire d'examiner attentivement les processus taphonomiques susceptibles d'affecter le matériel pollinique. Quand les résultats issus de ces analyses sont corrélables avec des niveaux archéologiques, il est possible de reconstituer l'environnement végétal de l'Homme préhistorique. Pour le site de Kalamakia, l'analyse des spéléothèmes était la seule possibilité pour reconstituer l'environnement végétal en connectant les résultats avec l'occupation humaine. L'enregistrement de la pluie pollinique dans les spéléothèmes permet de proposer des reconstitutions paléoenvironnementales et paléoclimatiques fiables au Weichselien ancien et au début du Pléniglaciaire en décrivant la structure de la végétation pendant le dernier glaciaire et des épisodes interstadiaires sur le littoral de la Grèce continentale. Les reconstitutions paléoenvironnementales proposées sont mises en relation avec les données fauniques pour appréhender les comportements de subsistance des Néandertaliens.

References

BAILEY, G.N.; GAMBLE C.; HIGGS H. (1983). Asprochaliko and Kastritsa: further investigations of Palaeolithic settlement and economy in Epirus (Northwest Greece). *Proceedings of the Prehistoric Society*, 49: 15-42.

DARLAS, A. (1994). Le Paléolithique inférieur et moyen de Grèce. *L'Anthropologie*, 98 (2-3): 305-328.

DARLAS, A. (1998). Le Paléolithique de la Grèce. *Arkeos*, 5: 19-27.

DARLAS, A.; LUMLEY, H. de (1998). Fouilles franco-helléniques de la grotte de Kalamakia (Aréopolis; Péloponnèse). *Bulletin de Correspondance Hellénique*, 122: 655–661.

FERRANTI, L.; ANTONIOLI, F.; MAUZ, B.; AMOROSI, A.; DAI PRA, G.; MASTRONUZZI, G.; MONACO, C.; ORRÙ, P.; PAPPALARDO, M.; RADTKE, U.; RENDA, P.; ROMANO, P.; SANSÒ, P.; VERRUBBI, V. (2006). Markers of the last interglacial sea-level high stand along the coast of Italy: Tectonic implications. *Quaternary International*, 145-146: 30-54.

HARVATI, K; DELSON, E. (1999). Conference Report: Paleoanthropology of the Mani Peninsula (Greece). *Journal of Human Evolution*, 36: 343-348.

HARVATI, K.; PANAGOPOULOU, E.; KARKANAS, P. (2003). First Neanderthal remains from Greece: the evidence from Lakonis. *Journal of Human Evolution*, 45: 465-473.

HUXTABLE, J.; GOWLETT, A.J.; BAILEY, G.N.; CARTER, P.L.; PAPACONSTANTINOU, V. (1992). Thermoluminescence Dates and a New Analysis of the Early Mousterian from Asprochaliko. *Current anthropology*, 33 (1): 109-114.

KOUMOUZELIS, M.; GINTER, B.; KOZLOWSKI, J.K.; PAWLIKOWSKI, M.; BAR-YOSEF, O.; ALBERT, R.M.; LITYNSKA-ZAJAC, M.; STORZEWICZ, E.; WOJTAL, P.; LIPECKI, G.; TOMEK, T.; BOCHEN-SKI, Z.M. (2001a). The Early Upper Palaeolithic in Greece: the excavations in Klisoura Cave. *Journal of Archaeological Science*, 28: 515-539.

KOUMOUZELIS, M.; KOZLOWSKI, J.K.; ESCUTE-NAIRE, C.; SITLIVY, V.; SOBCZYK, K.; VALLA-DAS, H.; TISNERAT-LABORDE, N.; WOJTAL, P.; GINTER, B. (2001b). La fin du Paléolithique moyen et le début du Paléolithique supérieur en Grèce: la séquence de la Grotte 1 de Klissoura. *L'Anthropologie*, 105: 469-504.

LEBRETON, V. (1997). *Etudes palynologiques des remplissages pléistocènes supérieurs de l'Abri Mochi (Baousse Rousse, Grimaldi, Ligurie italienne) et de la grotte de Kalamakia (Areopolis, Grèce)*. Mémoire de DEA, MNHN Paris, 59 p.

LEBRETON, V.; DARLAS, A.; CATTANI, L. (1998). Palynological analyses from Kalamakia Cave (Greece) and from Ca'Belvedere di Monte Poggiolo (Italy). *Arkeos*, 5: 85-100.

LEBRETON, V.; LARTIGOT, A.-S.; KARATSORI, E.; MESSAGER, E.; MARQUER, L.; RENAULT-MISKOVSKY, J. (2007). Potentiels et limites de l'analyse pollinique de spéléothèmes quaternaires: applications à la reconstitution de l'environnement végétal de l'Homme préhistorique sur le pourtour nord-méditerranéen. *Quaternaire*, sous presse.

LECERVOISIER, B. (2003). *Etude stratigraphique, sédimentologique, micromorphologique et paléoclimatique de remplissages de grottes du Pléistocène supérieur ancien de l'Europe méditerranéenne : Sites moustériens du Boquete de Zafarraya (Andalousie), de Madonna dell'Arma (Ligurie) et de Kalamakia (Laconie, Péloponnèse)*. Thèse de doctorat, MNHN Paris, 251 p.

LUMLEY, H. de; DARLAS, A. (1994). La grotte de Kalamakia (Aréopolis, Péloponnèse, Grèce). *Bulletin de Correspondance Hellénique*, 118: 535-559.

OKUDA, M.; YASUDA, Y.; SETOGUCHI, T. (2001). Middle to Late Pleistocene vegetation history and climatic changes at Lake Kopaïs, Southeast Greece. *Boreas*, 30: 73-82.

PAPAVASSILIOU, C. (1984). *Geological Map of Greece, 1:50.000, Mavrovoynion-Areopolis-Yerolimin Sheet*, Institute of Geology and Mineral Exploration.

QUEZEL, P.; BARBERO M. (1985). *Carte de la végétation potentielle de la région méditerranéenne au 1/2.500.000, feuille n°1: Méditerranée orientale*. Editions du CNRS.

SITTLER, C. (1955). Méthodes techniques physico-chimiques de préparation des sédiments en vue de leur analyse pollinique. *Revue de l'Institut français du Pétrole*, 10 (2): 103-114.

TZEDAKIS, P.C. (1993). Long-term tree populations in northwest Greece through multiple Quaternary climatic cycles. *Nature*, 364: 437-440.

TZEDAKIS, P.C. (1994). Vegetation change through glacial-interglacial cycles: a long pollen sequence perspective. *Philosophical Transactions of the Royal Society*, 345: 403-432.

TZEDAKIS, P.C. (1999). The last climatic cycle at Kopaïs, central Greece. *Journal of the Geological Society*, 156: 425-434.

TZEDAKIS, P.C. (2003). Timing and duration of Last Interglacial conditions in Europe: a chronicle of a changing chronology. *Quaternary Science Reviews*, 22: 763-768.

VOINCHET, P.; DARLAS, A. (1998). Dating stratigraphic levels in Kalamakia Cave (Greece). *Arkeos*, 5: 45-51.

WIJMSTRA, T.A. (1969). Palynology of the first 30 m of a 120 m deep section in northern Greece. *Acta Botanica Neerlandica*, 18: 511–527.

WIJMSTRA, T.A.; SMIT, A. (1976). Palynology of the middle part (30–78 m) of the 120 m deep section in northern Greece (Macedonia). *Acta Botanica Neerlandica*, 25: 297–312.

UPPER-PLEISTOCENE BIRD REMAINS FROM KALAMAKIA CAVE (GREECE)

Thierry ROGER

Laboratoire de Préhistoire du Lazaret, 33 bis, Boulevard Frank Pilatte, 06300 NICE, FRANCE

Andréas DARLAS

Ephorie de Paléoanthropologie-Spéléologie de la Grèce du Nord,
Navarinou 28, 55131 THESSALONIKI, GRÈCE, andreas.darlas@eps.culture.gr

Abstract: A study of the avifauna from Kalamakia Cave (Southern Greece) collected during the course of the excavations between 1993 and 2000 is presented. 95 bird remains belonging to 21 taxa, at least 39 individuals, are identified. The agents causing the accumulation of these bird remains in the cave and the contribution of birds to the reconstruction of the prehistric man are discussed. The high number of taxa in spite of the low number of remains makes the bird assemblage of Kalamakia one of the most diversified assemblages found in a Middle Paleolithic site of mainland Greece.
Key-words: Birds, Pleistocene, Middle Paleolithic, Paleoclimate, Greece

Résumé: Une étude de l'avifaune de la grotte de Kalamakia (Sud de la Grèce) récoltée lors des fouilles réalisées entre 1993 et 2000 est présentée. 95 restes d'oiseaux représentant au minimum 39 individus sont attribués à 21 taxons. Les agents responsables de la présence de ces restes d'oiseaux dans la grotte ainsi que l'apport de l'avifaune dans la reconstitution de l'environnement de l'homme préhistorique est discuté. Le nombre relativement important de taxons identifiés malgré malgré le faible nombre de restes récoltés fait du cortège d'oiseaux de Kalamakia l'un des plus diversifié trouvé dans un site du Paléolithique moyen de Grèce continentale.
Mots-clef: Oiseaux, Pléistocène, Paléolithique moyen, Paléoclimat, Grèce

INTRODUCTION

Kalamakia Cave is situated on the western coast of the Mani peninsula in the southern Peloponnese near the town of Areopoli (see fig. 8.1). The Cave belongs to a vast karstic system. Entrance of the cave opens in front of the Oitylo bay.

Excavations, undertaken since 1993 by Andreas Darlas and Henry de Lumley have allowed to define the stratigraphy of the Quaternary filling. It has been divided into seven stratigraphic units (Lumley and Darlas, 1994; Lecervoisier, 2003), see fig. 8.2.

The continental filling (units III, IV, V and VI) are covering the unit II, a shingle Tyrrhenian beach dated about one hundred and nine thousand years before present with Uranium-thorium methods (Lumley and Darlas, *op. cit.*). The unit III is composed of wind dune sands. The unit IV is angular gravel with sandy-clay matrix. The top of the unit IV has been dated to thirty six thousand years before present with Uranium-thorium methods (Lumley and Darlas, *op. cit.*). Between units III and IV exist a sedimentation gap. The unit V show blocks wrapped in a clay matrix. The unit VI is composed of clayey silts.

Consequently, the continental filling is earlier than Oxygene Isotopic stage 5. The relationship between the unit I (a stalagmitic floor) and the Tyrrhenian beach (the unit II) is unclear. From excavations provides a typical mousterian industry with 'Levallois Débitage' and Mousterian points. The macrofauna is composed of Caprines, Cervidae and Carnivores (Gardeisein, Tantralidou and Darlas, 1999). The *Dama dama* (fallow deer) and *Capra*

sp are dominant. Neanderthal remains have been discovered (Darlas and Lumley, 1998). The last excavation field took place in summer 2006.

MATERIAL AND METHODS

Excavation and sieving of sediments from units III to VI has permit to collect lots of bones of microvertebrates (Roger and Darlas, 1999) and among them birds. To identify our material, we have used the bird skeletons of the Regalia collection stored at the Institute of Human Paleontology, Paris, France and data from the literature: Tomek and Bocheński, 2000 for Corvids; Janossy, 1983; Kraft, 1972.

According to previous works (Roger and Darlas, *op. cit.*; Roger, 2004) and after a review of the material found between 1993 and 2000, 95 bird remains belonging to 21 species are identified.

Table 8.1 shows the percentage of minimum number of individuals (MNI) and figure 8.3 shows, for the whole site, the percentage of NMI for each bird's group (order) with, in brackets, the number of species for each group.

The most aboundant species is *Coturnix coturnix* with 31 remains. Follow *Alectoris graeca* with 26 remains, then *Columba livia/oenas* with 12 remains. Each of other species is representing by 1 to 4 remains belonging to 1 or 2 individuals at least. *Coturnix coturnix* is especially abundant in unit 4. Birds of prey are quite numerous with 5 species (*Accipiter nisus*, *Falco* cf. *vespertinus*, *Otus scops*, *Athene noctua* and *Strix aluco*) represented by 9

Fig. 8.1. Location of Kalamakia Cave in Greece

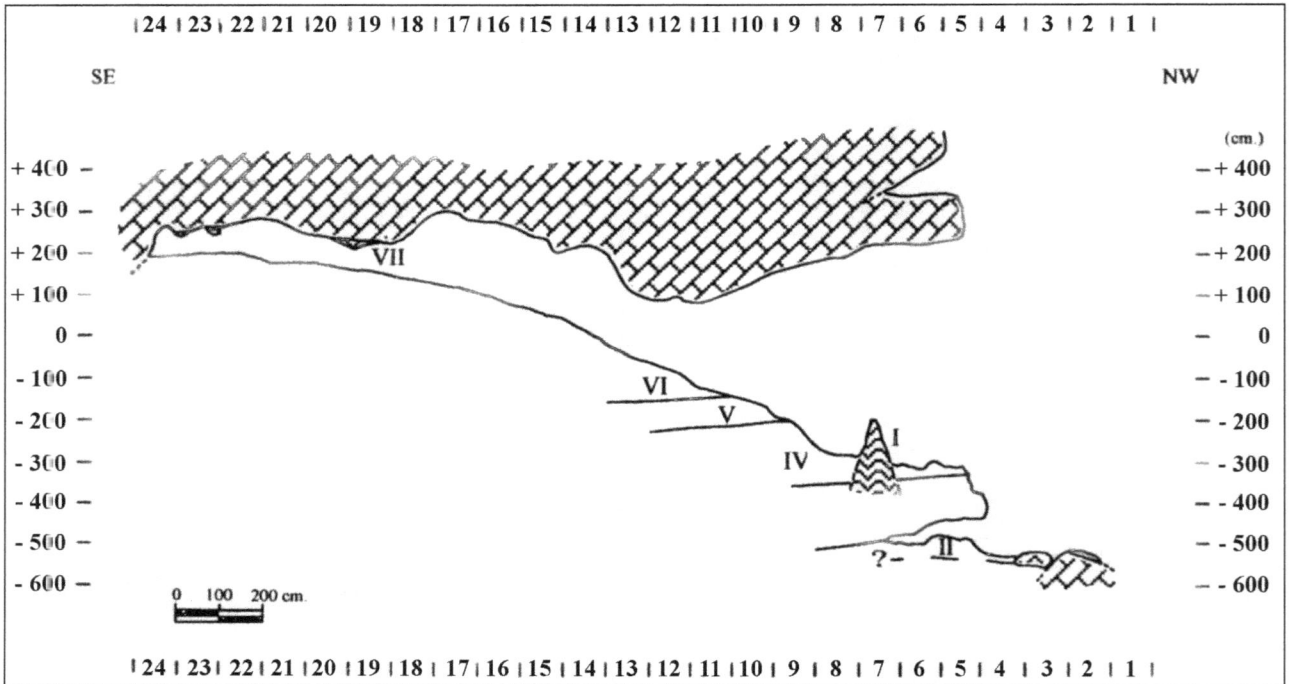

Fig. 8.2. Theoretical longitudinal section of Kalamakia Cave. Position of units I to VII (after Lebreton, 1999)

Tab. 8.1. Kalamakia Cave: distribution of birds. MNI = Minimum Number of Indivdual, NISP = Number of Identified Specimens

	unit VI	unit V	unit IV	unit III	Total
	NISP/MNI	NISP/MNI	NISP/MNI	NISP/MNI	NISP/MNI(*)
Order: Procelariiformes					
Puffinus puffinus				1/1	1/1
Order: Accipitriformes					
Accipiter nisus			1/1		1/1
Order: Falconiformes					
Falco cf. *vespertinus*			1/1		1/1
Order: Galliformes					
Alectoris graeca		13/3	12/2	1/1	26/6
Coturnix coturnix		3/1	28/7		31/8
Order: Charadriiformes					
Eudromias morinellus			1/1		1/1
Chlidonias sp.				1/1	1/1
Order: Columbiformes					
Columba livia/oenas		6/2	5/1	1/1	12/4
Order: Strigiformes					
Otus scops			4/1		4/1
Athene noctua	1/1				1/1
Strix aluco			2/1		2/1
Order: Apodiformes					
Apus apus			1/1		1/1
Apus cf. *pallidus*			1/1		1/1
Order: Passeriformes					
Hirundo rustica			1/1		1/1
Certhia sp.		1/1			1/1
Turdus cf. *philomenos*		1/1			1/1
Corvus corone		1/1	1/1		2/2
cf. *Corvus monedula*	1/1	2/1			3/2
cf. *Pica pica*	1/1		1/1		2/2
Pyrrhocorax pyrrhocorax			1/1		1/1
Emberiza citrinella			1/1		1/1
	2/2	28/11	61/22	4/4	95/39

(*) total MNI is the sum of MNIs from each unit.

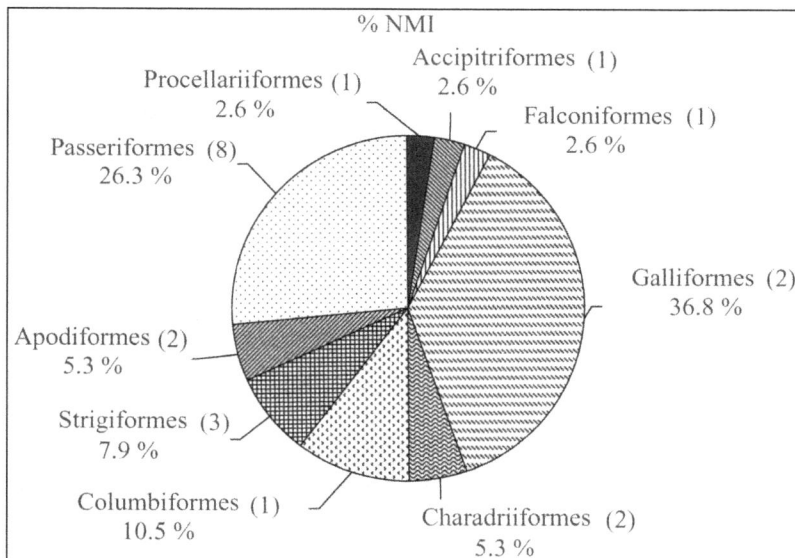

Fig. 8.3. Kalamakia: representation of MNI for bird's groups

remains. Passeriformes are quite numerous (8 species) but their MNI and number of species are certainly under-estimated due to difficulties to identify the small one's. Many remains belonging to small Passeriformes are left unidentified. We point out the presence of two small waders, *Chlidonias* sp. in unit III and *Eudromias morinellus* in unit IV, and also a sea bird, *Puffinus puffinus*, in unit III.

SYSTEMATIC

No morphological characters are given when bone of the fossil representative do not differs significantly from bone of living species. Habitat and distribution are taken from Birguides LTD. (2004), Handrinos and Akriotis, 1997.

Classe *AVES*, Linnaeus, 1758

Ordre *PROCELLARIIFORMA* Fürbinger, 1988

Famille *PROCELLARIIDAE* (Boie, 1826)

Genre *Puffinus* Brisson, 1760

Puffinus puffinus (Brünnich, 1764), Manx Shearwater
Material: 1 distal part of humerus.

Formerly, the *Puffinus puffinus* species included tree sub-species: *P. p. puffinus*, *P. p. mauretanicus* et *P. p. yelkouan*. Nowadays, these sub-species are considered as valid species: *P. puffinus*, the Manx Shearwater; *P. mauretanicus*, the Balearic Shearwater and *P. yelkouan*, the Mediterranean Shearwater.

Unfortunately, despite osteological studies in the literature (Walker, Wragg and Harrison, 1990), our materiel is too poor to make distinction between these species.

We choose, as formely, to consider these tree species as belonging to *Puffinus puffinus* sensus-lato and attribute our material to that species.

Manx Shearwater is common in Greek waters. It nests in hole or cavity on rock.

Ordre *ACCIPITRIFORMA* (Viellot, 1816)

Famille *ACCIPITRIDAE* (Viellot, 1816)

Genre *Accipiter* Brisson, 1760

Accipiter nisus (L., 1758), Sparrowhaws
Material: 1 distal part of femur.

Sparrowhawk occurs in wooded areas at all altitudes. Females mainly prefer more open landscapes with more patchy cover. In Greece, Sparrowhawk is quite widely distributed over much of the mainland, but it occurs more regularly in northern and central Greece and less so in the Peloponnese.

Ordre *FALCONIFORMA* Sharpe, 1874

Famille *FALCONIDAE* Vigors, 1824

Genre *Falco* Linnaeus., 1758

Falco cf. *vespertinus* Linnaeus, 1766, Red-footed Falcon
Material: 1 proximal part of coracoidum.

Red-footed-Falcon avoids closed forests, mountains, arid or desert zones. In Greece, Red-footed-Falcon is very common passage migrant in spring but scarce in autumn. It occurs in open habitat such hill slopes with phrygana or margins of wetlands.

Ordre *GALLIFORMA* Temminck, 1820

Famille *PHASIANIDAE* Vigors, 1825

Genre *Alectoris* Kaup, 1829

Alectoris graeca (Meisner, 1804), Rock Partridge
Material: 2 proximal parts of carpometacarpus, 1 coracoideum, 2 distal parts of coracoideum, 5 proximal parts of coracoideum, 1 proximal part of femur, 6 distal parts of humerus, 1 proximal part of humerus, 1 proximal part of scapula, 1 part of sternum, 1 distal part of tarsometatarsus, 3 proximal parts of ulna.

In Southern Europe, it lives from sea level to mountains. It avoids forest and humid grounds. Rock Partridge is widespread all over the Greece.

Genre *Coturnix* Bonnaterre, 1791

Coturnix coturnix (Linnaeus, 1758), Common Quail
Material: 10 proximal parts of carpometacarpus, 10 proximal parts of coracoideum, 2 distal parts of humerus, 2 proximal parts of humerus, 1 distal part of radius, 1 proximal part of scapula, 1 distal part of tarsometatarsus, 1 distal part of ulna, 1 proximal part of ulna.

Common Quail is common all over the mainland Greece. It is locally resident but above all it is passage migrant species from early March to early May and from late August to mid October. It lives in steppic environment and phrygana.

Ordre *CHARADRIIFORMA* (Huxley, 1867)

Famille *CHARADRIIDAE* Leach, 1820

Genre *Eudromias* Brehm,CL 1830

Eudromias morinellus (Linnaeus, 1758), Eurasian Dotterel
Material: 1 proximal part of coracoideum.

Eurasian Dotterel is a very rare passage migrant in Greece. It have been recorded fewer than 25 times in Greece (Handrinos and Akriotis, 1997). The points of passage are infrequently on the coast and must be open flat and treeless. It frequents semi-desert including shrubby steppe.

Famille *STERNIDAE* Vigors, 1825

Genre *Chlidonias* Rafinesque, 1822

Chlidonias sp.
Material : 1 ulna.

Ordre *COLUMBIFORMA* (Latham, 1790)

Famille *COLUMBIDAE* (Illiger, 1811)

Genre *Columba* L., 1758

Columba livia/oenas, Rock Dove / Stock Dove.
Material: 1 proximal part of carpometacarpus, 1 distal part of ulna, 1 tarsometatarsus, 2 distal parts of tibiotarsus, 3 ulnars.

Morphological studies do not allow to make a distinction between *Columba livia*, the Rock Dove and *Columba oenas*, the Stock Dove. Biometrical studies show that *Columba livia* is smaller on average than *Columba oenas* but the overlapping of bones size is wide. Our material is too few to allow a distinction between these species.

Unfortunately, their habitats are differents: the Rock Dove lives in rocky environment whereas the Stock Dove prefers the forest.

Cortege of birds at Kalamakia are in favour to rocky and steppic environment so we consider our material belonging to *Columba livia* for the environmental reconstruction.

Ordre *STRIGIFORMA* (Wagler, 1830)

Famille *Strigidae* Vigors, 1925

Genre *Otus* Pennant, 1769

Otus scops (Linnaeus, 1758), European Scops Owl
Material: 1 distal part of carpometacarpus, 2 distal parts of tarsometatarsus, 1 distal part of humerus.

Scops Owl breeds in west Palearctic in warm dry lowlands in middle and lower middle latitudes, mainly continental temperate and Mediterranean, but also steppe and oceanic. It avoids both closed forest and extensive open tracts.

Scops Owls have a very widespread distribution all over the Greek mainland and on almost all of the islands. They are numerous in open woodland from sea level to middle altitudes.

Genre *Athene* Boie, 1822

Athene noctua *(Pontoppidan, 1763), Little Owl*
Material: 1 distal part of femur.

It natural habitat is in moderate and warm European regions. It is not a forest species, it tends even to avoid margins or enclaves between forest (Birguides LTD., 2004). In Greece, Little Owl is very common on the mainland.

Genre *Strix* L., 1758

Strix aluco Linnaeus, 1758, Tawny Owl
Material: 1 proximal part of tarsometatarsus, 1 proximal part of femur.

Tawny Owl occurs in a wide variety of wooded habitats, whether coniferous, deciduous or mixed, in temperate, steppic and Mediterranean environment. In Greece, the species is widely distributed and quite common on the mainland.

Ordre *APODIFORMA* Peters, 1940

Famille *APODIDAE* (Hartert, 1897)

Genre *Apus* Scopoli, 1777

Apus apus (Linnaeus, 1758), Common Swift
Material: 1 humerus.

Apus cf. *pallidus* (Shelley, 1870), Pallid Swift
Material: 1 proximal part of humerus.

The species is present in Greece from late March to late October. Pallid Swift is generally confined to coastal areas and low altitudes.

Ordre *PASSERIFORMA* (Linnaeus, 1758)

Famille *HIRUNDINIDAE* Vigors, 1925

Genre *Hirundo* Linnaeus, 1758

Hirundo rustica Linnaeus, 1758, Barn Swallow
Material: 1 distal part of humerus.

Barn swallow is wide all over the Greece. It is a migrant species in Greece from early March to late May and from mid August to mid October. It lives in open environment from sea level until 1000 meters.

Famille *CORVIDAE* Vigors, 1825

Genre *Pica* Brisson, 1760

cf. *Pica pica* (Linnaeus, 1758), Common Magpie
Material: 1 proximal part of femur, 1 distal part of humerus.

Genre *Pyrrhocorax* Tunstall, 1771

Pyrrhocorax pyrrhocorax (Linnaeus, 1758), Red-billed Chough
Material: 1 distal part of tarsometatarsus.

Red-billed Chough is now absent from the Peloponnese but they were recorded in the past (Niethammer, 1943

Tab. 3.2. Percentage of Galliformes bones found at Kalamakia Cave. CO: coracoid, SC: scapula, HU: humerus, UL: Ulna, RA: radius, CMC: carpometacarpus, ST: sternum, FE: femur, TMT: tarsometatarsus

	CO	SC	HU	UL	RA	CMC	ST	FE	TMT
Alectoris - Kalamakia	30,8	3,8	26,9	15,4	0,0	7,7	3,8	7,7	3,8
Coturnix - Kalamakia	35,48	0	12,9	6,5	6,5	32,3	3,2	0	3,2

apud Handrinos & Triantaphyllos, 1997). It is common to highest altitudes in Greece but in winter, it usually descend to lower areas. It lives in caves or rocky open areas with cliff.

Genre *Corvus* Linnaeus, 1758

cf. *Corvus monedula* Linnaeus, 1758, Western Jackdaw
Material: 2 proximal parts of femur, 1 distal part of humerus.

Corvus corone Linnaeus, 1758, Carrion Crow
Material: 2 distal parts of tarsometatarsus.

Famille *TURDIDAE* Bonaparte, 1838

Genre *Turdus* L., 1758

Turdus cf. *philomenos* Brehm, 1831, Song Trush
Material: 1 proximal part of humerus.

Song Trush is very widespread as winter visitor in Greece, from early October to late March. It lives in all kind of habitat with some bushes or trees. It breeds only on the mountain along the northern border of the country.

Famille *CERTHIIDAE* Leach, 1820

Genre *Certhia* Linnaeus, 1758

Certhia sp.
Material: 1 proximal part of humerus.

Morphological and biometrical studies do not allow to make a distinction between the two species of European Treecreepers, the Short-Toed Treecreeper *Certhia brachydactyla* and the Common Treecreeper *Certhia familiaris*.

Famille *EMBERIZIDAE* Vigors, 1831

Genre *Emberiza* Linnaeus, 1758

Emberiza citrinella L., 1758, Yellowhammer
Material: 1 proximal part of humerus.

Nowadays, Yellowhammer is common to the north and parts of the central mainland of Greece. It is absent from Peloponnese and Sterea Hellas.Yellowhammer nest always above 800-900 meters altitude except in winter where it moves to lower altitudes. Wintering Yellowhammers lives in open lowland areas and other open habitats.

TAPHONOMIC REMARKS

Bird's bones show no cutmark and no roasting mark. So, there is no direct evidence of hunting or consumption by humans. There is no digestion trace too apart from a femur of Rock Partridge which shows what it could be a very light digestion trace.

Nevertheless, it is likely that smaller species were raptor's prey. Other species which live in rocky environments like *Columba* sp. or *Corvus* sp. might die a natural death in the cave.

Concerning *Coturnix coturnix* and *Alectoris graeca,* their abundance compared to other birds is striking. These species are relatively poorly- flying birds so they are species most likely to be hunted by humans. In two other greek sites – Kephalari (Reisch, 1976) and Klisoura Cave 1 (Tomek, T.; Bocheński, M., 2002)- Rock Partridge have been hunted by humans. Rock Partridge from layer D2 of Kephalari show cutmarks. Bones from others Kephalari's layers show no cutmarks. At Klisoura, this species have no cutmark but roasting marks. Moreover, the most numerous skeletal elements are humeri, coracoids and tibiotarsi like Kephalari's Rock Partridge which comes from layers where this species shows no cutmark.

At Kalamakia, the most numerous skeletal elements of Rock Partridge are coracoids, humeri and ulnas (table 8.2).

In common Quail, it is coracoids, humeri and carpometacarpi. So, results is quite different, it is difficult to conclude.

To sum up, hunting by humans or by raptor and especially noctural bird of prey due to absence of high digestion trace is possible for these two species.

Weesie (1988) reports that *Coturnix coturnix* is one of the favorite preys for raptors. Even if there is no digestion trace, may be abundance of this species in the unit IV could be linked to presence of five species of bird of prey in this unit ?

PALAEO-ENVIRONMENTAL ET PALAEO-CLIMATOLOGICAL RECONSTRUCTION

Bird species are grouped according to their climato-ecological group *sensus* Vilette (1983) and their Minimum Number of individuals (fig. 8.4A and 8.4B).

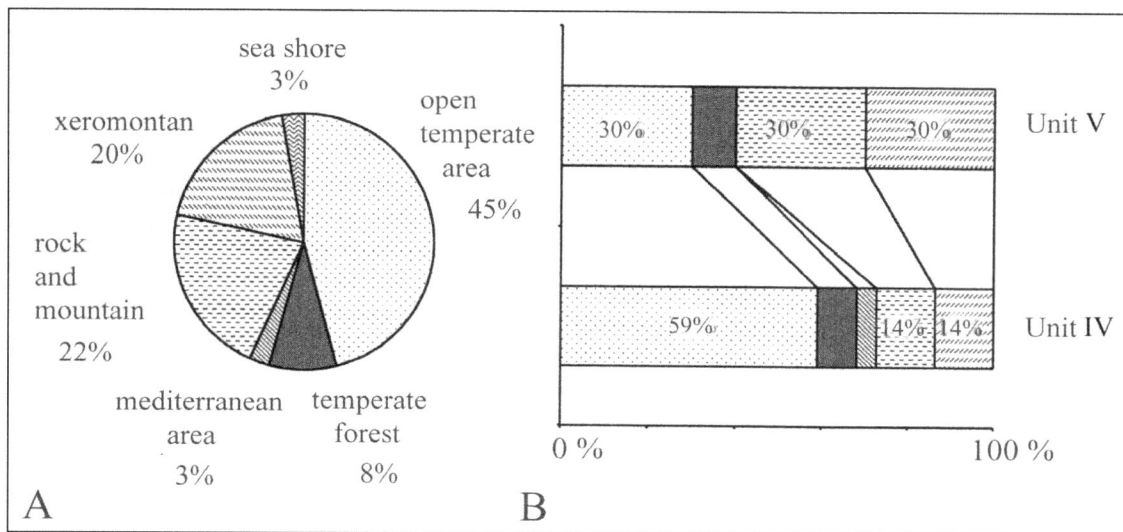

Fig. 8.4. Kalamakia: representation of climato-ecological groups. A – whole site; B – Units IV and V

We notice there are no "cold" species, except the dotterel, *Eudromias morinellus*, but the species is considered here as migrant passage so it's migrant passage's habitat who is used. There are only one Mediterranean species, *Apus* cf. *pallidus*, represented by a single remain.

Taken as a all, birds show that the surroundings of Kalamakia are mostly composed of open environment (fig. 8.4A). The climate is temperate. Some wooded areas exist.

Is there a evolution of environment or climate during the filling of Kalamakia cave?

Only units IV and V are considered because units III and VI are too poor in bird's remains to permit a valid environmental and climatological reconstruction. There is no drastic change in climate or environment between unit IV and V (fig. 8.4B). Environment is very open under temperate climate. Nevertheless, we observe a decrease of MNI of open temperate areas species between these units. It's due to the common quail, *Coturnix coturnix* which goes from 7 individuals at least in unit IV to 1 individuals in unit V. Consequently the xeromontan species and rocky and montains environment species increase. So, may be, environment from the unit V is drier than environment from the unit IV.

CONCLUSION

Study of bird bones found during the excavation of Kalamakia Cave between 1993 and 2000 has permit to identify 95 bird remains belonging to 21 species. The Galliformes are the most numerous. Birds show a very open environment under temperate climate. There is no sign of cool period. These results are according with rodents study (Roger and Darlas, 1999) even if cortege of rodents show a mediterranean climate more pronounced.

Bird bones from Upper pleistocene of Kalamakia Cave are not numerous but the cortege of species is quite diversified. It bring new data about Upper pleistocene avifaunas of mainland Greece which are scarce yet.

Acknowledgment

Thanks to the Departemental Laboratory of Prehistory of Lazaret, Nice and the National Museum of Natural History of Paris for the financial support, to Prof. H. de Lumley, all the staff of Lazaret, Eleni Psathi,Vincent Lebreton, Philippe Vilette for their support and advice and thanks to all the staff of the Kalamakia excavations.

References

BIRDGUIDES LTD. (2004). *BWPi: The Birds of the Western Palearctic on interactive DVD-Rom.*1 DVD. Oxford/Upton Magna: Oxford University Press/Bird Guides, 2004.

DARLAS, A; LUMLEY H. de (1998), Fouilles franco-helléniques de la grotte de Kalamakia (Aréopolis, Péloponnèse). *Bulletin de Correspondance Hellénique*, 122: 655-661.

GARDEISEIN, A.; TANTRALIDOU, K.; DARLAS, A. (1999). Faunals remains from Kalamakia (Peloponnese, Greece). In: CRUZ, A.R.; MILLIKEN, S.; OOSTERBECK, L.; PERETTO C., Eds., *Human Population Origins in the Circum-Mediterranean Area: Adaptations of the Hunter-Gatherer Groups to Environmental Modifications*. Arkeos, 5: 111-120.

HANDRINOS, G.; AKRIOTIS, T. (1997). The Birds of Greece. C. Helm – A & C Black, London: 336 p.

JANOSSY, D. (1983). Humeri of Central European Smaller Passeriformes. *Fragmenta mineralogica et palaeontologica* 11: 85-112.

KRAFT, E. (1972). *Vergleichend morphologische Untersuchungen an Einzelknochen Nord- und Mitteleuropäischer kleinerer Hühnervögel.* Dissertation Institut für Palaeoanatomie, Domestikationsforschung und Geschichte der Tiermedizin, München: 195 p.

LEBRETON, V. (1999). Palynological analyses from Kalamakia Cave (Greece) and Ca' Beveldere di Monte Pogiolo (Italy). In CRUZ, A.R.; MILLIKEN, S.; OOSTERBECK, L.; PERETTO C., Eds., *Human Population Origins in the Circum-Mediterranean Area: Adaptations of the Hunter-Gatherer Groups to Environmental Modifications.* Arkeos, 5: 85-100.

LECERVOISIER, B. (2003). *Etude stratigraphique, sédimentologique, micromorphologique et paléoclimatique de remplissages de grottes du Pléistocène supérieur ancien de l'Europe méditerranéenne: Sites moustériens du Boquete de Zafarraya (Andalousie), de Madonna dell'Arma (Ligurie) et de Kalamakia (Laconie, Péloponnèse).* Thèse de Doctorat du Muséum National d'Histoire Naturelle, Paris (unpublishing). 252 p.

LUMLEY, H. de; DARLAS, A. (1994). Fouilles franco-helléniques de la grotte de Kalamakia (Aréopolis, Péloponnèse). *Bulletin de Correspondance Hellénique,* 118: p. 535-558.

REISCH, L. (1976). Beobchtungen an Vogelknochen aus dem Spätpleistozän der Höhle von Kephalari (Argolis, Griechenland). *Archäologisches Korrespondenzblatt,* 6: 261- 265.

ROGER, T. (2004). *L'avifaune du Pléistocène moyen et supérieur du bord de la Méditerranée européenne : Orgnac 3, Lazaret (France), Caverna delle Fate, Arma delle Manie (Italie), Kalamakia (Grèce), Karain E (Turquie): Paléontologie, taphonomie et paléoécologie.* Thèse de doctorat MNHN, Paris: 317 p. (unpublishing)

ROGER, T.; DARLAS, A. (1999). Etude préliminaire des microvertébrés du Pléistocène supérieur de la Grotte de Kalamakia (Aréopolis, Grèce). In CRUZ, A.R.; MILLIKEN, S.; OOSTERBECK, L.; PERETTO C., Eds.,.- *Human Population Origins in the Circum-Mediterranean Area: Adaptations of the Hunter-Gatherer Groups to Environmental Modifications.* Arkeos, 5: p. 121-137.

TOMEK, T.; BOCHEŃSKI, Z.M. (2000). *The comparative osteology of European Corvids (Aves: Corvidae), with a key to the identification of their skeletal elements.* Z. Bocheński (ed.), Kraków: 102 p.

TOMEK, T.; BOCHEŃSKI, Z.M. (2002). Bird scraps from a Greek table: The case of Klisoura Cave. *Acta zoologica cracoviensa,* 45: special issue, p. 133-138.

VILETTE, P. (1983) – Avifaunes du Pléistocène final et de l'Holocène dans le sud de la France et en Catalogne. Atacina, 11: 1-190.

WALKER, C.A.; WRAGG, G.M.; HARRISON, C.J.O. (1990). A new shearwater from the Pleistocene of the Canary Islands and its bearing on the evolution of certain Puffinus shearwaters. *Historical Biology,* 3 (3): 203-224.

WEESIE, P.D.M. (1988). The Quaternary Avifauna of Crete, Greece. *Palaeovertebrata,* Montpellier, 18 (1): 94 p.

MICROVERTÉBRÉS, PALÉO-ENVIRONNEMENT ET PALÉOCLIMAT DE LA GROTTE DE KALAMAKIA (PÉLOPONNÈSE, GRÈCE)

Thierry ROGER

Laboratoire de Préhistoire du Lazaret, 33 bis, Boulevard Frank Pilatte, 06300 NICE, FRANCE,
troger@lazaret.unice.fr

Andréas DARLAS

Ephorie de Paléoanthropologie-Spéléologie de la Grèce du Nord, Navarinou 28, 55131 THESSALONIKI, GRÈCE,
andreas.darlas@eps.culture.gr

Abstract: *Excavations between 1993 and 2000 at Kalamakia Cave, a Middle Paleolithic site of Greece, provided abundant microvertebrate assemblage. This assemblage is composed of 59 species at least and is useful to know environment and climate during the continental filling. No sign of coolest period could be put in evidence. Environment was mainly open and rather dry under a temperate mediterranean climate.*
Key words: *Microvertebrate, Middle Paleolithic, Palaeoclimat, Palaeoenvironment, Greece*

Résumé: *Les fouilles effectuées entre 1993 et 2000 dans la grotte de Kalmakia, un site du Paléolithique moyen de Grèce, ont livré de nombreux restes de microvertébrés. L'étude du cortège des microvertébrés de la grotte de Kalamakia constitué d'au moins 59 espèces permet de mieux connaître l'environnement, le climat et leur évolution au cours de son remplissage. Aucun signe de refroidissement climatique n'est perceptible. L'environnement était principalement ouvert et assez sec sous un climat méditerranéen bien marqué.*
Mots- clef: *Microvertébrés, Paléolithique moyen, Paléoclimat, Paléo-environnement, Grèce*

INTRODUCTION

La grotte de Kalamakia se situe dans le Sud du Péloponnèse sur la commune d'Aréopolis. Elle est située en bord de mer au pied d'une falaise haute de 25 mètres de haut, à la limite sud de la baie d'Itylo (voir fig. 9.1).

Le remplissage de la grotte a une épaisseur de 7 mètres environs. La grotte est fouillée presque chaque année depuis 1993. La fouille est localisée à l'entrée de la grotte. Elle s'est achevée en 2006.

Sept ensembles stratigraphiques ont été définis (Lecervoisier 2003):

L'ensemble stratigraphique 0 est constitué par une couche de calcaire à algue rouge épais de quelques centimètres. Cette formation s'est déposée à une profondeur de 30 mètres environ lors de la transgression du sous-stade isotopique 5.5 (120.000 ans B.P.).

L'ensemble stratigraphique II est constitué par une calcarénite rose à galets et coquilles d'une épaisseur variant d'une douzaine de centimètres à un mètre. La comparaison de cette formation, similaire à une formation en Crète, permet de la dater de 95 Ka (sous-stade isotopique 5.3).

L'ensemble stratigraphique III est constitué de sables limoneux-argileux. Il s'est déposé durant le sous-stade isotopique 5.2 et jusqu'au stade 4 inclus.

Les ensembles stratigraphiques IV et V sont constitués par des argiles limoneuses brun-rouges riches en matériel archéologique. D'après les datations au carbone 14, ces ensembles sont au moins antérieur à 40.000 ans. Ils ont dû se déposer lors de la première moitié du stade isotopique 3.

L'ensemble stratigraphique VI est constitué de limons argileux presque exempt de matériel archéologique. Il a dû se déposer alors que l'entrée de la grotte était obstruée, entre 40.000 ans B.P. et l'époque sub-actuelle.

L'ensemble stratigraphique VII correspond à des fragments de planchers stalagmitiques probablement sub-actuel (stade isotopique 1).

La relation entre un pilier stalagmitique I-S-1 (dénommé aussi ensemble I) et la plage thyrénienne(ensemble II) n'est pas clairement définie.

La fouille a livré une industrie moustérienne (Darlas et de Lumley 1998; de Lumley et Darlas, 1994) et de nombreux restes de grands mammifères (Gardeisen *et al.* 1999) dont l'étude se poursuit actuellement (Psathi, *pers. com.*). Le cortège des grands mammifères se compose de dix-sept espèces (Psathi, *op. cit.*). Les espèces les plus abondantes sont *Rupicapra rupicapra*, le daim puis *Capra* sp., le bouquetin. Les carnivores sont peu abondants mais bien représentés (sept espèces).

L' étude palynologique (Lebreton et *alii*, 1999 et ce volume)a été possible uniquement au niveau du pilier stalagmitique I-S-1. Cette étude met en évidence la présence de taxons méditerranéens xériques et de steppes associée à des essences d'arbres tempérés et thermophiles.

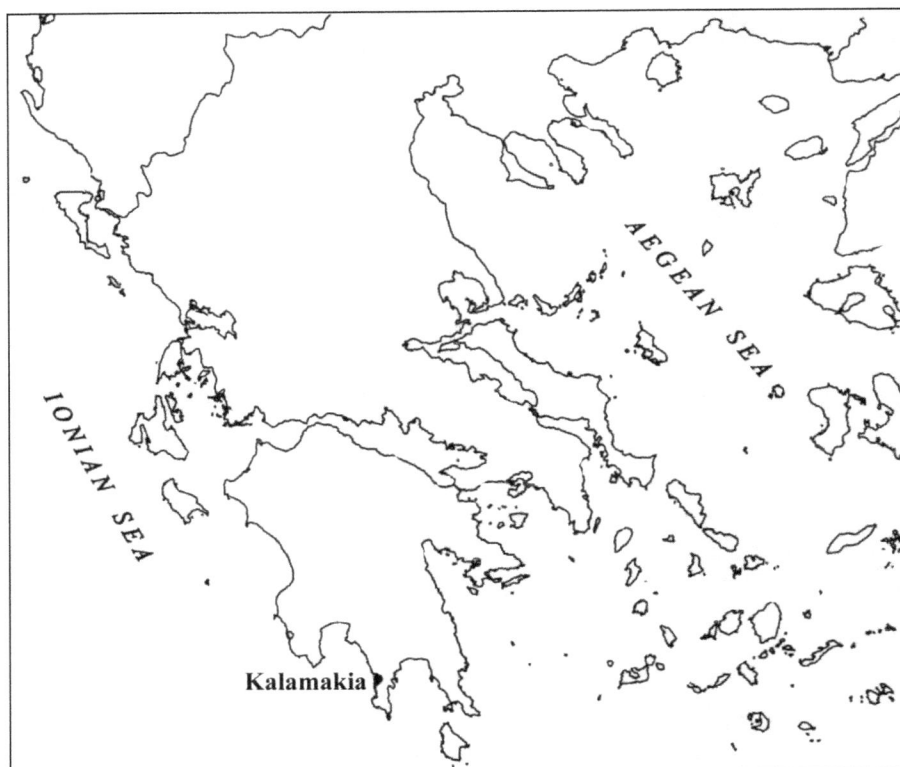

Fig. 9.1. Localisation de la grotte de Kalamakia en Grèce

MATÉRIEL ET MÉTHODES

Les microvertébrés sont récoltés à la fouille pour les restes les plus gros (e. g. oiseaux par exemple) et suite au tamissage à l'eau du sédiment à l'aide de deux tamis superposés dont la maille est d'un diamètre de 2 mm pour le petit tamis et de 4 mm pour le plus gros tamis. Les refus de tamis sont ensuite séchés puis triés.

Depuis les premiers travaux sur les microvertébrés de Kalamakia (Desclaux *in* de Lumley et Darlas 1994; Roger 1997; Roger et Darlas 1999), la totalité du matériel découvert entre 1993 et 2000 a été étudiée ce qui permet de compléter la liste faunique et ainsi donc de pouvoir effectuer, d'après les microvertébrés, une reconstitution plus précise du climat et de l'environnement à l'époque du remplissage de la grotte de Kalamakia L'étude paléontologique exhaustive du matériel ne sera pas abordée ici. Une étude plus détaillé des restes d'oiseaux est disponible chez Roger et Darlas (ce volume). Seul les conclusions de cette étude seront rappelées ici.

Le tableau 9.1 présente le nombre de reste (NR) et le nombre minimum d'individu (NMI) des espèces de microvertébrés de la grotte de Kalamakia par ensemble stratigraphique. Pour les amphibiens et reptiles, seul le NR est calculé.

Le cortège des microvertébrés se compose de 59 espèces au minimum. Les groupes des reptiles et oiseaux sont taxonomiquement les plus diversifiés avec 21 taxons pour chacun d'entre eux. Il suit le groupe des rongeurs avec 9 taxons, puis les Chiroptères et Insectivores (3 taxons), et enfin les Amphibiens (2 taxons). Le groupe le plus abondant est de loin celui des rongeurs avec 7051 restes déterminés, suivi par les reptiles (453 restes), les amphibiens (115 restes), les oiseaux (95 restes), les insectivores (62 restes) et les chiroptères (5 restes).

Il est à noter chez les Rongeurs l'abondance du campagnol de Thomas, *Microtus thomasi,* une espèce endémique à la région balkanique, suivie dans une moindre mesure par le mulot rupestre, *Apodemus mystacinus.* Chez les Amphibiens, l'abondance de restes de crapaud commun, *Bufo bufo,* dans l'ensemble IV, comparée aux autres ensembles est remarquable.

DONNÉES ÉCOLOGIQUES ACTUELLES DES ESPÈCES DE MICROVERTÉBRÉS DE LA GROTTE DE KALAMAKIA.

Seules les données sur les espèces présentant un intérêt pour la reconstruction paléo-environnementale et paléoclimatique sont signalées ici. Les données concernant les Reptiles et Amphibiens sont tirées de Gruber (1992) et de Gasc *et al.* (1997). Les données sur les oiseaux sont disponibles chez Roger et Darlas (ce volume, p. 69).

– Les Amphibiens:

– *Bufo bufo* (Linnaeus, 1758) – le crapaud commun.

Tab. 9.1. Kalamakia: distribution des microvertébrés

	ensemble VI NR/NMI	ensemble V NR/NMI	ensemble IV NR/NMI	ensemble III NR/NMI	Total NR/NMI
Amphibiens					
Bufo bufo	1	4	106		111
Rana sp.		1	2	1	4
total	1	5	108	1	115
Reptiles					
Testudo sp.		11	40	24	75
Scincidae indet.		2			2
cf. *Tarentola* sp.	1				1
Lacertidae indet.	9	20	12		41
Lacerta sp.	2	66	16		84
Anguis fragilis	8	14	55		77
Pseudopus cf. *apodus*	4	8			12
Pseudopus sp.		4		1	5
Eryx jaculus		6	9		15
Hierophis gemonensis		3	2		5
cf. *Dolichophis caspius*			1		1
Malpolon monspessulanus	5	3	15		23
Malpolon sp.			6		6
Coronella sp.	4	6	13		23
Coronella cf. *austriaca*	2				2
Elaphe quatuorlineata	3	3	18		24
Zamenis longissima	1	1	3		5
Zamenis cf. *situla*		2	2		4
cf. *Telescopus* sp.	2	2			4
Natrix natrix	1	2	25		28
Vipera sp.		9	7		16
total	42	162	224	25	453
Oiseaux					
Puffinus puffinus				1/1	1/1
Accipiter nisus			1/1		1/1
Falco cf. *vespertinus*			1/1		1/1
Alectoris graeca		13/3	12/2	1/1	26/6
Coturnix coturnix		3/1	28/7		31/8
Eudromias morinellus			1/1		1/1
Chlidonias sp.				1/1	1/1
Columba livia/oenas		6/2	5/1	1/1	12/4
Otus scops			4/1		4/1
Athene noctua		1/1			1/1
Strix aluco			2/1		2/1
Apus apus			1/1		1/1
Apus cf. *pallidus*			1/1		1/1
Hirundo rustica			1/1		1/1
Certhia sp.		1/1			1/1
Turdus cf. *philomenos*		1/1			1/1
Corvus corone		1/1	1/1		2/2
cf. *Corvus monedula*	1/1	2/1			3/2
cf. *Pica pica*	1/1		1/1		2/2
Pyrrhocorax pyrrhocorax			1/1		1/1
Emberiza citrinella			1/1		1/1
total	2/2	28/11	61/22	4/4	95/39
Chiroptères					
Myotis sp.		1/1			1/1
Myotis blythii		2/1	1/1		3/2
Rhinolophus hipposideros			1/1		1/1
total		3/2	2/2		5/4
Insectivores					
Erinaceus sp.			1/1		1/1
Talpa sp.		11/3	9/3	1/1	21/7
Crocidura suaveolens	2/2	5/3	29/10	4/4	40/19
total	2/2	16/6	39/14	5/5	62/27
Rongeurs					
Sciurus vulgaris	2/2	5/1	7/1	1/1	15/5
Myoxus glis	7/2	38/8	117/15	15/3	177/28
Apodemus sp.	4/2	13/4	18/6	3/2	56/14
Apodemus mystacinus	83/25	436/103	647/160	72/24	1238/312
Cricetulus migratorius				1/1	1/1
Microtus arvalis	2/1	29/16	1/1		32/18
Microtus guentheri	1/1	15/8	7/4	2/1	25/14
Microtus thomasi	190/98	2126/1059	2306/1199	765/395	5387/2751
Chionomys nivalis	3/2	21/14	15/9		39/25
total	296/133	2693/1213	3177/1395	867/427	7051/3168

Le crapaud commun a une distribution européenne très vaste. Bien qu'il préfère les environnements forestiers, il se rencontre aussi dans les environnements ouverts (Gasc *et al.* 1997). Un point d'eau lui est nécessaire uniquement en période de reproduction.

– Les Reptiles:

– Testudo sp.

Testudo hermanni habite les terrains chauds et secs, maquis, dunes et plateaux calcaires.

Testudo graeca occupe les collines et les régions sèches couvertes de broussailles.

– *Lacerta* sp.

Les lézards affectionnent les endroits brousailleux bien ensoleillés. Ils se rencontrent à toutes les altitudes entre 0 et 2000 mètres.

– *Anguis fragilis* Linnaeus, 1758 – l'orvet fragile.

L'orvet fragile affectionne les lieux humides et broussailleux avec des pierres et avec des troncs d'arbres en décomposition.

– *Pseudopus apodus* Pallas, 1775 – l'orvet des Balkans.

Actuellement, cette espèce a une distribution européenne exclusivement balkanique. Elle se rencontre dans les régions littorales et dans les guarrigues et maquis.

– *Eryx jaculus* (Linnaeus, 1758) – le boa des sables occidentale.

Le boa des sables occidental se rencontre dans tout le Sud de la péninsule balkanique, la Turquie, le Proche-orient et l'Afrique du Nord (Gruber 1992). Il affectionne les contrées arides à sol meuble ou sableux avec une végétation rare. En Grèce, cette espèce est représenté par la sous espèce *Eryx jaculus turcicus* (Gruber 1992).

– *Hierophis gemonensis* (Laurenti 1768) – la couleuvre des Balkans.

La couleuvre des Balkans occupe des biotopes très variés, des pentes d'éboulis brousailleuses aux bois clairsemés. Elle est connue sur la côte adriatique de l'ex-Yougoslavie, la Grèce continentale et quelques îles de la mer Egée.

– *Dolichophis caspius* (Gmelin, 1789) – la couleuvre de la Caspienne (= *Coluber caspius* Gmelin, 1789)

La couleuvre de la Caspienne est absente en Europe de l'Ouest. Elle se rencontre de la Hongrie au Kazakhstan dans les steppes ouvertes et les collines à végétation arborée.

– *Malpolon monspessulanus* (Hermann 1804)

D'après Carranza (2006), les populations balkaniques actuelles de *Malpolon monspessulanus* représentées par les deux sous-espèces *Malpolon m. insignitus* et *M. m. fuscus* ont une origine différente des populations de l'ouest de l'Europe qui appartiennent à *M. m. Monspessulanus*.

Ces deux pools de populations se différencient ostéologiquement d'après la morphologie de l'os basio-occipital. Malheureusement, nous ne disposons pas de cet élément squelettique dans notre matériel.

Cette espèce a besoin pour se reproduire d'une température moyenne minimale au mois de Juillet de 22°C (Saint-Girons 1982).

– *Coronella* cf. *austriaca* Laurenti, 1768

La coronelle lisse occupe les contrées dégagées et bien ensoleillés offrant de nombreux abris. Elle occupe toute l'Europe, la Turquie et l'Iran.

– *Elaphe quatuorlineata* (Lacépède 1789) – la couleuvre à quatre bandes.

La couleuvre à quatre bandes se rencontre en Europe exclusivement en bordure de la côte méditerranéenne de l'Italie à la Turquie.

– *Zamenis longissima* (Laurenti 1768) – la couleuvre d'Esculape.

La couleuvre d'Esculape a besoin d'une certaine humidité et aime les climats uniformes sans grandes variations thermiques (Gruber 1992).

– *Zamenis situla* (Linnaeus 1758) – la couleuvre léopard.

Cette espèce est en Europe une espèce presqu'exclusivement balkanique. Elle se rencontre aussi au Sud de l'Italie, en Sicile et à Malte.

– *Telescopus* sp.

Actuellement, le genre Telescopus est présent en Europe par une seule espèce, *Telescopus fallax*, la couleuvre chat. Cette espèce dans tous les pays de l'est du pourtour méditerranéen. Elle se rencontre sur les pentes sèches et bien ensoleillées. Son alimentation est spécialisée en Lacertidés.

– *Natrix natrix* (Linnaeus, 1758) – la couleuvre à collier.

La couleuvre à collier est commune dans toute l'Europe. Elle habite à proximité d'une étendue d'eau ou sur des territoires assez humides.

– *Vipera* sp.

Deux espèces de vipères sont suceptibles d'être rencontrées dans le Péloponnèse: la vipère ammodyte, *Vipera ammodytes*, et la vipère d'Asie mineure, *Vipera xanthina*. Elles affectionnent les biotopes dégagés et bien ensoleillés.

– Les mammifères:

– *Myotis blythii* (Tomes 1857) – le petit murin.

Le petit murin affectionne les biotopes boisés ouverts. En hiver, il se réfugie dans les grottes et les galeries. Il peut être observé au Sud de l'Europe et au Nord de l'Afrique.

– *Rhinolophus hipposideros* (Bechstein 1800) – le rhinolophe fer-à cheval.

Le petit rhinolophe fer à cheval affectionne les environnements boisés. Il occupe en été les entrées de grottes. Il se rencontre des îles britanniques à la péninsule arabique ainsi qu'en Asie centrale et en Afrique, du Maroc au Soudan.

– *Erinaceus* sp.

Actuellement, le seul Erinacéidé présent en Grèce est *Erinaceus concolor*. Son écologie ne diffère pas de l'écologie de *Erinaceus europaeus*. Il habite les forêts déciduales et les prairies humides. Cependant, il a été signalé comme abondant dans les steppes boisés du Sud de la Russie.

– *Crocidura suaveolens* (Pallas 1811) – la crocidure pygmée.

La crocidure pygmée est très commune en Grèce où Poitevin (1984) signale que, au Sud, elle peut représenter 100 % des Soricidés retrouvés dans les pelotes de réjections de rapaces. Elle affectionne les terrains plutôt secs et découverts.

– *Sciurus vulgaris* Linnaeus, 1758 – l'écureuil d'Europe.

L'écureuil d'Europe fréquente les forêts de conifères et de feuillus et surtout les bois assez jeunes et sombres. Il est présent dans toute l'Europe hormis en islande, dans les îles de la méditerranée et dans les zones montagneuses les plus hautes.

– *Myoxus glis* (Linnaeus 1766) – le loir.

Le loir fréquente de préférence la forêt de feuillus et le maquis. Les biotopes rocheux et les bocages lui conviennent également (Marquet 1989). Il est très sédentaire. Son domaine vital est estimé à 200 mètres environ.

Le loir se rencontre en Europe du Nord de la péninsule ibérique à l'Asie mineure. Il est plutôt méridional – il est très commun en Italie- alors qu'au Nord, il n'est abondant que dans certianes régions et selon les années.

Considéré comme un animal de climat tempéré doux, le Loir a pu supporter néanmoins des climats très rigoureux comme l'atteste sa présence au sein d'une association arctique à Lemmings en France dans la grotte de la Garenne à Gisey-sur-Ouche (Chaline 1972).

– *Apodemus* sp. de taille moyenne

Actuellement, deux espèces de taille moyenne du genre *Apodemus* se rencontrent en Grèce, *Apodemus flavicollis* et *Apodemus sylvaticus*. Elles occupent les endroits tempérés boisés.

– *Apodemus mystacinus* (Danford and Alston 1877) – le mulot rupestre.

Le mulot rupestre affectionne, d'où son nom, les karsts, les pentes d'éboulis. Il peut aussi se rencontrer dans des bois clairsemés. Il est très commun en Grèce et dans toute la péninsule balkanique. Il a actuellement une distribution européenne restreinte à la région balkanique mais son aire de répartition était beaucoup plus vaste au Pléistocène inférieur où il est signalé ainsi en France au Vallonnet (Pasquier 1974).

– *Cricetulus migratorius* (Pallas 1773) – le hamster migrateur.

Le domaine de prédilection du hamster migrateur est actuellement constitué par les collines abruptes et boisées dans les steppes arbustives. Il n'est pas très répandu en Europe. Il existe à l'est de la Grèce dans les zones qui possèdent son biotope de prédilection. Il est présent aussi en Ukraine, Syrie et Turkménistan.

– *Microtus arvalis* (Pallas 1778) – le campagnol des champs.

Le campagnol des champs se rencontre dans les milieux d'espaces découverts secs et les prairies mésophiles. Il n'est pas présent sur la bordure méditerranéenne occidentale mais se rencontre sur le pourtour méditerranéen oriental.

– *Microtus guentheri* (Danford and Alston 1880) – le campagnol levantin.

Le campagnol levantin affectionne les milieux relativement secs et ouverts en domaine méditerranéen. Il habite ainsi les prairies sèches, les endroits semi- désertiques mais aussi les zones cultivées. Actuellement, il se rencontre en Libye, Israël, Liban ainsi qu'en Turquie et à l'est de la Bulgarie et de la Grèce où Ondrias (1966) le signale en Attique et en Théssalie.

– *Microtus thomasi* (Barrett-Hamilton 1903) – le campagnol de Thomas.

Le campagnol de Thomas est une espèce endémique à la péninsule balkanique. Il occupe les biotopes ouverts et assez secs, les oliveraies et les alpages en altitude. En Grèce, elle se rencontre au sud- est en Attique et Eubée et au nord- ouest et au sud du Péloponnèse. En Laconie, ce campagnol a été observé au mont Taygète au abord d'une forêt de conifère à 1700 mètres d'altitude (Giagia 1985).

– *Chionomys nivalis* (Martins 1842) – le campagnol des neiges.

Les endroits ensoleillés en haute montagne constituent le biotope de prédilection du campagnol des neiges. Il est capable de vivre à des altitudes élevées puisqu'il est signalé dans les Alpes à 4700 mètres, près du sommet du Mont-blanc.

Il peut se rencontrer aussi jusqu'au bord de la Méditerranée dans des biotopes rocailleux situés peu au

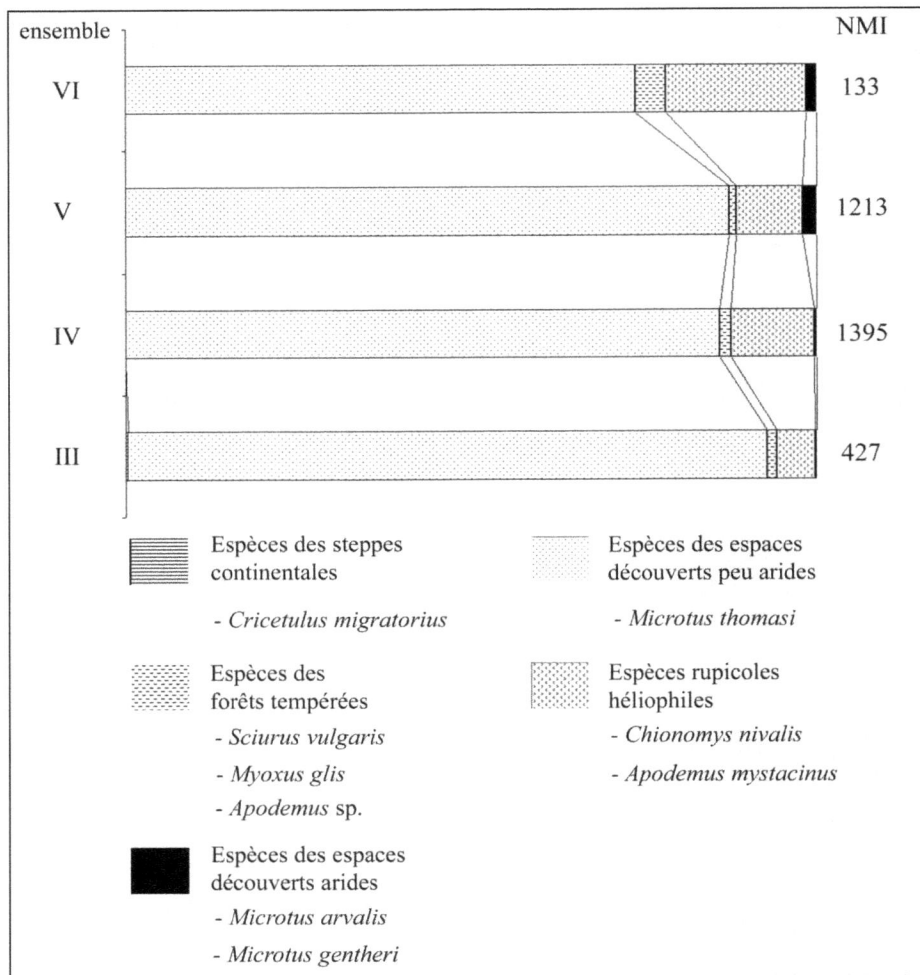

Fig. 9.2. Kalamakia: représentation des groupes climato-écologiques d'après l'étude des rongeurs

DISCUSSION

Les rongeurs regroupés selon le nombre minimum d'individu en catégorie climato-écologique (figure 9.2) selon les données de Marquet (1989), Chaline (1972) et Niethammer et Krapp (1982) donne une image de l'environnement et du climat à l'époque du remplissage de Kalamakia relativement uniforme et conforme à ce qui est déjà signalé chez Roger et Darlas 1999: l'environnement est ouvert et relativement sec avec quelques zones boisées plus humides. Le climat est tempéré méditerranéen.

La présence de *Cricetulus migratorius* dans l'ensemble III et la légère augmentation de l'abondance de *Microtus arvalis* et *Microtus gentheri* dans l'ensemble V indique peut-être un climat plus sec durant ces périodes par rapport à l'ensemble IV. Les espèces des forêts tempérées

sont toujours faiblement représentés. Elles sont légèrement plus abondante dans l'ensemble VI. Nous remarquons l'absence d'espèce de rongeur typique de climat froid.

Les oiseaux (Roger & Darlas, ce volume) indiquent que l'environnement est ouvert sous un climat tempéré. Tout comme chez les rongeurs, il n'y a pas d'espèces d'oiseaux indiquant un moindre rafraichissement climatique. L'influence méditerranéenne est peu marquée d'après l'avifaune. La relative abondance d'*Alectoris graeca* dans l'ensemble V et celle de *Coturnix coturnix* dans l'ensemble IV indique peut-être un climat plus sec dans l'ensemble V.

Rongeurs et oiseaux indiquent donc un environnment et un climat similaire avec peut-être un climat plus sec durant le dépôt de l'ensemble V, mais les rongeurs montrent une influence méditerranéenne beaucoup plus marquées que les oiseaux.

Le cortège des reptiles qui est constitué de nombreuses espèces inféodées à la zone méditerranéenne en Europe (cf. données écologiques actuelles ci-dessus) indique un

dessus du niveau de la mer. Il s'installe surtout sur les versants rocheux, les cônes d'éboulis, les bois clairs et les collines ensoleillées à condition que des éléments rocheux émergent au dessus du sol.

environnement similaire mais l'aridité de l'environnement et l'influence méditerranéenne du climat est très fortement marquée. Là encore, l'abondance relative d'*Anguis fragilis* et de *Natrix natrix* plaide en faveur d'un climat moins sec et un environnement plus humide dans l'ensemble IV.

Le cortège des amphibiens est peu important mais l'abondance de *Bufo bufo* dans l'ensemble IV est remarquable et indique peut-être là encore un milieux plus humide, sauf si éventuellement cette abondance ait dû à un biais de prédation.

CONCLUSION

Les résultats obtenues par l'étude des microvertébrés indique que le remplissage de la grottte de Kalamakia s'est déposé sous un climat méditerannéen relativement bien marqué sous un environnement ouvert et assez sec. Quelques zones plus humides, boisées, existaient au alentour de la grotte. Aucun signe d'un moindre refroidissement climatique n'est perceptible, néanmoins il est probable que durant le dépôt de l'ensemble IV le climat soit moins sec et que les zones plus humides soient plus étendues.

Il est à remarquer que les grands mammifères dont l'étude est actuellement en cours pourraient indiquer un climat un peu plus humide et peut-être un environnement plus fermé à partir de l'ensemble IV par l'apparition du chevreuil, une augmentation nette de l'effectif du cerf élaphe ainsi que celle, moins nette, du sanglier (Psathi, *pers. com.*).

Remerciements

Nous tenons à remercier P. Brunet-Leconte pour la détermination du Campagnol souterrain ainsi que S. Bailon pour l'aide apportée à la détermination des restes d'Amphibiens et de Reptiles. Je n'oublie pas le Laboratoire départemental de préhistoire du Lazaret, Nice, France et le Muséum d'Histoire Naturel de Paris pour leur soutien financier.

Bibliographie

CHALINE, J. (1972). *Les rongeurs du Pléistocène moyen et supérieur de France (systématique, biostratigraphie, paléoclimatologie)*. CNRS Cahiers de Paléontologie, 410 p.

CARRANZA, S.; ARNOLD, E.N.; PLEGUEZUELOS, J.M. (2006). Phylogeny, biogeography, and evolution of two Mediterranean snakes, *Malpolon monspessulanus* and *hemorrhois hippocrepis* (Squamata, Colubridae), using mtDNA sequences. *Molecular Phylogenetics and Evolution*, 40: 532-546.

DARLAS, A; LUMLEY H. de (1998). Fouilles franco-helléniques de la grotte de Kalamakia (Aréopolis, Péloponnèse). *Bulletin de Correspondance Hellénique*, 122: 655-661.

GARDEISEIN, A.; TANTRALIDOU, K.; DARLAS, A. (1999). Faunals remains from Kalamakia (Peloponnese, Greece). In: CRUZ, A.R.; MILLIKEN, S.; OOSTERBECK, L.; PERETTO C., Eds., *Human Population Origins in the Circum-Mediterranean Area: Adaptations of the Hunter-Gatherer Groups to Environmental Modifications*. Arkeos, 5: 111-120.

GASC, J.-P. *et alii* (Eds.) (1997). Atlas of Amphibians and Reptiles in Europe. Societas Europaea Herpetologica & Muséum National d'Histoire Naturelle (IEGB/SPN), Paris: 496 p.

GIAGIA, E.-B. (1985). Karyotypes of "44-chromosomes" Pitymys species (Rodentia, Mammalia) and their Distribution in Southern Greece. *Saütierkundliche Mitteilunge*, t.32, p. 169-173.

GRUBER, U. (1992). *Guide des serpents d'Europe, d'Afrique du Nord et du Moyen-Orient*. Delachaux et Niestlé ed., 248 p.

LEBRETON, V.; DARLAS A.; CATTANI, L. (1999). Palynological analyses from Kalamakia Cave (Greece) and Ca' Belvedere di Monte Pogiolo (Italy). In CRUZ, A.R.; MILLIKEN, S.; OOSTERBECK, L.; PERETTO C., Eds., *Human Population Origins in the Circum-Mediterranean Area: Adaptations of the Hunter-Gatherer Groups to Environmental Modifications*. Arkeos, 5: 85-100.

LECERVOISIER, B. (2003). *Etude stratigraphique, sédimentologique, micromorphologique et paléoclimatique de remplissages de grottes du Pléistocène supérieur ancien de l'Europe méditerranéenne: Sites moustériens du Boquete de Zafarraya (Andalousie), de Madonna dell'Arma (Ligurie) et de Kalamakia (Laconie, Péloponnèse)*. Thèse de Doctorat du Muséum National d'Histoire Naturelle, Paris (unpublishing). 252 p.

LUMLEY, H. de; DARLAS, A. (1994). Fouilles franco-helléniques de la grotte de Kalamakia (Aréopolis, Péloponnèse). *Bulletin de Correspondance Hellénique*, 118: p. 535-558.

MARQUET, J.C. (1989): Paléoenvironnement et chronologie des sites du domaine atlantique français d'âge Pléistocène moyen et supérieur d'après l'étude des rongeurs. Thèse de doctorat d'état., Université de Bourgogne, 637 p.

NIETHAMMER, J. (1982). *Handbuch der Saügetiere Europas*. J. Niethammer et Krapps eds., Akadennische Verlagsgesselleschalft (Wiesbaden), vol. 2/I, 649 p.

ONDRIAS, J.-C. (1966). The taxonomy and geographical distribution of the rodents of Greece. *Saütierkundliche Mitteilungen*, t. 14, sonderheft, fasc. 1, p. 1-136.

PASQUIER, L. (1974). *Dynamique évolutive d'un sous-genre de Murinae, Apodemus (Sylvaemus). Etude biométrique des caractères dentaires des populations fossiles et actuelles d'Europe occidentale*. Thèse de doctorat, Université de Montpellier II.

POITΞVIN (1984). Biogéographie et Ecologie ddes Crocidures Méditerranéennes. Mémoire des travaux de l'école pratique des hautes études, institut de Montpellier, n°14, 100 p.

ROGER, T. (1997). *Contribution à l'étude des microvertébrés de la grotte de Kalamakia (Aréopolis, Grèce)*. Mémoire de DEA, MNHN, Paris, 91 p.

ROGER, T.; DARLAS, A. (1999). Etude préliminaire des microvertébrés du Pléistocène supérieur de la Grotte de Kalamakia (Aréopolis, Grèce). In CRUZ, A.R.; MILLIKEN, S.; OOSTERBECK, L.; PERETTO C., eds. lits.- *Human Population Origins in the Circum-Mediterranean Area: Adaptations of the Hunter-Gatherer Groups to Environmental Modifications.* Arkeos, 5: p. 121-137.

SAINT-GIRONS, H. (1982). Reproductive cycles of male snakes and their relationships with climate and female reproduction cycles. *Herpetologica*, 38: 5-16.

FIRST PALEOLITHIC RESEARCHES IN THE R. MACEDONIA (FYROM): THE CAVE GOLEMA PESHT NEAR THE VILLAGE ZDUNJE – PRELIMINARY RESULTS

Ljiljana SALAMANOV-KOROBAR

National Institution Museum of Macedonia, Skopje, R. Macedonia (FYROM),
ljiljasalamanovkorobar@yahoo.com

Abstract: The cave Golema Pesht is situated near the village Zdunje, 65 km SW from the capital city Skopje at 460 m above sea level. The trial excavation was undertaken in 1999, while the systematic researches, on a relatively small area, continued during 2003 and 2004.
The cave is 31 m long, 18,5 m wide; the entrance is on SE. At 11 m from the entrance, on 1,05 m depth, at 6 m² in 6 geological layers a rich quartz industry (more than 6000 lithic artifacts), fauna material and traces of fireplaces have been found. The rock of the cave has not been reached yet. Ceramics dating from the later prehistoric periods have not been found. The preliminary results from the researches at this site in the continental part of Central Balkan will be presented.
Key words: Cave Golema Pesht, Middle Paleolithic, quartz

Résumé: La grotte de Golema Pesht (la Grande Grotte) est localisée à 460m au-dessus du niveau de la mer, a proximité du village de Zdunje, a 65 km de la capitale Skopje. Un sondage a été entrepris en 1999, et des fouilles systématiques, de faible étendue, en 2003 et 2004. La grotte mesure 31 m de long et 18.5 m de large, avec une entrée au sud-est. A 11 m. de l'entrée, a 1.05 m de profondeur, une zone exposée sur 6 m² et comprenant 6 couches géologiques produit une riche industrie sur quartz (plus de 6000 artefacts), de la faune et des vestiges de foyers. Le sol vierge n'a pas encore été atteint. Aucun indicateur chronologique de type poterie, attestant d'une occupation préhistorique récente, n'a été observe. Cette présentation fera état des résultats préliminaires des recherches menées sur ce site continental du S-E des Balkans.
Mots-clefs: Grotte Golema Pesht, Paléolithique Moyen, quartz

The investigations of the Paleolithic in R. Macedonia (FYROM) (SE Europe) have started relatively late, and up to 1999 no archeological excavations from the aspect of this period were carried out. There is also an absence of archeological literature (Salamanov-Korobar 1996, 244-7; 2005 a, 11,13; 2005b, 15,23).

The only available data from the early and mid 20th century come from chance finds. There are two artifacts form SW part of the country: one from the vicinity of the village Krstoar, the other from the village Bukovo, near Bitola, and they are not kept in our country. They were discovered by the French soldier E. Patte (Patte 1918, 232, 234).

In 1953-1965, paleontological researches were undertaken in the cave Makarovec, near Veles in central part of the country (Garevski 1969, 59-63, 69-73; 1994, 20). Five stone artifacts were discovered, roughly attributed to the Upper Paleolithic.

Since 1998, projects for surveying the caves, rock shelters and open air sites have been carried out, in order to discover potential Paleolithic sites. In various regions of the country 43 sites were surveyed:

– In 1998, along the course of the river Babuna, near the town of Veles, 10 caves and rock shelters were surveyed (Salamanov-Korobar & Djuricic 2005, 9-13, 20, 21; Djordjevic 2005, 23-25);

– In 1999, investigations along the course of the river Treska, Poreche region, near the town of Makedonski

Brod were carried out. Test trenches were made only in one of the 19 recorded caves and rock shelters (Salamanov-Korobar & Djuricic 2005, 13-20; Djordjevic 2005, 25-27);

– In 2001, 14 sites in the southern, eastern and north-eastern micro regions of the country were surveyed, but open air sites were not found (Salamanov-Korobar 2006, 18).

The first systematic excavations were carried out in 2003 and 2004 in the cave Golema Pesht, at the village of Zdunje in the region of Poreche, 65 km SW from the capital city Skopje (see: Map). The cave consists of conglomerates, dolomites and breccia, and belongs to the type of dry caves. It is located at 460 m above sea level (Fig. 10.1). It consists of one large room, 31 x 18.5 m. The entrance is wide 12 m and 3.5 m high and is oriented to SE (Fig. 10.2).

The first data originate from the excavations in 1999. The test trench, 2 x 2 m, was located at 6 m from the cave entrance (Fig. 10.3). From the geological and archeological aspect, 19 layers up to the depth of 3 m were registered, but the bottom of the cave has not been reached yet. It is supposed that the entire deposit in the cave, down to the bedrock, may reach a depth of 8-9 m.

It was not possible to make cultural and chronological determination of the available repertoire of stone finds. In the layers 2-6, 198 stone artifacts were discovered, more precisely, 4 cores, 19 tools (endscrapers, sidescrapers, notched tolls and retouched flakes) and 175 unretouched flakes were distinguished.

In the layers 16-18/19, 36 stone artifacts, i.e. 2 cores, 1 tool and 33 unretouched flakes were registered. Preliminary survey of the stone artifacts point to a Paleolithic chipped-stone technique. The insufficient number of distinctive features as well as the very small sizes of the cores and the tools made us to suppose that they might originate from the Epipaleolithic Period (Salamanov-Korobar & Djuricic 2005, 18).

In the campaigns from 2003 to 2004, at 11m from the entrance, in an area of 6 m^2, in 6 geological layers excavated to a depth of 1.05 m (unit A1) 6.300 stone artifacts and 4.900 remains of animal bones were discovered (Fig. 10.3).

There are no big variations in the stratigraphic sequences in the new trench in comparison with the basic stratigraphy, so that the layers from the test trench completely correlate with the layers from the new/second trench (Fig. 10.4).

1. Recent powdery layer of 15 to 20 cm.

2. Light yellow sediment with a large concentration of small dolomite debris, 3-5 cm in size. The layer has a variable depth of 5 to 15 cm.

3. In the third layer is visible a small concentration of small debris (3-5 cm in size). In comparison with the previous layer, again predominates the small dolomite debris with sharp and partly rounded edges, but in this layer appear blocks with sharp edges, of 30 x 40 cm in size. The greatest depth of this light yellow layer is 30 cm.

4. Layer 4 has a variable depth of 10 to 16 cm in the test trench but 10 to 25 cm in the second trench. The concentration of debris is drastically reduced in comparison with the previous layer. The interstices in which is encountered angular and rarely partly rounded debris, 5-7 cm in size, are filled with a fine, very small-grained structure of 0.005 mm. This friable and soft layer has a gray-brown color and includes a large concentration of archaeological material.

5. Layer 5 is divided into an upper level, 5a, and a lower one, 5b. Their division is caused by ash, which originates from fireplaces; the ash was registered both in tests and in systematic excavation. Layer 5a has a dark brown color. In terms of structure, it is sandy and has a little dolomite debris and a great concentration of finds. In layer 5b again appears a fine fraction, but of reddish color, while the concentration of debris, 5-7 cm in size, increases and shows sharp and partly rounded edges. The variable depth is 15-35 cm.

6. Pale yellow sediment with a larger concentration of angular and rounded debris, 1-3 cm in size, but the interstices are filled with a fine fraction. The variable depth is 5 to max. 18 cm.

The primary raw material is quartz, more precisely milky quartz and rock crystal. Small percentages of other types are encountered: rhyolite, basalt, and jasper (Salamanov-Korobar & Djuricic Djordjevic, 1999, 8; Salamanov-Korobar 2005c, 4; Sirakova et al. 2005, 13, 22, 24).

From the technological aspect, various phases were noted through which the lithic material passed: from its gathering to discarding of the tools. The assemblage includes pebbles, cores, fragments of cores, first flakes with cortex, which were the most numerous – more than 50 %; second flakes with cortex – less than 50%, flakes without cortex, small flakes, chips, debris, and indeterminate flakes (Inizan et al. 1992, 33-63; Karavanic 2004, 81-85). The hypothesis is that we are dealing with a workshop, based on the phases represented in manufacture and based on the large concentration of finds in a small and limited space.

In the lithic material from geological layers 6 and 5 are represented denticulated tools with semi-abruptes and/or abruptes retouch (Fig. 10.11 and 10.14) and tools with notches (Fig. 10.9, 10.10 and 10.13). It should be stressed that there is a lack of sidescrapers – one convex sidescraper of rock crystal, (very small, 3 cm) and one transversal sidescrapers of basalt. Only few examples of perforators and atypical perforators are present. One bifacial point and two unfinished bifacial pieces are registered in the assemblage. The bifacial points were found in the layer 5b/6. There are remains of pebble cortex and covering retouch on dorsal and ventral sides. It is made of milky quartz with a size of 45 x 25 x 13 mm (Fig. 5). The dominant group in the assemblage is the small retouched flakes with marginal or semi-abrupt and irregular retouch. The cortical (total) flakes with continuous semi-abrupt retouch on the ventral side are characteristic (Fig. 10.12). The assemblage contains: Levallois cores and unretouched Levallois flakes and points (Fig. 10.7e). The presence of micro-cores is significant. The cores bear Levallois (Fig. 10.7a and c) and discoid (Fig. 10.7b and d) conceptions characteristic for the Middle Paleolithic, Mousterian (Pohar 1978, 26-58; 1979, 12-32; Sirakov 1972, 26-32; Gacov et al. 1983, 13-28; Sirakov et al. 1993, 1-17; Karavanic 1992, 15-32; 1995, 7-9; Sirakova et al. 2005, 2,4,7,9,14,19).

A contact zone of ca. 15 cm exists in the upper level of layer 5, noted as 5a, and in the lower level of layer 4, where Middle Paleolithic and Upper Paleolithic elements are mixed. Here, in this zone is the greatest concentration of finds.

In layers 4 and 3 the Upper Paleolithic conception is evident where cores with single-platform (Fig. 10.8a), double-platform (Fig. 10.8c), and cores with changed orientation (Fig. 10.8b) predominate. The presence of micro-cores is significant. Two fragments of microblades were discovered, few perforators, endscrapers and splintered pieces, denticulated and notched pieces, formed on small flakes, but retouched flakes are dominant.

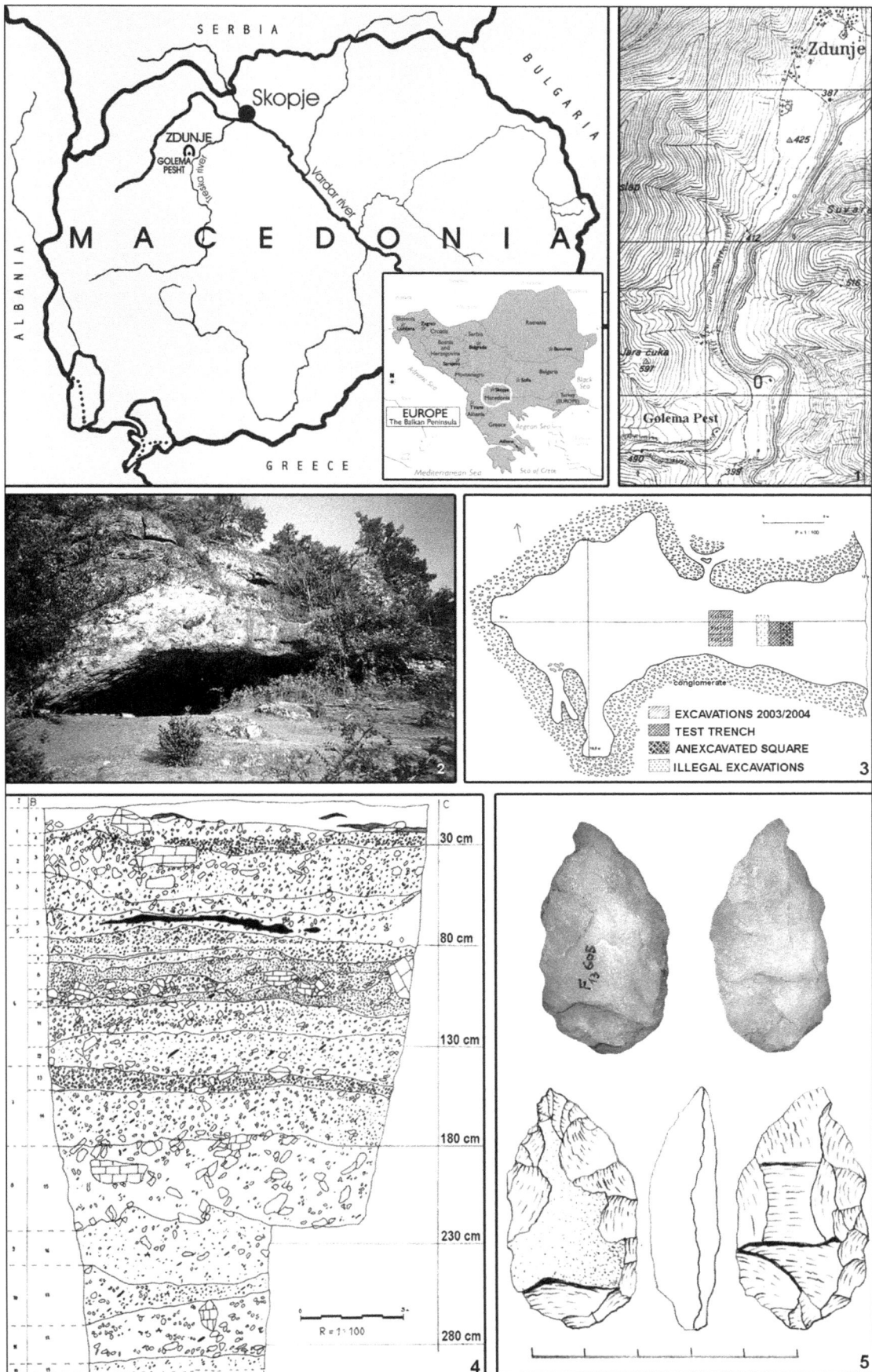

Fig. 10.1. Golema Pesht: site location; a view of the cave enterance; ground plan of the cave; section, quartz tool

Both in the lower layers, 6 and 5, and in the upper layers, 4 and 3, the small sizes of the artifacts are emphasized. Finds smaller than 3 cm predominate, but there is a small number of standard size finds, larger than 3 cm.

Future excavations will confirm whether this is a question of Denticulated Mousterian and/or Micromousterian in layers 6 and 5, but small artifacts are present also in layers 4 and 3 (Bordes 1968, 102,119; Kuhn 1995, 44-54, 120-123; Mayer & Rolland 2001, 40-3). Small tools and cores are able to be explained with the use of small pebbles, which are of local origin. They are present even today, everywhere around the cave and in its vicinity.

From the preliminary archeozoological report the presence of the following fauna types is confirmed: *Cervus elaphus* (deer), *Capreolus capreolus* (roe deer), *Capra ibex* (alpine goat), *Sus scrofa* (wild boar), *Crocuta spelaea* (hyena), *Ursus* sp. (bear), *Castor fiber* (beaver), carnivorous animal in a size of a marten, *Carnivora* indet., *Aves* indet. (birds), *Testudo* sp. (tortoise). The majority of remains (80-90%) are from the deer, while all the other species are present in very small scale (1-3%) (Dimitrijevic 2005, 2). According to Dimitrijevic, the long bones were deliberately split lengthwise. Probably they were used as soft hammers or retouches in the working of lithic material in the chipped stone industry. The author believes that the large concentration of faunal remains in connection with the lithic material results from workshop activity (Fig. 10.6).

The microfauna is represented by 17 specimens. The analyzed material – 885 teeth, jaw fragments and postcranial skeletons remains, originates from layers 3, 4, 5 and 6.

According the analysed fosil association it could be said that open vegetation was dominant in the landscape. The forests were limited to small oases. Larger quantities of forest representatives are found in layer 4. Layer 4 is emphasized as having more moderate and moist climate. The fauna of the geological layer 2-5 is deposited in the period of the Upper Pleistocene (Marinska, 2003, 4; 2006, 2).

Several parameters should be distinguished. There are three distinct series of sediments in the cave Golema Pesht according to the stratigraphic profile and the finds. The first series of sediments from layer 2 to layer 6, unit A1, contains a great concentration of lithic and faunal material; the second series from the test trench is recorded with sterile sediments from layer 7 to layer 15; and, the third series, unit A2, from layer 16 to layers 18-19 of the test trench, contains both lithic and faunal materials, but more definite conclusions are expected from further excavations. It should be stressed also that in the first series, unit A1, from layer 2 to layer 6, the assemblage contains: Upper Paleolithic characteristics in the upper layers 3 and 4, and Middle Paleolithic characteristics in the lower layers 5 and 6.

From layer 5, whose upper level – 5a is divided from the lower level – 5b by fireplaces, which were noted both in tests and in systematic excavations, two samples of charcoal were sent for analysis. The dates in the level 5a were as follows: 47.100 ± 4.800 and <50.000 years ago. AMS analysis was carried out in the laboratory of the Physikalisches Institut der Universitat Erlangen-Nurnberg, Germany.

There are lot of varieties of the Middle Paleolithic cultures in the Balkans, but chronologically they are very close both in the continental parts and at the sea sides. They are registered in the caves, rock shelters and open air sites on several sites on the Balkans.

Vindija cave in the northwest of continental Croatia: the Late Mousterian industry from level G3 has been dated to over 42.000 years ago; the finds are characterized by high frequency of notched and denticulate pieces (36%), sidescrapers (30%) and dominant flake technology; there is no use of Levallois technique; a bifacial leaf piece is present in this level; high percentage of white quartz is utilized (76%) (Karavanic and Smith 1998, 226-230, 245; Richards *et al*. 2000, 7666; Rink *et al*. 2002, 943, 950; Blaser *et al*. 2002, 387-8, 393).

Mujina Pecina in Dalmatia in Croatia, close to the Adriatic coast: Late Mousterian/Micromousterian; presence of denticulate and notched pieces; the use of local small pebble row material – flint; similar with Eastern Adriatic and Pontinian sites in west-central Italy, dated to 50.000 - 40.000 years ago (Karavanic 2000, 777-8; Rink *et al*. 2002, 943, 946; Karavanic 2003, 36).

The late phase of the Middle Paleolithic in Pecina pod Lipom: in 4 rock shelters, out of a complex of 5, in the eastern part of Bosnia and Herzegovina, there are special facies of microliths made in Clactonian chipping-off technique. "Found here is not only microlithisation, but also frequent notches and jaggedness of the working edges of tools" (Kujundzic-Vejzagic 2001, 60-1).

In the rock shelter Crvena Stijena in Montenegro several types of Mousterian are determined, but general remark for the Middle Paleolithic assemblage is the micro size of the tools. Late Mousterian (layer XII) is determined in 40.777 ± 900. The analogies should be looked, perhaps, in the Denticulated Mousterian (layer XIII) and in Pontinian (layers: XXII, XXI and XVIII) (Bazler, 1975, 37, 45, 49-52, 80, 90, 118; 1979, 383-5).

Quartz finds are abundant at three Middle Paleolithic sites in Serbia: Petrovaradinska tvrdjava in Vojvodina, with about 2000 artifacts from two layers. In the upper layer there are Levallois cores and flakes, denticulated tools, retouched flakes, different types of sidescrapers and atypical endscrapers on flakes. A lot of specimens are made of quartz (Mihailovic 2006, 10-12). Hadzi-Proda-nova Pecina (SW Serbia): Typical Mousterian with flint artifacts in layer 6 and with quartz artifacts in the Middle

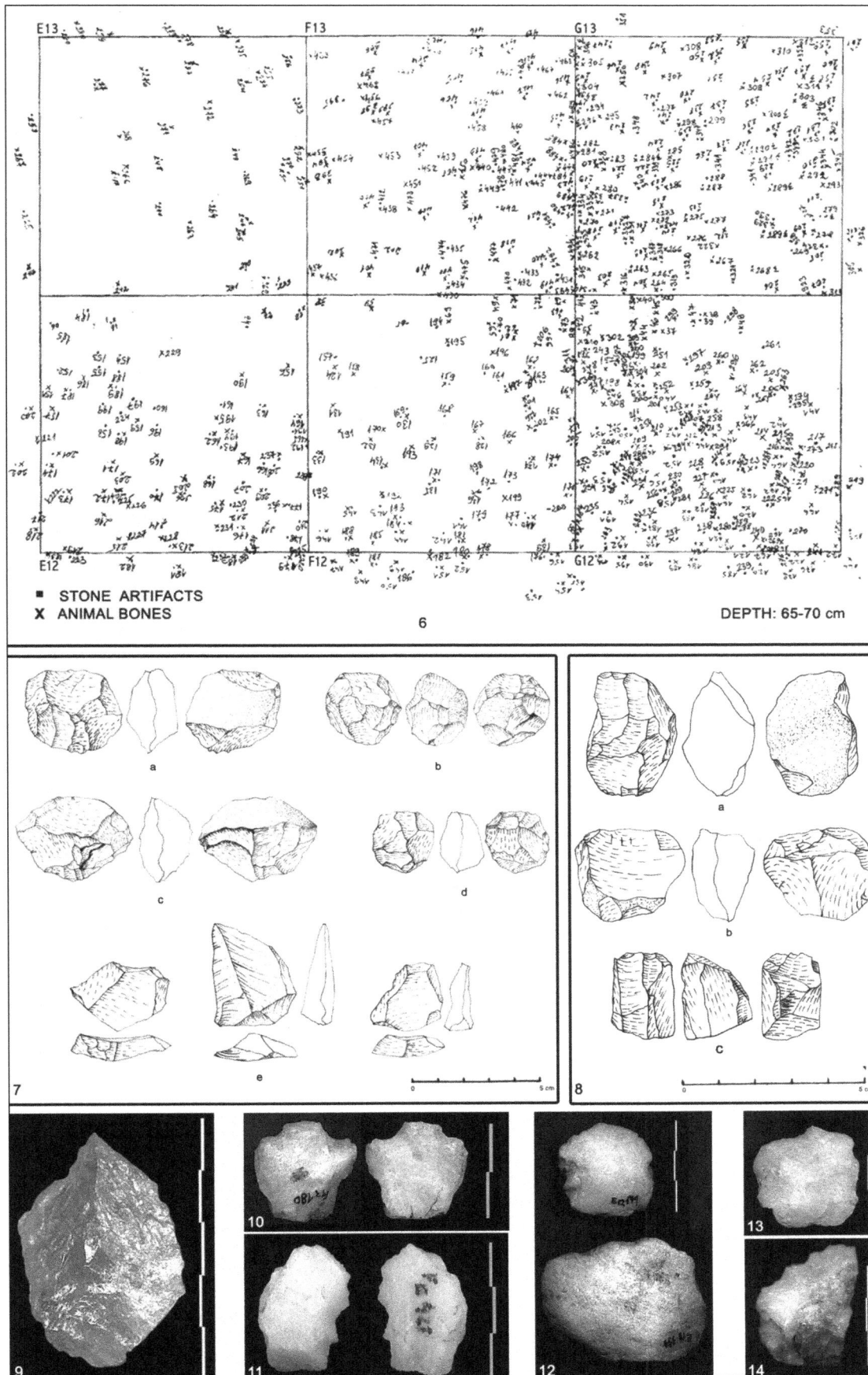

Fig. 10.2. Golema Pesht: Spatial distribution of the finds; quartz artifacts

Tab. 10.1.

Geological layers 6 and 5:	Geological layers 4 and 3:
– local small pebbles as row material	– local small pebbles as row material
– abundant quartz finds	– abundant quartz finds
– Levallois cores and flakes	– single-platforms, double-platforms and cores with change orientation
– discoidal cores	
– dominant retouched flakes	– dominant retouched flakes
– high frequency of notched and denticulated pieces	– high frequency of notched and denticulated pieces
– low frequency of sidescrapers, points and perforators	– low frequency of microblades, endscrapers, perforators and splintered pieces
– micro size of cores and tools	– micro size of cores and tools
– small participation of standard size of cores and tools	– small participation of standard size of cores and tools
– the majority of macrofaunal remains are from deer	– the majority of macrofaunal remains are from deer
– the long bones are intentionally chipped and probably used as a soft hammer	– the long bones are intentionally chipped and probably used as a soft hammer
– occupied by Neanderthals	– moderate and moist climate
– Upper Pleistocene	– Upper Pleistocene
– Mousterien is determined in 47.100±4800; < 50.000	

Paleolithic layer 5 (Mihailovic&Mihailovic 2006, 14-5). Balarica (eastern Serbia): lower stratigraphic complex with quartz artifacts prevailing over the flint artifacts; there are not products of the Levallois technique; the following tools are present: sidescrapers (many of them of the Quina type), retouched flakes and denticulated tools. The upper stratigraphic complex belongs to the Typical Mousterian with Levallois cores and flakes where the following tools are present: various types of sidescrapers, denticulated tools and perforators (Mihailovic in press).

In the rock shelter Asprochalico in Epirus, northwestern Greece, two Mousterian types are confirmed: layers 18-16 are confirmed in Levallois-Mousterian, about 100.000 year ago, while the layer 14 belongs to Micromousterien/Upper Mousterian > 39.900 year ago (Papagianni 1996, 147). It is characteristic for the layer 14 that 30% of the retouched flakes are used for making sidescrapers, and the percentage of the points is very small (Papaconstantinou & Vassilopoulou 1997, 461-3).

The number of sites with Middle Paleolithic finds in Bulgaria is significant. There are various types of Mousterian which have been studied thoroughly: Typical, with Levallois facies, non-Levallois facies, with Sharentian elements, Denticulated and Mousterian with leaf points. By the analysis of the chronology and cultural classification, the researchers of the Middle Paleolithic assemblages in Bacho Kiro, Temnata cave, Musselievo, Samuilica II, date them from 67.000-47.000 years ago (Sirakova & Ivanova 1994, 235-240; Taneva, 2002, 65). But, according to the latest researches in the cave Kozarnika (NW Bulgaria) the Middle Paleolithic is dated much earlier, even to 200.000 years ago (Information by Dr. Sirakova 2006; Sirakov & Guadeli, 2004, 11-12). Nevertheless, besides the various types of Mousterian and the dominant role of the Levallois-Mousterian with leaf points, in NE and N Bulgaria there is one facies of Micromousterian with denticulated retouch in the cultural group Dikilitash (group II), an open site near the coastal town of Varna, and Devetashka cave (group IIb) Lovech region, dated about 50.000-45.000 years ago (Ivanova & Taneva, 1996, 18).

According to the preliminary results of the researches undertaken in three campaigns in the cave Golema Pesht we may say that there are some more or less similar features with the other Middle Paleolithic sites on the Balkans.

The excavations in the cave Golema Pesht are not completed. These are only the first stages of the systematic researches. The analyzed assemblage will have a final statistical elaboration, but at the present stage we have only initial indicators (see Tab. 10.1).

Acknowledgments

This research was carried out with the support of the Ministry of Culture. I am grateful to Dr Svoboda Sirakova, MA Ivo Krumov, MA Elka Atanasova, MA Margareta Marinska, (Bulgaria), Dr Vesna Dimitrijevic, MA Ljiljana Djuricic (Serbia) who helped me with the preliminary analysis of the archeological and the zoological material and MA Nedeljko Djordjevic (FYROM) for the geological interpretations. I am also grateful to Dr Dusan Mihailovic (Serbia) and Dr Ivor Karavanic (Croatia) for our discussion suggestions about this material. I would also like to express my gratitude to my co-workers and students: Miroslav Dimovski, Mihail Stojanovski, Vasilka Dimitrovska, Magdalena Katmerova, Jasmina Glavincevska, Tamara Tomovska, Donco Naumovski, Jane Krstevski, Viktor Simonovski, Zivko Grcev (FYROM) for their participation in the field excavation, and also to the inhabitants of the villages Zdunje and Blizansko, Ilija Kostadinovski and Dimce Miloeski.

References

BAZLER, DJ., (1975). Stariji liticki periodi u Crvenoj Stjeni, In BAZLER, DJ., ed. – *Crvena stijena – zbornik radova*. Niksic: Zajednica kulturnih ustanova, p.11-120.

BAZLER, DJ. (1979). Nalazišta paleolitskog i mezolitskog doba u Crnoj Gori. In BAZLER, DJ., ed. – *Praistorija jugoslovenskih zemalja* I. Sarajevo: Centar za balkanološka ispitivanja ANUBIH, p.383-5.

BLASER, F. [*et al.*] (2002) L'industrie du site nèandertalien de la groptte de Vindija (Croatie): une rèvision des matieres premières lithiques. *L'Anthropologie*. 106, p. 387-398.

BORDES, F. (1968) *The Old Stone Age*. New York-Toronto: World University Library

DIMITRIJEVIC, V. *Paleolitska stanica Golema Pest (selo Zdunje, Zapadna Makedonija) – fauna, Preliminarni arheozooloski izvestaj*, [Manuscript – Report] 2005. Arhiva na Muzejot na Makedonija, Skopje, p. 1-5.

DJORDJEVIC, N. (2005) Geolosko-geomorfoloski opservacii po tecenieto na Babuna i Treska. *Macedoniae Acta Archaeologica* 16, Skopje, p. 23-27.

GACOV, I. [*et al.*] (1983) Tipologia na kamenite oradia ot ranniot i sredniot paleolit, *Arheologia* 1-2, Sofia, p. 13-28.

GAREVSKI, R. (1969) *Stratigrafsko i paleontolosko znacenje na pleistocenskata fauna od pesterata Makarovec vo klisurata na rekata Babuna vo okolinata na Titov Veles*. Skopje: Posebno izdanie 6, Prirodonaucen Muzej, 73 p.

GAREVSKI, R.; MALEZ, M., (1994) Razvoj na reljefot vo kvarterot. In *Arheoloska karta na Republika Makedonija*, Tom 1, Skopje: Makedonska Akademija na Naukite i Umetnostite, Muzej na Makedonija – Arheoloski oddel, Skopje, p. 14-21.

INIZAN, M-L.; ROCHE, H.; TIXIER, J. (1992) *Tehnology of Knapped Stone*, Préhistoire de la Pierre taillée Tome 3, Paris: CREP

IVANOVA, S.; TANEVA, S. (1996) Srednopaleolitni ansambli ot kolekciite na fonda na NAM. *Godisnik na Department Arheologia*. II-III, Sofia, p. 7-49.

KARAVANIC, I. (1992) Predlog osnovnoga strukovnog nazivlja za srednji i mladji paleolitik. *Opuvscula Archaeologica* 16. Zagreb, p.15-35.

KARAVANIC, I. (1995) Strukovno nazivlje za donji i srednji paleolitik, In *Opuvscula Archaeologica* 19, p.7-9.

KARAVANIC, I. (2000) Research on the Middle Palaeolithic in Dalmatia, Croatia, In *Antiquity* 74, p.777-778.

KUHN, S. (1995) *Mousterian lithic tehnology, An Ecological perspective*, Princeton: Princeton University Press

KUJUNDZIC-VEJZAGIC, Z. (2001) Pecina pod lipom – Paleolitsko staniste na Glasinackoj visoravni. *Glasnik Zemaljskog muzeja Bosne i Hercegovine u Sarajevu.* Arheologija, NS 48/49 (1996-2000), p.33-89.

MALEZ, M. (1975) Vindija, Nalazista paleolitskog i mezolitskog doba u Hrvatskoj. In BASLER DJ. ed. – *Praistorija jugoslovenskih zemalja* I, Sarajevo, p.270-273.

MARINSKA, M. – *Drebnite bozainici (Insectivora, Lagomorpha, Rodentia) ot peserata Golema pest, s. Zdune, Makedonia* [Manuscript-Report] 2003. Arhiva na NU Muzej na Makedonija, Skopje, p. 1-4.

MARINSKA, M. – *Drebnite bozainici (Insectivora, Lagomorpha, Rodentia) ot peserata Golema pest, s. Zdune, Republika Makedonia. Predvaritelni rezultati* [Manuscript-Report] 2006. Arhiva na NU Muzejot na Makedonija, Skopje , p. 1-3.

MAYER, C.C.; ROLLAND, N. (2001) Understanding of Middle palaeolithic assamblage tupology. *Antquity* 75, p. 39-43.

MIHAILOVIC, D. (2006) Petrovardinska tvrdjava – paleolitsko nalaziste. *Arheoloski pregled Srpskog arheoloskog drustva* 1 (2003), p. 9-12.

MIHAILOVIC, D. (in press) *New data about the Middle Palaeolithic of Serbia*. In A. Darlas, D. Mihailović (eds.) – *The Palaeolithic of the Balkans*, Session C33, XV UISPP Congresss, Lisbon – Portugal, 4th to 9th Septembre 2006

MIHAILOVIC, D.; MIHAILOVIC, B. (2006) Paleolitsko nalaziste Hadzi Prodanova pecina kod Ivanjice, *Arheoloski pregled srpskog arheoloskog drustva* 1 (2003), p.13-16.

PAPACONSTANTINOU, V., VASIIILOPOULOU, D. (1997) The Middle Palaeolithic Industries of Epirus (chapter 24), In: BAILEY, G.N. ed. – *Klithi: Palaeolithic settlement and Quaternary landscapes in northwest Greece*. Vol. 2, Cambridge, p.459-480.

PAPAGIANI, D. (1996) Middle Palaeolithic Occupation and tehnology in NW Greece: Evidence from open-air sites, In *XIII U.I.S.P.P. Congress Proceedings* vol. 2, Forli, p. 147-152.

PATTE, E. (1918) Coup-de poing en Quartzite, des environs du Monastir. *Bulletin de la Société préhistorique* française XV/4, p. 232-234.

POHAR, V. (1978) Tipologija in statisticna obdelava mlajsepaleolitskih kamenih orodnih inventarjev. *Porocilo o raziskovanju paleolita, neolita in eneolita v Sloveniji* 6, p.7-42.

POHAR V. (1979) Tehnika izdelave in tipologija staro in srednje paleolitskega kamenega orodja. *Poročilo o raziskovanju paleolita, neolita in eneolita v Sloveniji* 7. p.15-80.

RICHARDS, P.M. [*et al.*] (2000) Neanderthal diet at Vindia and Neanderthal predation: The evidence from stable isotopes. *Proceedings of the national Academy of Sciences* 97, p. 7663-66.

RINK, W.J. [*et al.*] (2002) ESR and AMS – based ^{14}C Dating of Mousterian levels at Mujina Pecina,

Dalmatia, Croatia. *Journal of Archaeological Science* 29, p.943-952.

SALAMANOV-KOROBAR, Lj. (1996) Terminot "Chipped Stone Industry" vo makedonskata arheologija. *Macedoniae Acta Archaeologica* 14, p. 241-247.

SALAMANOV-KOROBAR, LJ. (2005a) Surovini za izrabotka na delkani kameni alatki, *Zbornik – Arheologija* 2, Muzej na Makedonija, Skopje, p.7-13.

SALAMANOV-KOROBAR, LJ. (2005b) Paleolitska terminologija vo makedonskiot jazik, *Zbornik – Arheologija* 2, Muzej na Makedonija, Skopje, p.15-23.

SALAMANOV-KOROBAR, LJ. – *Izvestaj za arheoloskike iskopuvanja i istrazuvanja 1999-2005 od lokalitetot "Golema Pest" kaj selo Zdunje, Porece,* [Report] 2005c. Archiva na NU Museum of Macedonia, Ministry of culture, Skopje, p. 1-14 (unpublished).

SALAMANOV-KOROBAR, LJ. (2006) Rekognosciranje na paleolitsko-mezolitski lokacii vo Makedonija – 2001, *Macedonia Acta Archaeologica* 17, Skopje, p. 9-20.

SALAMANOV-KOROBAR, LJ.; DJURICIC, LJ. (2005) Paleolitsko-mezolitski lokacii po tecenieto na Babuna i Treska, *Macedoniae Acta Archaeologica* 16, Skopje, p. 9-21.

SALAMANOV-KOROBAR, Lj; DJURICIC, Lj; DJORDEVIC, N. – *Arheoloskogeoloski prospekcii i probni iskopuvanja po tecenieto na reka Treska,* [Manuscript-Report] 1999. Arhiv na NU Museum of Macedonia, Skopje, p. 1-14.

SIRAKOV, N. (1972) Tehnologia, tipologia na kamenite izdelia ot paleolita i nomenklatura na bulgarski ezik. *Arheologia* 3, p. 20-32.

SIRAKOV, N. [*et al.*] (1993) Tipologia na kamenite orudia od kasnia paleolit, *Arheologia* 3, Sofia, p. 1-17.

SIRAKOV, N.; GUADELLI, Z-L. (2004) Razkopki na paleolitnoto nahodiste Kozarnika, Belogradcisko, In *Arheologiceski otkritia i razkopki prez 2003*, XLIII., Nacionalna arheologiceska konferencia, BAN, Arheologiceski institut s muzea, Sofia, p. 11-13.

SIRAKOVA, B.; KRUMOV, I.; SALAMANOV-KOROBAR, Lj. – *Analiza na kameniot materijal od pesterata Golema Pest, kaj selo Zdunje,* [Manuscript-Report] 2005. Arhiv na NU Museum of Macedonia, Skopje, p.1-24.

SIRAKOVA, S.; IVANOVA, S. (1994) Hronologia na paleolitnite kulturi na teritoriata na Bulgaria. *Godisnik na Department Arheologia – NBU*, I, Sofia, p. 234-248.

TANEVA, S. (2002) Istoria na paleolitnite izsledvania v Bulgaria. *Godisnik na Arheologiceskia institut s muzea – BAN*, tom II, Sofia, p. 63-69.

TOPOGRAFSKA KARTA, ZDUNJE, MAKEDONIJA, 174-1-4 [Cartographic material] / Narodna odbrana, Vojnogeografski institut, Scale 1:25.000, Skopje: Republicka geodetska uprava Skopje, 1978.

NEW DATA ABOUT THE MIDDLE PALAEOLITHIC OF SERBIA

Dušan MIHAILOVIĆ

Faculty of Philosophy, Department of Archaeology, Čika Ljubina, 18-20, 11000 Belgrade-Serbia

Abstract: Within last few decades in the central Balkans commenced the investigations of few multi-layered Middle Palaeolithic sites. In Hadzi-Prodanova pecina near Ivanjica have been investigated horizons with 'Quartz' and Typical Mousterian, in Velika Balanica and Mala Balanica near Sicevo were encountered many horizons with Typical Mousterian and Charentian and at Petrovaradin fortress near Novi Sad were investigated two horizons with stone industry including Charentian and Levallois elements as well as backed bifacial tools. This initial investigations give us opportunity to comprehend at least in general the periodization and cultural differentiation of Middle Palaeolithic industries in this part of the Balkans.
Keywords: Middle Palaeolithic, Mousterian, Balanica, Petrovaradinska fortress, Hadzi Prodanova Pecina, lithic industry

Résumé: Durant ces dernières décennies, les fouilles de quelques sites à plusieurs horizons du Paléolithique moyen ont été effectuées dans les Balkans centraux. Dans la Grotte de Hadži Prodan, près de la ville d'Ivanjica, on a exploré les horizons livrant l'industrie moustérienne "de quartz" et celle du Moustérien Typique; sur les sites de Velika Balanica et de Mala Balanica, près de Sićevo, ont été attestés de nombreux horizons avec l'industrie Moustérienne Typique, ainsi que celle de type Charentien; enfin, dans la Fortresse de Petrovaradin, près de la ville de Novi Sad, on a exploré deux horizons livrant une industrie aux éléments Charentiens et Levallois et aux outils bifaciaux à dos. Les explorations initiales permettent d'envisager, au moins à grands traits, la périodisation et la différenciation culturelle des industries du Paléolithique moyen dans cette région des Balkans.
Mots-clés: Paléolithique Moyen, Moustérien, Balanica, la Forteresse de Petrovaradin, Hadzi Prodanova Pecina, l'industrie lithique

Only until few years ago very little was known about the Middle Palaeolithic of the central Balkans. Even though the first finds had been discovered at few sites in the vicinity of Vršac already in the end of the 19th century (Mihailović 1992), first scientific excavations were conducted by B. Gavela in the 1950s. On that occasion relatively small amount of the Middle Palaeolithic finds was collected in the Risovača cave and in the Pećina pod Jerininim brdom in the central Serbia (Gavela 1988) (fig. 11.1). These investigations were not published in full detail and today is difficult to trace down the material and documentation. From that time until the mid-1990s there were many attempts to discover Middle Palaeolithic in the central and southwestern Balkans but good results have been achieved only in Montenegro in the Bioče cave near Podgorica (Žižić and Srejović 1987) and at Mališina Stijena near Pljevlja (Radovanović 1986). At that time in Serbia were conducted systematic excavations only in the Smolućka cave near Tutin where have been discovered many Middle Palaeolithic horizons containing about hundred artifacts (Kaluđerović 1985). At other sites have been found, almost as a rule, up to five chipped stone artifacts (Cigan-Irig, Pećina pod Crvenim Stijenama, Pećurski kamen – Kaluđerović 1993; Mihailović *et al.* 1997).

When owing to the favorable circumstances the investigations of the Middle Palaeolithic in Serbia has been resumed in 2003 it was not expected that even three multilayered sites from this period would be discovered within a short period of time including Hadži Prodanova Pećina in western Serbia (Mihailović and Mihailović 2006), Petrovaradin fortress in Vojvodina (Marković *et al.* 2004; Mihailović 2006) and Velika Balanica in southern Serbia. When we add to this the site Golema Pesht in the vicinity of Skopje (Shalamanov-Korobar, this volume) it is clear that initial requirements for compre-

hension of the cultural conditions in the Middle Palaeolithic in the central Balkans are satisfied. Of course, it should be emphasized that excavations at these sites have just started so in this review we are going to present only the preliminary results of those investigations.

HADŽI PRODANOVA PEĆINA

Hadži Prodanova Pećina is situated 6 kilometers to the north of Ivanjica (southwestern Serbia) some twenty meters above the Rašćanska River. The cave entrance is high and it continues into around twenty meters long corridor, which opens into a large room whose floor is covered with thick deposits of guan. Rescue archaeological excavations at this site were conducted in 2003 and 2004 and the reason for them was the restoration of the church of St. Archangel Michael situated at the plateau in front of the cave. At the beginning there was almost no indications for the existence of Palaeolithic site (as there had previously been found only the bones of the Ursus spelaeus). First trench was opened at the very entrance to the cave and only later the excavations extended to include the plateau in front of the cave. Until the end of excavations the plateau was investigated to the depth of 4.5 meters.

Several cultural and geological horizons were distinguished in the stratigraphy of the Hadži Prodanova Pećina. Immediately under the surface layer occurred the layer of brown sediment with eboulis that contained the Epigravettian finds (layer 2) while the Middle Palaeolithic artifacts were registered in the layer of brown sediment with coarse eboulis (layer 5a) on top of the level with large rock fragments and in layers 5b, 5c and 5d characterized by somewhat darker sediment.

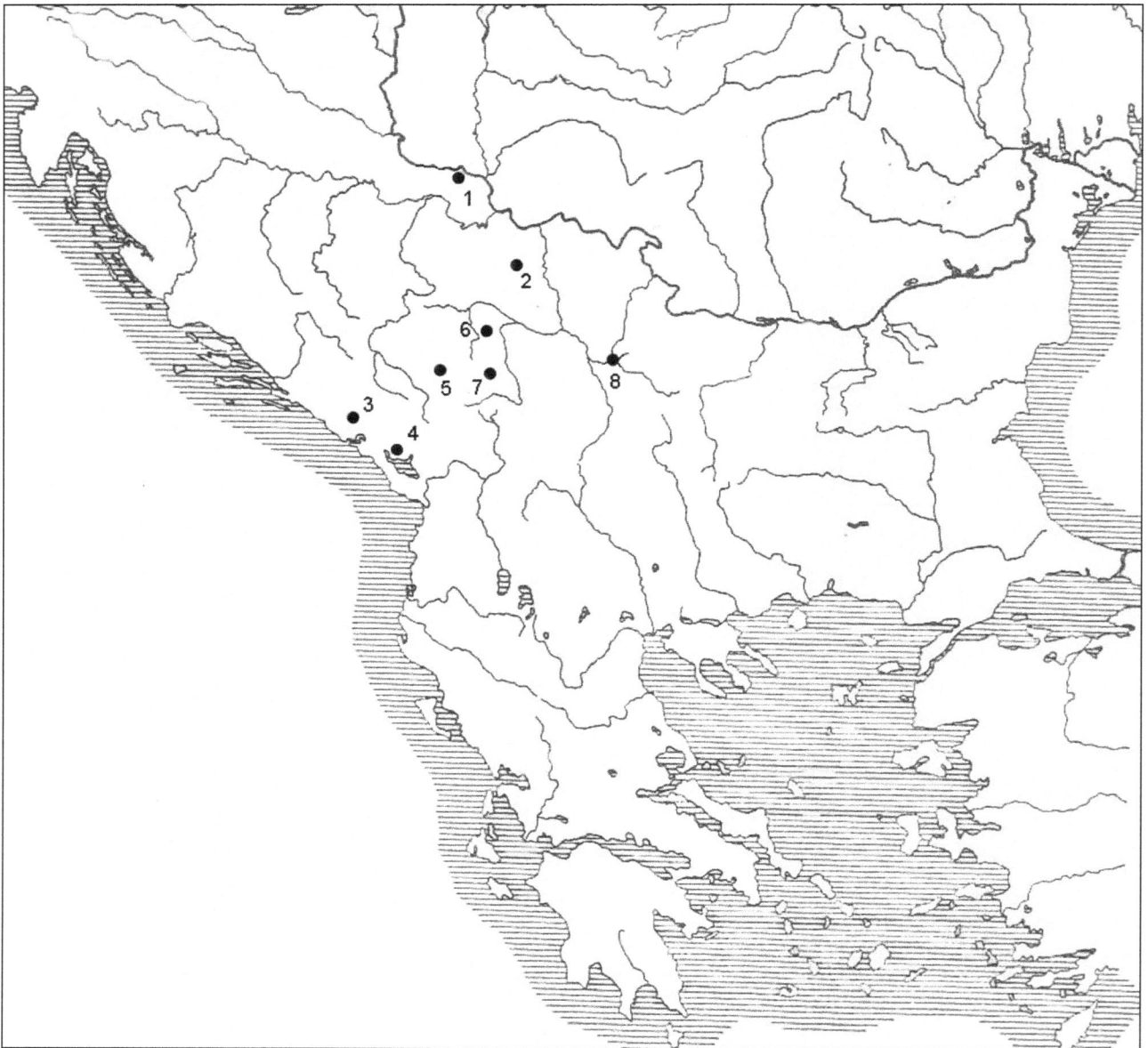

Fig. 11.1. Middle Palaeolithic sites in the central Balkans: 1 – Petrovaradin fortress, 2 – Risovača, 3 – Crvena Stijena, 4 – Bioče, 5 – Mališina Stijena, 6 – Hadži Prodanova Pećina, 7 – Smolućka Pećina, 8 – Velika Balanica and Mala Balanica

The number of finds discovered at Hadži Prodanova Pećina is small (hardly over a hundred of chipped stone artifacts in total) but their character is such that it makes possible general cultural determination. On the other hand, this material is very useful when the explanation of the activities of the Middle Palaeolithic communities.

In the layer 5d only few flint artifacts have been discovered in the lower part of the sequence. These finds were not sufficient for any cultural determination but they suggested that finds could be expected at the greater depth (total thickness of the plateau exceeds 10 meters). On the other hand, in the layer 5b and 5c were registered many artifacts including the Levallois flakes and blades, retouched tools of flint and certain amount of the quartz artifacts while in layer 5a were found quartz finds and

many bones of the *Ursus spelaeus*. All in all, the material from the upper layer (fig. 11.2: 1-3) could be attributed to the so-called Quartz or Cave Mousterian while the finds from the lower horizon (fig. 11.2: 4-8) could be related to the Typical Mousterian encountered at many sites in the neighboring regions. The chronology of the Middle Palaeolithic layers is not known at this moment but it could be assumed that layer 5c could be earlier than the isotopic phase 4 to which eventually could be dated the level of large rock fragments in in the substratum of the layer 5a.

In Hadži Prodanova Pećina could be rather clearly perceived the activities of the Palaeolithic communities. It is obvious that the cave was used as short-term habitation where the tools brought from other places (retouched flint

94

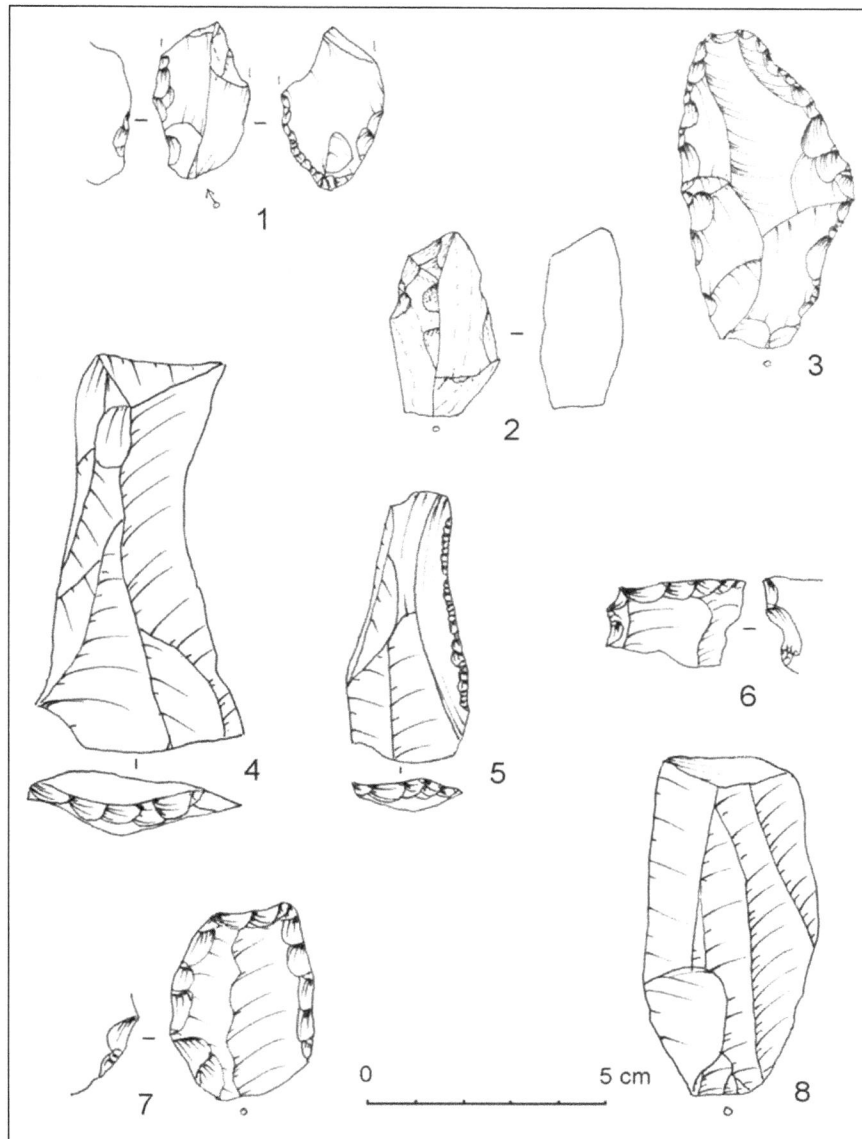

Fig. 11.2. Chipped stone artefacts from Hadži Prodanova Pećina

tools and Levallois blades) had been used to the maximum while the quartz artifacts, which obviously had temporary purpose were produced on the spot. One artifact made of rock crystal was found in layer 5a (fig. 11.2: 1) while a few quartz crystals were found at the boundary of layer 4. It is impossible to conclude for the time being whether the quartz crystals reached the cave in a natural way or the people brought them to the cave. The deposits of this raw material were encountered at few kilometers distance from the site – in the village Lise and at the location Gliječ that is about 7 km to the south.

PETROVARADIN FORTRESS

Middle Palaeolithic at Petrovaradin fortress near Novi Sad was discovered almost by chance when the authors of the rescue excavations tried to establish the depth of the

parent rock. On that occasion the Palaeolithic finds were discovered in the layers of loess at the very top of the plateau immediately behind the building of the Novi Sad City Museum. After that the systematic archaeological excavations were organized at this site in the 2003 and 2004. The excavations comprised a large area of almost 80 square meters.

Petrovaradin fortress is situated high above the Danube bank on the eastern slopes of Fruška gora and excavations revealed that the site covers almost the entire Petrovaradin plateau. In the course of the rescue excavations almost 2000 artifacts were collected and these finds were encountered within two loess layers immediately above the rocky base. Considering the homogeneity of the industry and the fact that contact zone between the two layers is considerably disturbed it is not impossible that both layers belong to the same habitation horizon. On the

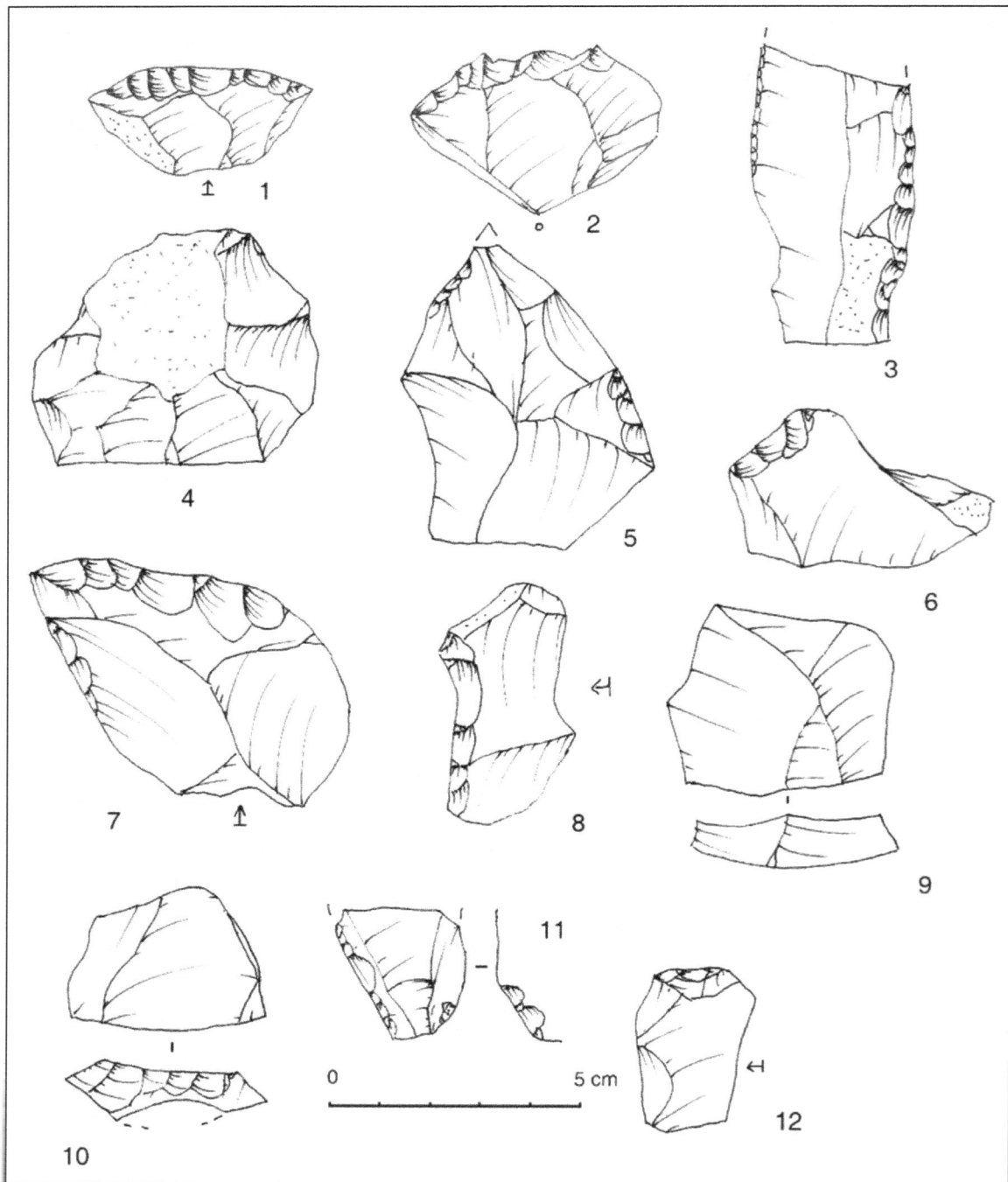

Fig. 11.3. Chipped stone artefacts from Petrovaradin fortress

basis of malacological investigations and investigations of the magnetic susceptibility it is assumed that lower layer could belong to the loess subhorizon L1L2 that was formed in the early phase of the last glacial (OIS 4) while for the upper layer was concluded that it is palaeosoil in the initial phase of formation and that it could belong to OIS 3 (Marković et al. 2004).

In the industry from Petrovaradin fortress prevail the flakes made of low quality raw material and there are also many specimens made of quartz (fig. 11.3). In the upper horizon were encountered Levallois cores and flakes. Among the tools are prevailing plain retouched flakes and denticulated tools and there were also registered different types of sidescrapers (mostly transversal) and atypical endscrapers on flakes. On the whole the industry has the characteristics of middle European Charentian of the Tata-Erd type but it differs from it on the basis of the presence of the Levallois elements and the fact that massive bifacially flaked backed sidescrapers were found in the each horizon (fig. 11.4). Quantity and character of the finds as well as the area of their distribution clearly

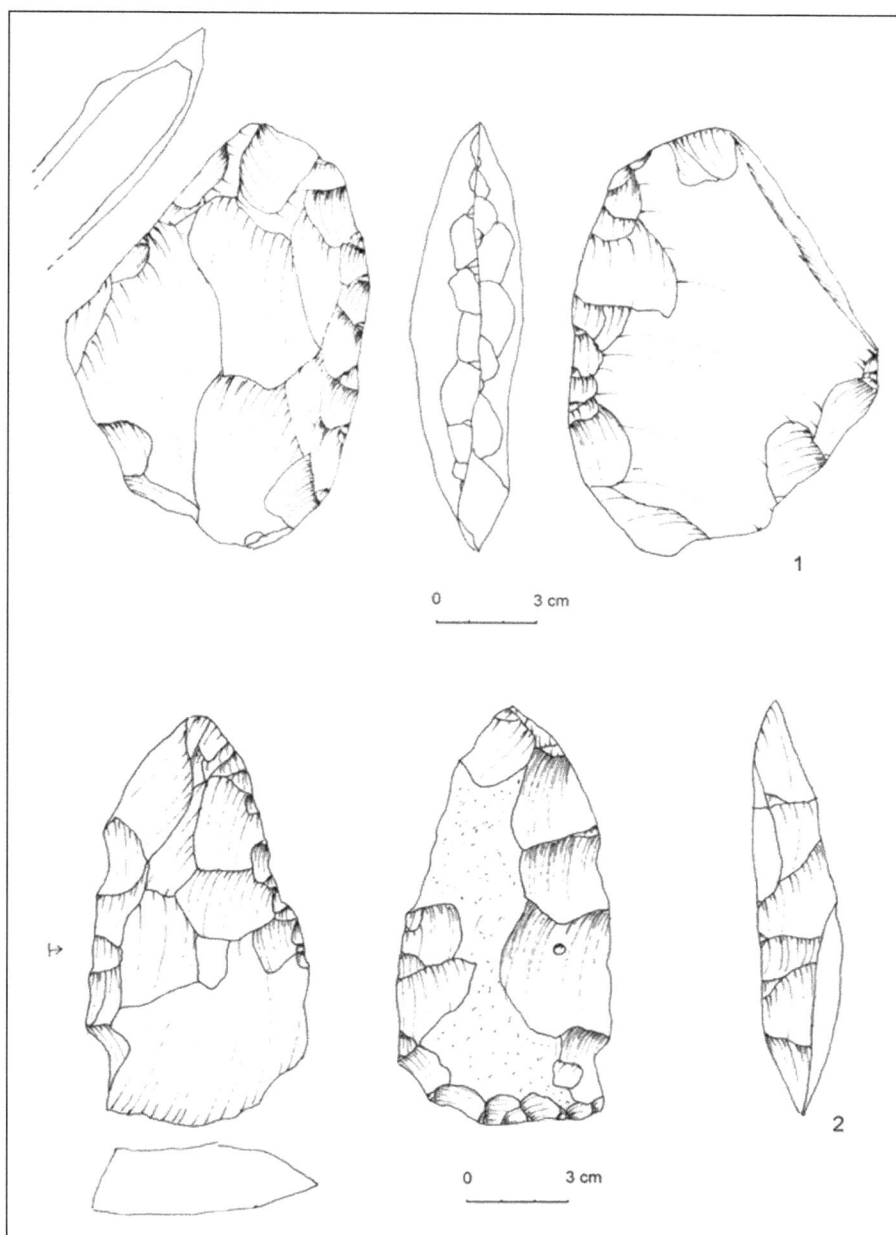

Fig. 11.4. Chipped stone artefacts from Petrovaradin fortress

indicate that Petrovaradin fortress was the base camp. About the character of settlement the conclusions could be drawn only on the basis of the chipped stone artifacts as the bones were not preserved. It is assumed on the basis of the spatial distribution of finds that center of the settlement was at the very top of the Petrovaradin plateau. This area will soon be available for investigations when the works on installation under the museum building start.

BALANICA CAVE COMPLEX

The Palaeolithic finds within Balanica cave complex were discovered in 2002 in the course of site survey of the line of the motorway from Niš to the Bulgarian border. On that occasion were discovered few chipped stone artifacts in a profile of a trench dug at the entrance of the cave by those searching for valuables (Mihailović 2004) The archaeological test excavations were undertaken in the late autumn of 2004 and included only a couple of square meters. Then it turned out that layers with the Middle Palaeolithic finds occur from the very surface of the ground. Until the end of the first season five habitation horizons from which we collected over 1.000 artifacts and many mostly fragmented and burned animal bones were investigated within these few squares. During subsequent excavations in 2005 and 2006 substantially larger area (of approximately 20 square meters) was investigated. Several thousands of finds were registered and it was concluded that cultural layers exist also inside the cave.

97

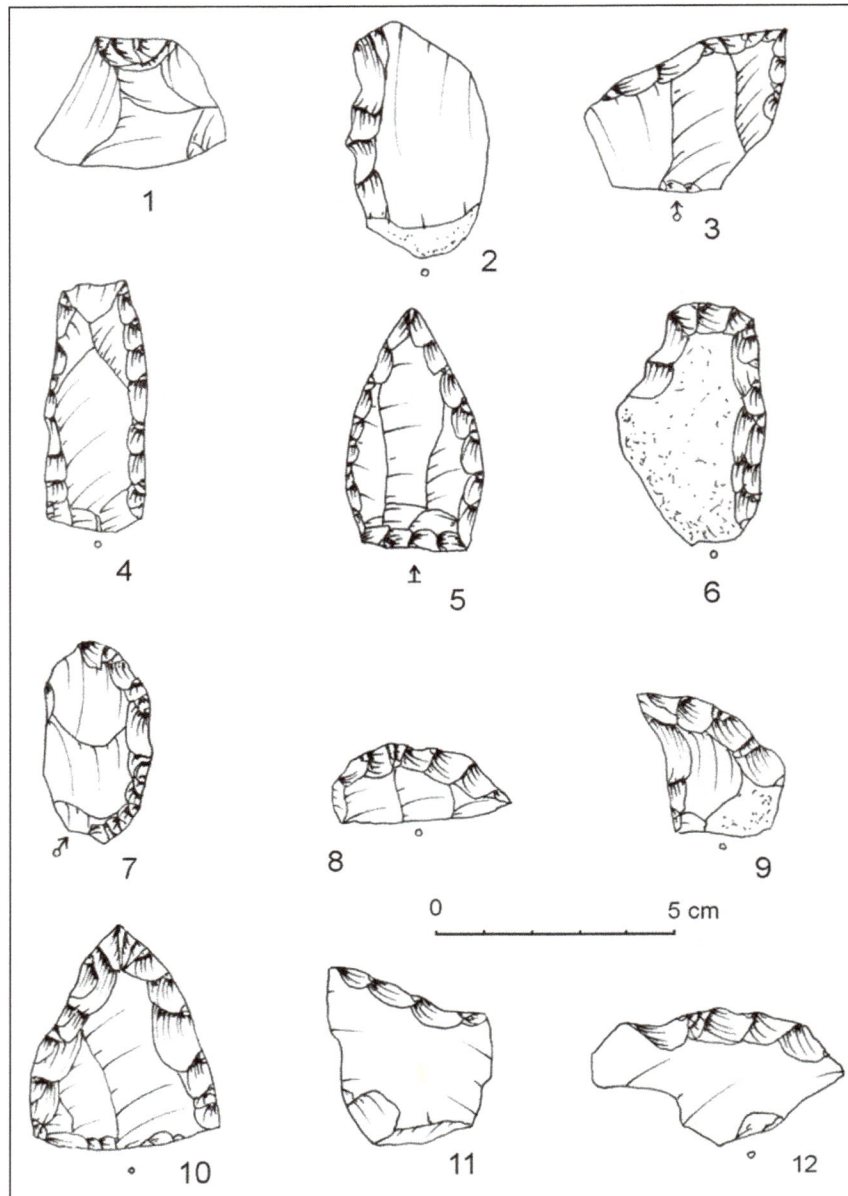

Fig. 11.5. Chipped stone artefacts from Velika Balanica

Velika Balanica was genuine base camp, living site, intensively and frequently inhabited within prolonged period of time. Not far away is another cave (Mala Balanica), which was probably the part of the same cave complex. In 2005 in the upper layer of this cave were discovered the Middle Palaeolithic artifacts mostly made of quartz, transversal sidescrapers and plenty of well-preserved animal bones. The fact that two habitations dating from the approximately same period but of differ-rent function occur next to each other offers a unique opportunity to comprehend the way of life of the Neanderthal man.

The lower stratigraphic complex of Velika Balanica incluce layers with somewhat darker sediment and rich in organic remains. From these layers was collected industry with the quartz artifacts prevailing but the flint artifacts were also registered (fig. 11.5: 8-12). There were no products of the Levallois chipping technique. Among the tools are prevailing short and broad transversal sidescra-pers (many of them of the Quina type), retouched flakes and denticulated tools. In the upper stratigraphic complex including layers with reddish and brown sediment with debris was registered the Typical Mousterian with the Levallois cores and flakes, various types of sidescrapers, denticulated tools and perforators (fig. 11.5: 1-7). The quartz is present in considerably smaller quantity than in the lower layers and there are indications that raw materials were obtained also from the near by site and flint deposit Kremenac near Niš for which was assumed already in the 1990s to had been a Palaeolithic site It is interesting that zones of activities in various horizons do not overlap and while in the late phase the entrance zone of the cave was intensely inhabited in the earlier period the activities were confirmed more towards the cave interior. The analysis of the samples from Velika Balanica has not been completed yet. Only after that the chronology of the site will be known and it will be possible to comprehend the factors, which had the impact on the deposition of the finds as well as the character of activities taking place in the cave.

CONCLUDING REMARKS

Having no intention to give final judgment about anything (as this will be premature at this moment) we would like to draw attention to certain implications of the more recent discoveries of the Middle Palaeolithic in the central Balkans. It turned out, however, that the phenomena from the neighboring regions could be expected in many regions of Serbia. Thus is understandable the occurrence of the Charentian elements at Petrovaradin as well as the occurrence of the Typical Mousterian in the upper layers of Velika Balanica and in layer 5c of Hadži Prodanova Pećina. Nevertheless, we distinguished also the phenolmena, which throw the entirely new light on the cultural circumstances in the Middle Palaeolithic of the central Balkans.

At Petrovaradin fortress was encountered the elements of different Middle Palaeolithic facies, which usually do not occur together in the neighboring regions. In the industry from this site that despite stratigraphic perplexities could be considered homogeneous the Charentian component is prevailing but there were also registered the products of the Levallois chipping technology as well as the elements, which only conditionally could be associated with the industries with backed bifaces in the central and western zones of the Carpathian basin. We do not think that industries from Petrovaradin have any direct relations with Micoquian and Bábonyien of the middle Europe (Bosinski 1967; Ringer 2001). It is evident, however, that occurrence of these finds is not accidental and they almost certainly along with other indicators bear witness to the cultural merging and certain degree of cultural unity within the entire territory of the Carpathian basin.

It is also important that more recent investigations confirmed that Charentian industries also occur in the central Balkans. The Charentian elements are well documented at Petrovaradin fortress (where they are the prevailing component) as well as at Velika Balanica. We would like to remind you that until only couple of years ago this industry type had not been confirmed in the central and eastern Balkans. Whether it is a regional facies or an earlier horizon, which could perhaps be paralleled with the Charentian industries in the south Pannonia (from the sites Tata and Erd – Gabori-Czank 1968; Moncel 2003) and northwestern Croatia (Ivanova 1979; Simek and Smith 1997) will be known only after precise dating of these two sites.

In addition, it should also be emphasized that the quartz finds are very abundant at all three investigated sites. In contrast to Petrovaradin fortress and Velika Balanica where the quartz artifacts occur in the Charentian context, these finds at Hadži Prodanova Pećina could be associated exclusively with the character of activities in the settlements. Rather great importance for understanding the occurrence of the quartz industries in the Balkans will have the future investigations at Golema pesht in Macedonia considering the fact that quartz finds are signifycantly predominant at this site (Shalamanov-Korobar, this volume). In any case, only after the analyses of all the materials and samples gathered during the systematic investigations of these sites it will be possible to comprehend more thoroughly the cultural evolution and way of life of the Neanderthal communities in this area of the Balkans.

References

BOSINSKI, G. (1967) *Die Mittelpaläolithischen Funde im Westlichen Mitteleuropa,* Köln – Graz: Böhlau Verlag. p. 206.

GAVELA, B. (1988) *Paleolit Srbije.* Beograd: Centar za arheološka istraživanja.

IVANOVA, S. (1979) Cultural differentiation in the Middle Palaeolithic on the Balkan Peninsula. In KOZŁOWSKI, J.K. ed. *Middle and Early Upper Palaeolithic in Balkans.* Warszawa-Krakow: Zeszity Naukowe Uniwersytetu Jagiellonskiego. p. 13-33.

KALUĐEROVIĆ, Z. (1985) Istraživanja Smolućke pećine 1984-1985. *Novopazarski zbornik 9.* p. 5-18.

KALUĐEROVIĆ, Z. (1993) Palaeolithic in Serbia in the Light of the recent Research. *Starinar.* N.S. XLII (1991). p. 1-8.

MARKOVIĆ, S.B.; MIHAILOVIĆ, D.; OCHES, E.A.; JOVANOVIĆ, M.; GAUDENYI, T. (2004) The Last Glacial climate, environmet and the evidence of Palaeolithic occupation in Vojvodina province, Serbia: an overview. *Antaeus.* 27. p. 147-152.

MIHAILOVIĆ, D. (1992) *Orinjasijenska kremena industrija sa lokaliteta Crvenka-At u blizini Vršca.* Beograd: Centar za arheološka istraživanja.

MIHAILOVIĆ D. (2004) Istraživanja pećinskih arheoloških nalazišta u slivu Timoka i Nišave. *Zbornik radova Odbora za kras i speleolologiju SANU.* 8. P. 135-144.

MIHAILOVIĆ, D. (2006) Petrovaradinska tvrđava – paleolitsko nalazište. *Arheološki pregled Srpskog arheološkog društva.* 1(2003), p. 9-12.

MIHAILOVIĆ, D.; ĐURIČIĆ, LJ.; KALUĐEROVIĆ, Z. (1997) Istraživanje paleolita na području istočne Srbije. In LAZIĆ, M. ed. – *Arheologija istočne Srbije.* Beograd: Centar za arheološka istraživanja. p.33-44.

MIHAILOVIĆ, D.; MIHAILOVIĆ, B. (2006) Paleolitsko nalazište Hadži Prodanova pećina kod Ivanjice.

Arheološki pregled Srpskog arheološkog društva. 1 (2003). p. 13-16.

RADOVANOVIĆ, I. (1986) Novija istraživanja paleolita i mezolita u Crnoj Gori. *Glasnik Srpskog arheološkog društva.* 3. p. 63-76.

RINGER, A. (2001) Le complexe techno-typologique du Babonyien-Szélétien en Hongrie du Nord. In CLUQUET, D. ed. *– Les industries à outils bifaciaux du Paléolithique moyen d'Europe occidentale.* Liege: E.R.A.U.L. 98. p. 213-220.

SHALAMANOV-KOROBAR, LJ. (this volume) First Palaeolithic Researches in the R Macedonia (FYROM): the Cave "Golema Pesht" Near Village Zdunje.

SIMEK, J.F.; SMITH, F.H. (1997) Chronological changes in stone tool assemblages from Krapina (Croatia). *Journal of Human Evolution* 32, p. 561-575.

ŽIŽIĆ, O.; SREJOVIĆ, D. (1987) Bioče – paleolitsko nalazište. *Arheološki pregled (1986),* 36.

THE GRAVETTIAN SITE ŠALITRENA PEĆINA NEAR MIONICA (WESTERN SERBIA)

Bojana MIHAILOVIĆ

National Museum, Belgrade-Serbia

Abstract: The new investigation of Šalitrena Pećina, near Mionica (western Serbia), has shown that this site presents very rich Gravettian site. During the excavation in 2004. we found some hearths, more than 7000 chipped stone artefacts and numerous animal bones in layer 4. Gravettian points, bilaterally retouched micropoints with thinned distal part and thinned base, pointed blades and numerous backed bladelets with double truncation represent the chipped stone collection. The assemblage from the layer 4 in Šalitrena cave shows many similarities with Gravettian industries from the sites in Eastern Balkans (Temnata, Kozarnika) and Central Europe (Pavlov, Willendorf II).
Keywords: Šalitrena Pećina, Gravettian, Upper Palaeolithic, lithic industry, backed bladelets

Résumé: Les études récentes de Šalitrena Pećina près de Mionica (Serbie occidentale) ont démontré qu'il s'agit d'un site Gravettien extrêmement riche. Lors des fouilles effectuées en 2004, dans la couche 4 ont été découverts des foyers, plus de 7000 artefacts de pierre taillée et de nombreux os animaux. La collection d'artefacts contient des pointes gravettiennes, des micropointes retouchées bilatéralement amincies dans la partie distale et basale, des lames appointées et de nombreuses lamelles à dos bitronquées. La collection livrée par la couche 4 de Šalitrena Pećina révèle une assez grande similitude avec les industries Gravettiennes provenant des sites situés dans les Balkans orientaux (Temnata, Kozarnika) et de ceux de L'Europe centrale (Pavlov, Willendorf II).
Mots-clés: Šalitrena Pećina, Gravettien, Paléolithique Supérieur, l'industrie lithique, lamelles à dos

Šalitrena Pećina is the first Gravettian site registered so far in the territory of the central Balkans. It is situated in the village Brežđe, in the canyon of the Ribnica river, around 6 km far from Mionica and around 100 km southwest of Belgrade (Fig. 12.1).The cave is located on the left river bank at 277 meters above sea level. The cave entrance is approximately 20 m above the present-day river course and it is around 20 meters wide. The area of the cave is around 600 square meters and its total length is around 135 m. (Đurović 1998: 270). The cave entrance is facing west and it is divided by a rock into two passages, which merge in the interior into one area.

Šalitrena Pećina has been discovered in the process of site surveying of the Ribnica river valley carried out by a group of young amateur explorers from Valjevo, the town in the northwestern part of the Republic of Serbia. The finds of pottery fragments and stone artifacts initiated the test archaeological excavations, which were conducted by the Institute of Archaeology in Belgrade and Petnica Science Center in 1983, 1985 and 1995 (Jež, Kaludjerović 1985, Kaludjerović 1991, 1-8) but they were mostly directed to the investigations of the Early Neolithic (Starčevo) layer.

After five years interval the Office for Protection of Cultural Monuments in Valjevo conducted two small-scale rescue archaeological excavations in the years 2000 and 2001. First systematic excavations of this site started the National Museum in Belgrade in 2004 within its planned long-lasting project 'Culture and Art in the Paleolithic and Mesolithic in Serbia'.

EXCAVATIONS IN 2004 AND STRATIGRAPHIC SITUATION

In the course of excavations of Šalitrena Pećina in 2004 we investigated the area of 32 square meters in total. An average depth of the excavated sediment was around 80 cm. The works in 2004 were carried out in the entrance section of the cave where the stratigraphic situation is rather clear. The following layers have been distinguished:

Layer 1 – Surface layer. Gray, dusty sediment containing the mixed material from many different periods. The surface layer is disturbed as a consequence of exploitation of saltpeter that started already in the time of First Serbian Rebellion.

Layer 2 – Starčevo layer. Dark gray compact sediment with fragments of pottery of the Starčevo provenance, flint and bone artifacts (Jež 1985, 43-46; Šarić 2002). Large amount of pits, stone structures, fireplaces and various dug out features in this layer suggest dynamic activities of the Neolithic people in this area.

Layer 3 – Pleistocene layer. Light yellow compact sediment, which is because of the difference in the sediment structure divided into two horizons – geological horizon 3a with coarse debris and geological horizon 3b with rather fine debris. There are flint artifacts and numerous, mostly fragmented faunal remains were encountered in both horizons.

Layer 4 – Pleistocene layer. Dark brown, loose, sporadically black sediment. Few thousands of stone artifacts, large amount of animal bones and few fireplaces were encountered in this layer.

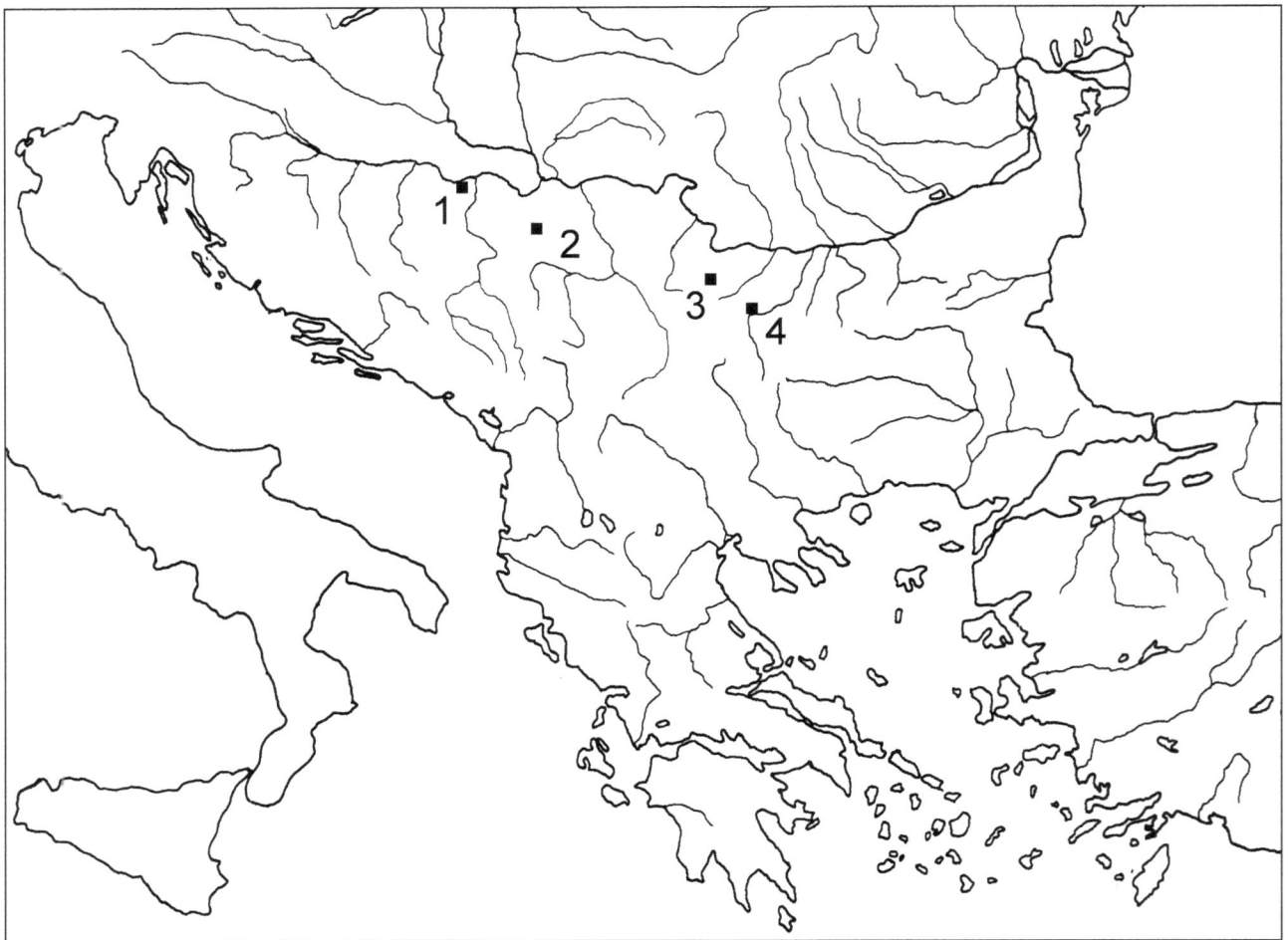

Fig. 12.1. Gravettian and Epigravettian sites in the northern Balkans, mentioned in the text:
1- Kadar, 2 – Salitrena Pecina, 3 – Kozarnika, 4 – Temnata

CHIPPED STONE INDUSTRY FROM THE LAYER 4

Over 7.000 chipped stone artifacts have been discovered in the layer 4 of Šalitrena Pećina. As this report is of preliminary character we are going to present here just basic data about the raw materials, products of chipping and characteristic types of tools.

Raw materials

On the basis of the macroscopic characteristics of the minerals it could be concluded that flint of various kinds (gray, green, brown and red) is basic and dominant raw material for the tool production. The most frequent are the kinds of local origin, exploited from the deposits in the immediate vicinity of the site (Šarić 2002, 11-12). The mass use of local flint is also indicated by large quantity of cores, which were exploited on the spot, in the cave interior or in the area in front of the cave. There were also encountered the tools made of higher quality flint, which was, judging by the absence of cores, probably obtained from somewhat greater distance. The chalcedony in addition to flint was also used as raw material for chipped

stone artifacts. It should be particularly emphasized that rather large amount of artifacts made of the so-called light white stone have also been found. It is well-known that this raw material had been intensively used for production of chipped and even also ground stone artifacts in the considerably later period – first of all in the Vinča culture (Antonović 1997).

Technology of manufacture

Despite the fact that flakes are prevailing among the finds, the most of culturally and chronologically relevant types have been made on blades. There were encountered the cores for blades and bladelets but also the cores of small size intended for flaking the microbladelets. We found the single-platform cores often made on larger massive flakes but there were also atypical two-platform cores. There were also registered the burin-like cores, established on the narrower side of the raw material or larger flake. Among the cores for microbladelets were encountered small, more or less elongated prismatic cores but the conical cores have also been found. In the process of flaking, the cores for bladelets and microbladelets have often been rejuvenated as it is confirmed by large quantity

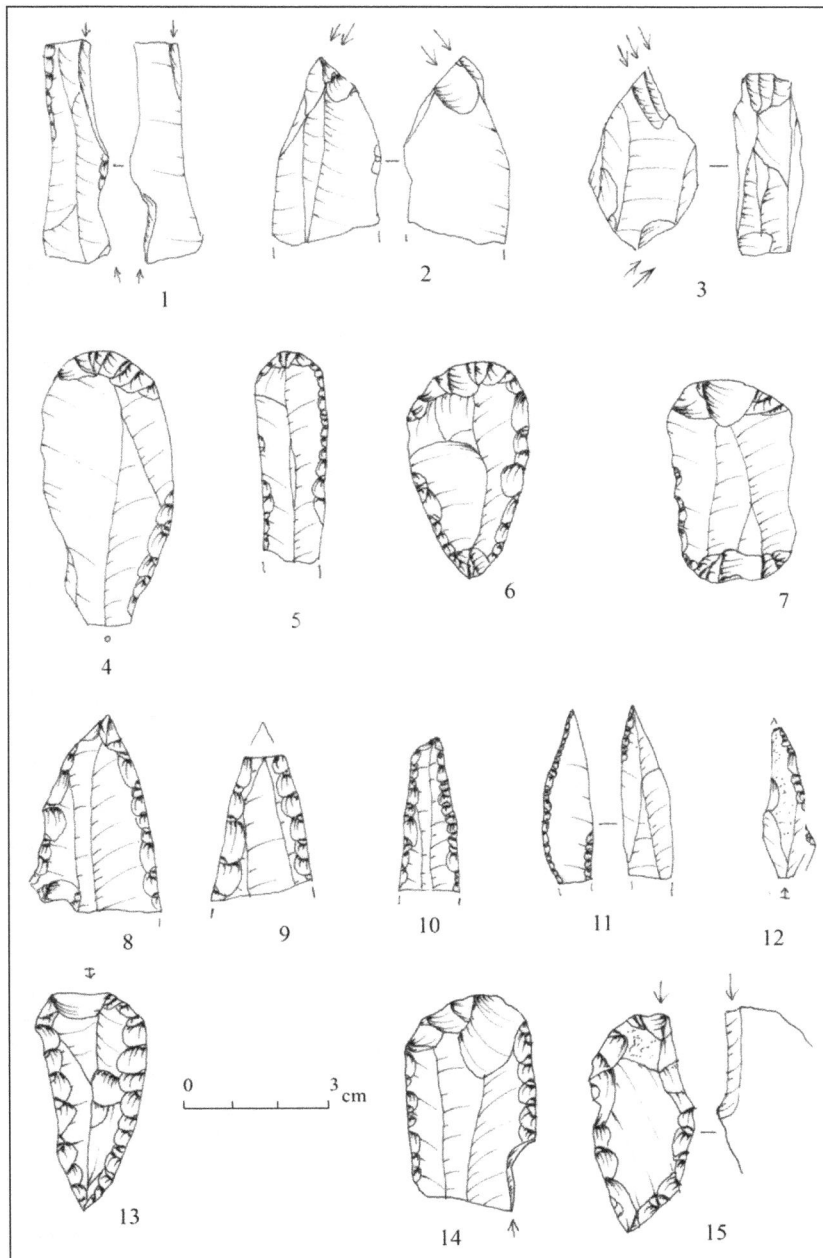

Fig. 12.2. Chipped stone industry from layer 4 at Šalitrena Pećina

of discovered rejuvenation blades. The flakes were chipped from asymmetrical and globular cores.

Retouched tools

In this work we would discuss in more details only those categories of tools, which we consider relevant for cultural and relative-chronological interpretation of the industry. They include the burins, endscrapers, retouched blades and points, backed and combined tools.

The burins are not so numerous in comparison with backed tools and endscrapers. Among them are well represented the burins on truncation (Fig. 12.2: 1),

dihedral burins and carinated burins (Fig. 12.2: 3). There were also identified angular burins (Fig. 12.2: 2) as well as multiple burins. Large amount of burin spalls bear witness to the fact that these tools have been produced at Šalitrena Pećina.

When the endscrapers at Šalitrena Pećina are concerned, they could be classified into two basic groups: endscrapers on blades (retouched or unretouched) and endscrapers on flakes. The nosed endscrapers are relatively numerous among the endscrapers on blades. Rather frequent are also the endscrapers on the blades, which have lateral or bilateral semi-abrupt retouch (Fig. 12.2: 4, 5).

When the endscrapers on flakes are concerned the prevailing types are simple arched endscrapers on the flakes over 25 mm, fan-shaped endscrapers and there are also many double endscrapers (Fig. 12.2: 7). There were also encountered the specimens made on somewhat thicker flakes – that resemble the carinated endscrapers of the Aurignacian type. It is absolutely evident that the microlithic – thumbnail and circular endscrapers are lacking and they could eventually indicate that this industry dates from the Epigravettian period as it has been assumed earlier (Jež, Kaluđerović 1985).

In the industry from Šalitrena Pećina also appear the retouched blades and retouched points. The blades are perhaps not so characteristic – prevailing are the specimens with lateral or bilateral shallow semi-abrupt retouch but the pointed blades are very distinct and they represent a differentiated and culturally and chronologically relevant category of tools. These points were usually made on larger and wider blades and have deep and semi-abrupt retouch (Fig. 12.2: 8-9). There were also the specimens on rather narrow blades and with shallow and semi-abrupt retouch (Fig. 12.2: 10).

According to the analysis of the material it seems that perforators at Šalitrena Pećina are not so numerous. We identified the perforators on the flakes with abruptly retouched tip as well as the perforators made on the blades and bladelets. Their tip is not distinguished and is retouched by direct or inverse semi-abrupt retouch (Fig. 12.2: 12). Specimen having on one edge the inverse and on the other direct semi-abrupt retouch (Fig. 12.2: 11) could be classified as projectil-point (fr. fléchette), frequent in the early phase of the Gravettian in the central Europe (Otte 1985, 484).

Considering other tool types, the retouched flakes, side-scrapers, splintered pieces and many combined tools are registered at Šalitrena Pećina. Among the combined tools are distinguished the endscrapers-points (Fig. 12.2: 13), the endscrapers-burins (Fig. 12.2: 14) and the points-burins (Fig. 12.2: 15).

For the industry from layer 4 at Šalitrena Pećina are particularly characteristic the backed points and bladelets. Their repertoire is highly standardized and includes the following tool types:

a) Abruptly retouched points on blades of rather large size with base retouched using shallow, surface retouch (Fig. 12.3: 1).

b) Abruptly retouched points of various dimensions with the tip in the axis of the tool. Very small specimens resemble the double points from somewhat later period (so-called Sauveterrian points). In most cases these points are on the top but also near the base made thinner by shallow surface retouch (Fig. 12.3: 3, 8-10) although there are also micropoints without ventral retouch on the distal end (Fig. 12.3: 8, 13-14). Predominant among the points with thinner base and tip are the bilaterally retouched points. They usually have one edge retouched by abrupt retouch and the other by semi-abrupt, marginal retouch.

c) Retouched truncations (Fig. 12.3: 15-25). Within this category of tools were encountered the specimens on the bladelets as well as the specimens on the microbladelets. Many tens of artifacts of this type have been found. Most of the bladelets are fragmented. On all specimens the retouched truncation is straight and almost always inversely retouched by semi-abrupt retouch (just few specimens deviate from this rule) while belowe the retouch, especially on the distal end, are sometimes visible shallow burin facets (Fig. 12.3: 21-22). Most of the specimens have one tool edge retouched by abrupt and the other by semi-abrupt retouch and there was also one specimen with denticulated working edge that greatly resembles denticulated points and the bladelets of Pavlovian type (Fig. 12.3: 24). It should be particularly emphasized that there were not found the preserved specimens with just one retouched truncation. All complete specimens have the retouch on both ends of the tool so they could be classified without any doubt in a group of double inverse retouched truncations that could be more or less elongated. From the typological point of view these tool types could be classified as rectangles.

d) Atypical shouldered points. There were encountered just one point with only proximal end retouched (Fig. 12.3: 5) and one specimen with continual abrupt retouch (Fig. 12.3: 4).

CULTURAL AND RELATIVE-CHRONOLOGICAL DETERMINATION

It was considered even until the last year that only Epigravettian and Middle Palaeolithic layers are present at Šalitrena Pećina. For the time being, however, there are no indications that there is the Middle Palaeolithic material at this site but future investigations will provide the decisive answer to this question. When the Epigravettian is concerned there is a possibility that horizons 3a and 3b actually date from that period. Within the layer 3 industry were encountered few thumbnail endscrapers and backed tools that, conditionally speaking, do have the Epigravettian characteristics. The investigations conducted last year revealed, however, that Šalitrena Pećina is an exceptionally important Gravettian site. This is indicated in the first place by the presence of backed points but also the complete repertoire of tools found in the layer 4 at Šalitrena Pećina.

Among the backed tools from Šalitrena Pećina there are no arched points and other types, which could be related to the Epigravettian. But there are many Gravettian points with thinner end and base, the truncated backed bladelets (rectangles), endscrapers on retouched and unretouched blades, angular burins on retouched truncations, double endscrapers on blades and larger flakes, retouched points

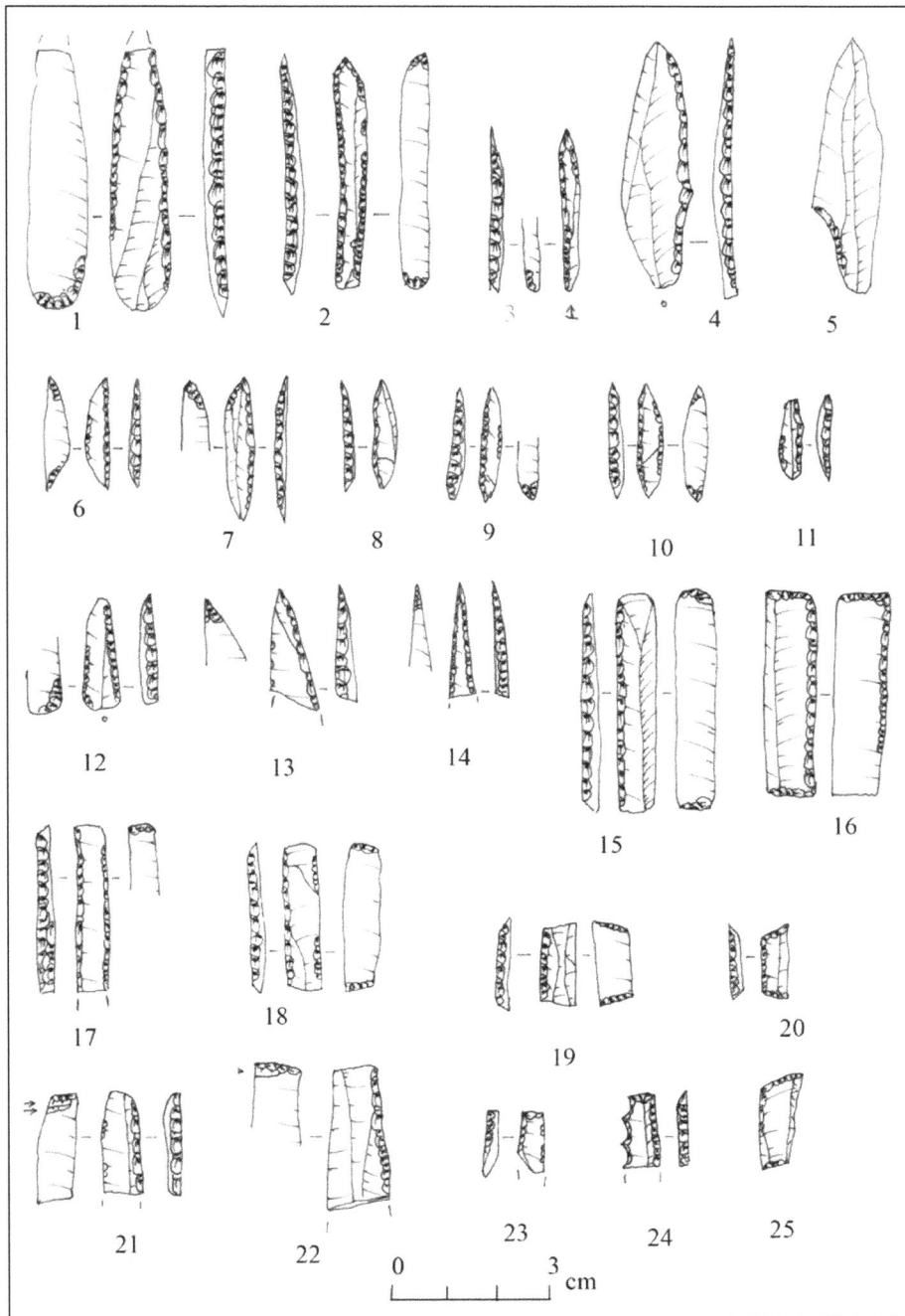

Fig. 12.3. Chipped stone industry from layer 4 at Šalitrena Pećina

and combined tools. These are the tools, which without any doubt could be associated with the Gravettian culture in the territory of Western Europe (Upper Perigordian) and central Europe (Willendorfian, Pavlovian).

The closest analogies with the industry from Šalitrena Pećina could be found in Bulgaria in the layers IX-IV of the cave Temnata dupka (Drobniewicz et al. 1992) and in the layer IVb of the cave Kozarnika (Tsanova 2003). Both these caves are located in the northern Bulgaria near the border with the Republic of Serbia. It is interesting that on the basis of the finds from Temnata was expressed in the

middle of the 1990s the hypothesis that these sites could testify that there was an intrusion of the eastern Gravettian in the area of the Balkans – already from the 30th millennium BP (Kozlowski 1996, 94-95; Kozlowski 1999, 320-321). Prior to these finds it had been considered that expansion of the backed tools industries in the regions of south Pannonia and the Balkan Peninsula happened much later, during the Epigravettian period (Schmider 1992: 390). In the late phase of Gravettian (which in fact chronologically corresponds with Epigravettian) was also ascribed the site Kadar in northern Bosnia (Montet White & Johnson 1976).

From the chronological point of view the industry from Šalitrena Pećina most probably dates from the advanced phase of Gravettian, i.e. to the period between 25th and 21st millennium BP. Among the finds from this cave are small in number the elements indicating slightly earlier date (e.g. Aurignacian elements and 'fléchettes') but also the elements suggesting somewhat later date (atypical shouldered points in the first place).

On the basis of preliminary study of the material a conclusion could be drawn that industry from Šalitrena Pećina even more than the finds from Temnata and Kozarnika has close parallels with the middle European Gravettian and in the first place with finds from Willendorf II in Austria and to somewhat lesser extent also with finds from the Bohemian sites, those which belong to the Pavlovian (Valoch 1996, Otte et al. 1996, Svoboda 1994). Whether the industry from layer 4 at Šalitrena Pećina is culturally and chronologically closer to the industry from layers 6-8 of Willendorf II or to somewhat later industry from the layer 9 at the same site (dated between 25.000 BP and 23.000 BP) still remains an unanswered question. At this moment we would not like to draw definite conclusions about that because Šalitrena Pećina is rather far from the middle European sites so it is quite possible that there are also certain chronological discrepancies. For the time being it is sufficient to say that Šalitrena Pećina is the richest Palaeolithic site discovered so far in Serbia and that as such it contains the affluent archaeological evidence about Gravettian, the culture, which has not been known in the areas of central and western Balkans until these days.

References

ANTONOVIĆ, D. (1997) Use of Light White Stone in the Central Balkans Neolithic, Starinar N.S. XLVIII, 33-39.

DROBNIEWICZ, B.; GINTER, B.; KOZLOWSKI, J.K. (1992) The Gravettian sequence, Temnata Cave – Excavations in Karlukovo Karst Area, Vol. 1 (J.K. Kozlowski, H. Laville, B. Ginter eds.), Krakow, 295-501.

ĐUROVIĆ, P. 1998 (ed.) Speleološki atlas, Srpska akademija nauka i umetnosti, Geografski institut "Jovan Cvijić", Zavod za zaštitu prirodne sredine, Geografski fakultet – Univerziteta u Beogradu, Biološki fakultet – Univerziteta u Beogradu, Beograd

JEŽ, Ž. (1985) Pregled neolitskih i eneolitskih kultura Gornje Kolubare, Istaživanja II – Saopštenja sa 6. skupa arheologa Srbije, Valjevo, 43-57

JEŽ, Ž.; KALUĐEROVIĆ, Z. (1985) Šalitrena pećina – paleolitsko i neolitsko nalazište, Arheološki pregled 25, 33-34.

KALUĐEROVIĆ, Z. (1985) Istraživanje Smolućke pećine 1984-1985, Novopazarski zbornik 9, 5-18.

KALUĐEROVIĆ, Z. (1991) Palaeolithic in Serbia in the Light of the Recent Research, Starinar N.S. XLII, 1-8.

KOZLOWSKI, J.K. (1996) L'origine du Gravettien dans le Sud-Est européen, The Colloquia of the XIII International Congress of Prehistoric and Protohistoric Sciences, Colloquium XI – The Late Aurignacian, Colloquium XII – The Origin of Gravettian (A. Palma di Cesnola, A. Montet White, K. Valoch eds.), Forli, 191-202.

KOZLOWSKI, J.K. (1999) Gravettian/Epigravettian sequences in the Balkans: environment, technologies, hunting strategies and raw material procurement, The Palaeolithic Archaeology of Greece and Adjacent Areas: Proceedings of the ICOPAG Conference, Ioannina, September 1994 (G. N. Bailey, E. Adam, E. Panagopoulou, C. Perles, K. Zachos eds.), British School at Athens Studies 3, 319-329.

MONTET-WHITE, A.; JOHNSON, A.E. (1976) Kadar: A Late Gravettian Site in Northern Bosnia, Yugoslavia, Journal of Field Archaeology Vol. 3 No. 4, 407-424.

OTTE, M. (1985) L'Gravettien en Europe, L'Anthropologie 89, No. 4, 479-503.

OTTE, M.; NOIRET, P.; CHIRICA, V.; BORZIAK, I. (1996) Rythme evolutif du Gravettien oriental, The Colloquia of the XIII International Congress of Prehistoric and Protohistoric Sciences, Colloquium XI – The Late Aurignacian, Colloquium XII – The Origin of Gravettian (A. Palma di Cesnola, A. Montet White, K. Valoch eds.), Forli, 213-226.

RADOVANOVIĆ, I. (1986)Vršac-At, paleolitsko nalazište, Arheološki pregled 25, 11-12.

SCHMIDER, B. (1992) Le Gravettien, La Préhistoire dans l'monde, (J. Garanger ed.), Nouvelle Clio, Paris, 379-396.

SVOBODA, J. (1994) The Pavlov Site, Czech Republic: Lithic Evidence from the Upper Palaeolithic, Journal of Field Archaeology Vol. 21 No. 1, 69-81.

ŠARIĆ, J. (2002) Artefakti od okresanog kamena sa lokaliteta Šalitrena pećina, Glasnik Srpskog arheološkog društva 18, 9-23.

TSANOVA, T. (2003) Le Gravettien en Bulgarie du Nord: Niveau IVb de la grotte Kozarnika, The Humanized Mineral World: Towards Social and Symbolic Evaluation of Prehistoric Technologies in South Eastern Europe (T. Tsonev, E. Montagnari Kokelj eds.), ERAUL 103, Liege-Sofia, 33-39.

VALOCH, K. (1996) L'origine du Gravettien de l'Europe Centrale, The Colloquia of the XIII International Congress of Prehistoric and Protohistoric Sciences, Colloquium XI – The Late Aurignacian, Colloquium XII – The Origin of Gravettian (A. Palma di Cesnola, A. Montet White, K. Valoch eds.), Forli, 203-212.

MIDDLE PALAEOLITHIC AND EARLY UPPER PALAEOLITHIC SUBSISTENCE PRACTICES AT VINDIJA CAVE, CROATIA

Dejana BRAJKOVIĆ

Institute for Quaternary Palaeontology and Geology, Croatian Academy of Sciences and Arts,
A. Kovačić 5, 10000 Zagreb – Croatia, dejbraj@public.srce.hr

Preston MIRACLE

Department of Archaeology, University of Cambridge, Cambridge CB2 3DZ- U.K., ptm21@cam.ac.uk

Abstract: Vindija Cave contains important Middle and Early Upper Palaeolithic lithic and faunal assemblages associated with remains of Neandertals that span the period from ca. 45 – 25 ka. The association in level G1 of Neandertal remains (directly radiocarbon dated to ca. 29 ka) and Early Upper Palaeolithic artifacts (e.g. bone points, lithic bifacial point, and other Aurignacian-type lithics) is particularly significant for different models of the Middle to Upper Palaeolithic transition, and the artefact and hominin assemblages have been studied in detail in recent years. In this paper we present the first results of new zooarchaeological analyses of Vindija. We focus on the ungulate remains from the F and G Complexes at Vindija, and discuss the significance of our results for palaeoecological reconstructions, taphonomy, and hominin subsistence practices.
Keywords: Vindija, Zooarchaeology, Neandertal, Middle Palaeolithic, Upper Palaeolithic

Résumé: La Grotte de Vindija contient des assemblages lithiques et fauniques datés du Paléolithique Moyen et du Paléolithique Supérieur Ancien et sont associés à des restes de Néanderthaliens, qui couvrent une période de environ 45 à 25 ka. L'association dans le niveau G1 de restes néanderthaliens (directement datés par radiocarbone de environ 29 ka) et d'artefacts du Paléolithique Supérieur Ancien (e.a. pointes osseuses, pointe bifaciale lithique et autres artefacts lithiques de type aurignacien) est particulièrement significative pour les différents modèles relatifs à la transition Paléolithique Moyen – Paléolithique Supérieur. Les assemblages archéologiques et osseux humains ayant été étudiés dans le detail ces dernières années, nous présentons dans cet article les premiers résultats des analyses zooarchéologiques menées à Vindija. Nous nous intéressons plus particulièrement aux restes des ongulés des complexes F et G de Vindija, et discutons leur implication pour les reconstructions paléoécologiques, la taphonomie et les techniques de subsistence des hominidés.
Mots-clés: Vindija, Zooarchéologie, Neandertal, Paléolithique Moyen, Paléolithique Supérieur

INTRODUCTION

The site of Vindija Cave, Croatia, has played a key role in recent discussions about Neandertal genetics (Krings *et al.* 2000; Green *et al.* 2006; Noonan *et al.* 2006), morphology (Ahern *et al.* 2004; Wolpoff *et al.* 1981), diet (Richards *et al.* 2000), and persistence in Europe (Higham *et al.* 2006). The site is also famous (or infamous, depending on your perspective) for an apparent association in Layer G1 of Neandertal remains dated to about 32.000 BP and a split-base bone point, a well known type fossil of the Aurignacian (Malez *et al.* 1980). Recent work by Karavanić (1995; Karavanić and Smith 1998) has significantly contributed to our understanding of the artefact assemblages from the site. What has been missing until now is a detailed analysis and discussion of the faunal remains, and the implications of zooarchaeological and taphonomic analyses for our understanding of Late Middle Palaeolithic and Early Upper Palaeolithic subsistence strategies and ecology at the site and in the wider region. Here we present the first results of the first detailed study of the zooarchaeology of the Vindija faunal assemblage (Brajković 2005). This study focuses on the ungulate remains, and here we limit discussion to those layers around the Middle to Upper Palaeolithic transition. We address three questions.

1. What changes are there in ungulate composition from OIS 4 to 2, from roughly 74.000 – 18.000 BP?

2. What component of the faunal assemblage can be attributed to hominins as compared to other bone accumulators active at the site?

3. Did hominin subsistence practices at Vindija change dramatically across the Middle-Upper Palaeolithic transition?

Vindija was systematically excavated from 1974-1986; the excavation methods seriously compromised the results, and the biases introduced by these methods must be considered in any discussion of the cave (Brajković 2005). Likewise, in parts of the cave the sediments from the G-Complex were severely cryoturbated postdepositionally (Malez and Rukavina 1975). As a result, often at the time of excavation it was impossible to make finer stratigraphic distinctions beyond "Layer G" or "Layers E+F". The degree of cryoturbation varied significantly among different parts of the cave; as has been pointed out on numerous occasions, sediments were not cryoturbated in the area of the main concentration of Neandertal fossils and Aurignacian bone points in Layer G1 (Karavanić *et al.* 1998; Miracle 1998). Further evidence of mixing, probably at the time of excavation or during the later curation of the faunal assemblages was also noted based on contrast in bone patina and/or clear remains of domestics found in Pleistocene strata (Brajković 2005). Remains that were clearly mixed have been excluded from all analyses.

Tab. 13.1. Species representation at Vindija in Layers H – E

Species	E	E/F	F	F/d+F/d/d	G1	G2	G3	G4	G5	G	H
Rupicapra rupicapra	X	X	X	X	X					X	X
Capra ibex	X	X	X	X						X	
Capreolus capreolus					X				X	X	
Cervus elaphus		X	X	X	X		X	X	X	X	X
Rangifer tarandus	X	X	X							X	
Alces alces	X	X	X	X	X	X	X	X	X	X	X
Megaloceros giganteus	X	X	X	X	X	X	X	X		X	X
Bison priscus	X	X	X	X						X	X
Bos primigenius	X	X	X	X	X		X		X	X	X
Stephanorhinus kirchbergensis		X								X	
Stephanorhinus sp.	X	X			X			X	X	X	X
NISP	15	79	33	18	25	3	35	9	10	296	35

We consider the remains from Layers H to E. Layers H – to G2 are associated with Middle Palaeolithic assemblages (Malez *et al.* 1980; Malez *et al.* 1984). We roughly correlate the deposition of Layer H with OIS 4 (ca. 74.000 – 60.000 BP), for which there is sedimentological and stratigraphic support (Malez and Rukavina 1979; Malez *et al.* 1984). The radiocarbon and U/Th dates of around 29.000–36.500 on Layer H are clearly too young, while a date of about 42.000 BP based on amino acid racemization and U/Th for Level G3 seems probable (Wild *et al.* 2001). Layer G1 has a lithic assemblage with Middle and Upper Palaeolithic elements and an Aurignacian bone tool assemblage. The most reliable dates on G1 come from the Neandertal remains themselves and suggest deposition about 32.000 BP (Higham *et al.* 2006). Layer F is associated with an Early Upper Palaeolithic lithic industry and has a range of ^{14}C dates; a date of about 27.000 BP seems likely (Wild *et al.* 2001). Finally Layer E has been dated to about 18.000 BP (Wild *et al.* 2001).

COMPOSITION OF THE UNGULATE ASSEMBLAGE

In Table 13.1 we compare composition of the ungulate assemblage at Vindija from Layers E to H. Owing to limitations in how the cave was excavated and the material conserved post excavation, only a minority of the remains can be assigned to finer stratigraphic units from Vindija, e.g. strata within the Layer G like G1 to G3. This is unfortunate, as the Neandertal fossils come from only some of the units within the Layer G – in particular G1 and G3. Be that as it may, our results show that the following species are present in Stratum G3 – red deer, elk, giant deer, and aurochs. The situation changes somewhat in Stratum G1 with the addition of chamois, roe deer, and rhino. These taxa can tolerate a wide range of conditions, and none of them is considered to be particularly indicative of cold conditions. Although chamois today is commonly found in "alpine" environments, we have shown that it is better described as adapted to broken terrain (Miracle and Sturdy 1991); it should not be considered a cold-climate indicator. Furthermore, taxa like roe deer suggest fairly well developed vegetative cover. In a preliminary summary of the Vindija faunal assemblages, Malez reconstructed climatic oscillations within Layer G – Strata G5, G3, and G1 contained "warmer" faunas while Strata G4 and G2 contained "colder" faunas (Malez and Ullrich 1982). Our new data do not support Malez's preliminary interpretation; the ungulate taxa do not suggest major fluctuations in regional environments during the deposition of Layer G. There are, however, suggestive changes as we move into Layer F. Ibex and bison are present in the lower portion of Layer F (F/d+F/d/d), while roe deer disappears. Likewise, the presence of reindeer is confirmed in the remainder of Layers F and E. Although these changes in the species list suggest somewhat cooler and perhaps more arid conditions in Layers E and F relative to G, the presence of Merck's rhino in Layer E/F (Figure 13.1)

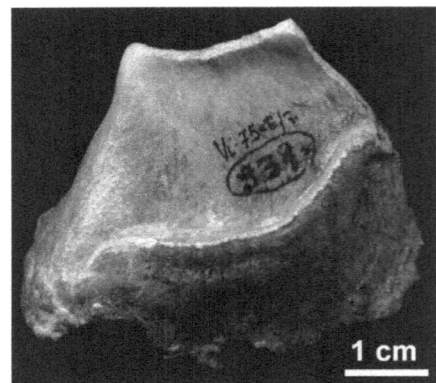

Fig. 13.1. Merck's rhino (*Stephanorhinus kirchbergensis*) upper dp^3 (Vi-931) from Layer E/F

Tab. 13.2. Relative frequency of ungulate species at Vindija by complex. Complex "E/F total" includes all remains from levels E and F and those marked "E/F". Complex "G upper" includes remains labeled G1, G2, G3, Gg, Fd+G, Fd-G and F/G. Complex "G lower" remains labeled G4, G5, Gd, G4-H, G5-H, Gd-H, and G/H. Complex "G total" includes all remains from "G upper" and "G lower" as well as those labeled only as "G"

	Complex						
Species	E	F	E/F total	G upper	G lower	G total	H
Chamois+Ibex	13.3%	11.8%	16.6%	3.6%	3.3%	4.5%	5.7%
Roe deer				3.6%	1.6%	1.4%	
Red deer		7.8%	15.9%	16.9%	23.0%	17.5%	25.7%
Reindeer	6.7%	2.0	2.1%			0.5%	
Elk+Giant deer	33.3%	43.1%	37.2%	56.6%	37.7%	48.6%	48.6%
Pig			2.1%	1.2%		1.8%	
Bos+Bison	40.0%	35.3%	22.8%	15.7%	16.4%	14.3%	14.3%
Rhino	6.7%		3.4%	1.2%	14.8%	4.1%	5.7%
NISP	15	51	145	83	61	440	35

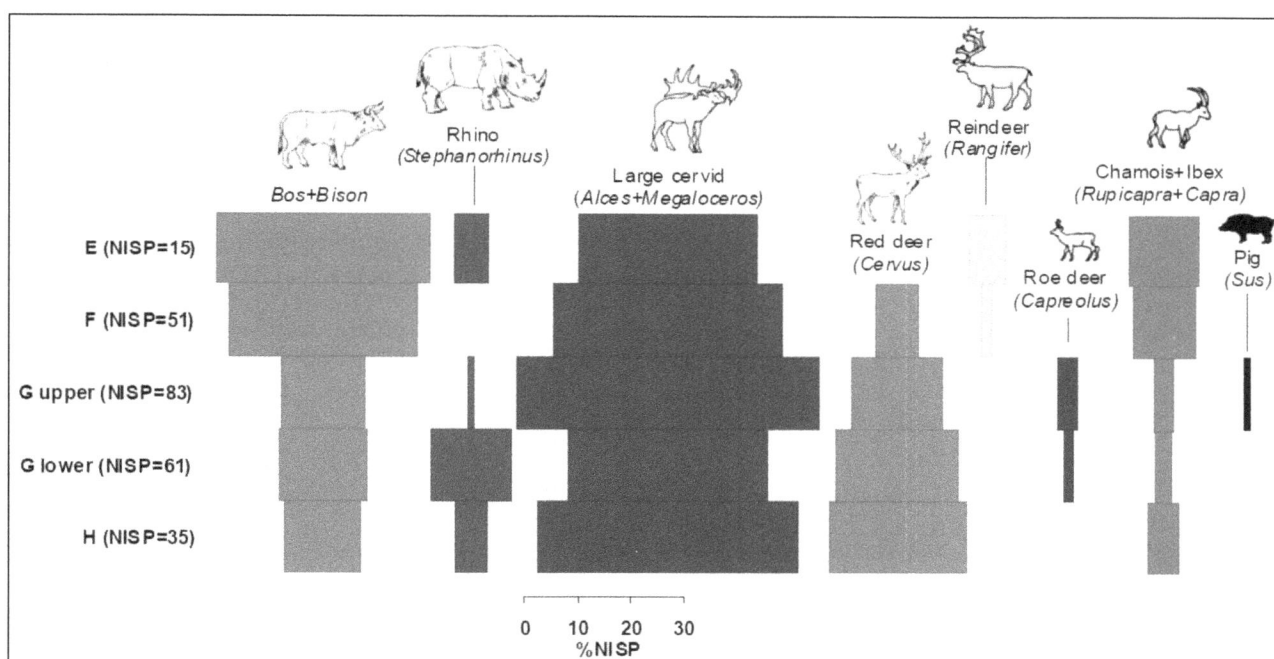

Fig. 13.2. Relative frequency of ungulate taxa at Vindija Cave from Layers H to E

indicates one of the following: a relatively more temperate phase during the sedimentation of these complexes, an environmental mosaic in the region that could have supported taxa adapted to both relatively "warmer" and "cooler" conditions, or post-depositional mixing. Resolution of this issue requires direct radiocarbon dating of faunal remains and other palaeoenvironmental analyses that can be conducted directly on the remains themselves.

In Table 13.2 and Figure 13.2 we have combined together some of the excavation layers into more inclusive complexes. Large cervids (elk and giant deer) dominate throughout the sequence with the exception of Layer E,

where they are second to *Bos/Bison*. Large bovids are present throughout; their relative frequency increases in Layers E and F relative to G. The frequency of red deer gradually falls from Layer H to F, and red deer is missing from Layer E. A few pieces of reindeer are present in Complex G, but cannot be assigned to any of the strata within G. The relative frequency of reindeer increases from Layer F to E. Roe deer and pig are present in small numbers in the G Complex. Rhino is represented mostly by tooth fragments; none of these are from the woolly rhino. Rhino is a minor contributor to all of the layers, although it is missing in F; the minor fluctuations in its relative frequency can be attributed to the effects of small sample sizes (Figure 13.3). From these data we conclude that the G complex accumulated under somewhat more temperate conditions relative to Layers E and F. This pattern fits well with the absolute dates on these complexes and other palaeoclimatic indicators, although we stress again that these contrasts were not particularly marked. The Zagorje region of northern Croatia appears to have provided biomes suitable for a range of larger mammals during OIS 4–2.

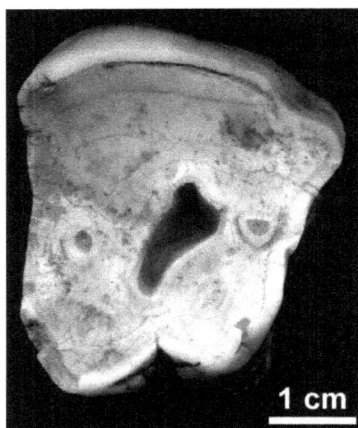

Fig. 13.3. Merck's rhino upper P^2 (Vi-947) from Layer Gd-H (G lower complex)

Our new data on the Vindija ungulate assemblage do not indicate significant climatic oscillations during the deposition of Layers H to E. The Layer G3 and G1 ungulates do not stand out from the rest of the assemblage. The Layer G3 and G1 Neandertals were deposited at Vindija during a more temperate oscillation within OIS 3. The ungulate fauna suggests a shift to somewhat cooler conditions during the accumulation of Layers F and E, caused in part by the onset of the LGM (OIS 2) roughly 24.000 BP. The presence of prairie/woodland rhino, aurochs, elk, and giant deer in the Layer E assemblage from Vindija suggests rather temperate conditions at the LGM. The absence of "cold-adapted" taxa among the ungulates suggests that their remains accumulated only during more temperate periods within OIS 4–2, perhaps because Neandertals only visited Vindija during such conditions, or that cold oscillations were not strongly expressed in northern Croatia.

COMPARISON TO CAVE BEARS

How does ungulate frequency compare to other evidence of the use of Vindija by hominins and other animals? Comparisons are limited owing to the lack of contextual data discussed above. One possible proxy is comparison to cave bears. Cave bears were the most common Pleistocene occupants of caves in the region (Miracle 1991), and their remains overwhelmingly dominate the Vindija faunal assemblages. Ungulates did not dwell in the cave, and we can be quite certain that their remains were brought to Vindija by hominins and/or other carnivores. Cave bears had a mostly vegetarian diet (Kurtén 1976), and it seems reasonable to assume that they did not accumulate ungulate remains at Vindija. Hence, comparison of the frequency of cave bears to ungulates should give us a rough indication of the frequency with which cave bears hibernated in the cave relative to carnivore and/or hominin use of the site.

In Figure 13.4 we compare the relative frequency of ungulate and cave bear teeth from Layers H to E at

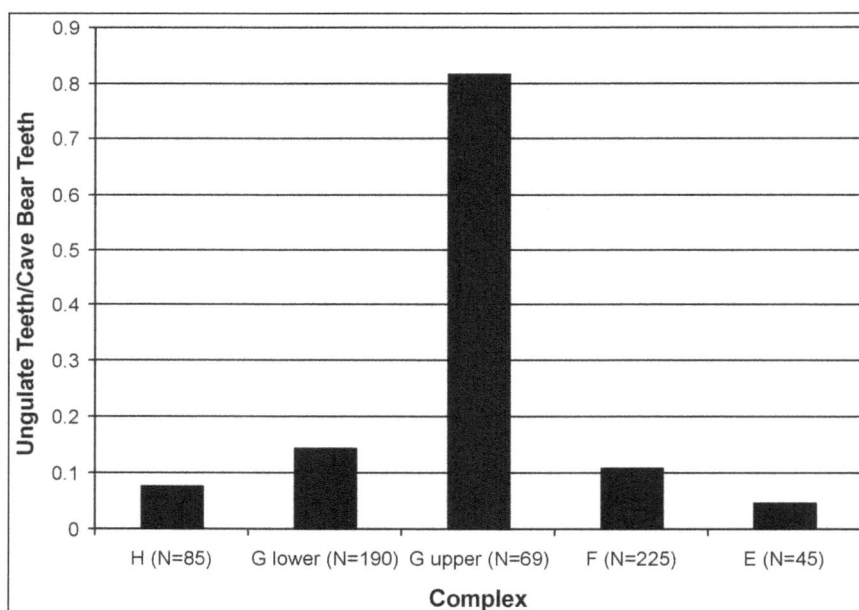

Fig. 13.4. Relative frequency of ungulate and cave bear teeth at Vindija Cave. "Ungulate Teeth" includes the NISP of all teeth identified to ungulates. "Cave Bear Teeth" includes the NISP of measurable cheek teeth identified to cave bear

Vindija. For the ungulates, we have included all teeth and teeth fragments, whereas for the cave bear we have included only those cheek teeth that were selected by Maja Paunović for measurement. The relative frequency of ungulate to cave bear remains is much higher in Complex G upper than in the remaining complexes, at the time that the majority of the Neandertal remains were deposited. During the accumulation of Layer H, Vindija served primarily as a cave bear den; the relatively low number of cave bear teeth suggests that their visits to the cave were sporadic. Within Complex G, the intensity of cave use by hominins increased. In Layer F the overall frequency of larger mammal remains falls, as does the relative frequency of ungulates to cave bears. This trend continues in Layer E and the frequency of ungulates relative to cave bears further drops. With the onset of the LGM, cave bears became the almost exclusive, although increasingly sporadic, users of Vindija. The relative and absolute frequency of cave bears at Vindija may thus provide some of the strongest evidence of inhospitable conditions associated with cold and arid climatic fluctuations.

TAPHONOMY

We studied in detail bone surface modifications on the Vindija ungulate remains. Detailed taphonomic analyses of the Vindija carnivores remain to be done. The surfaces of all remains were examined using a X10 hand lens using strong, low-angle artificial lighting. Bone surface modifications were identified using standard criteria (e.g. Binford 1981; Fisher 1995; Lyman 1994; Blumenschine *et al.* 1996). Identified carnivore modifications included tooth drags, punctures, pitting, crenulations of broken edges, and chemical etching/thinning from digestive acids (Figure 13.5). Particular care was taken to distinguish between surface scratches, most probably produced through trampling by cave bears, and cut marks produced by stone tools. Compared to the former, the latter were deeper in cross section, occurred in discrete groups, and/or could be related to anatomic features such as points of muscle/ligament attachment. Bone surfaces were relatively clean of calcium carbonate rinds. Bone surfaces were often weathered – between 40 – 50% of the identified ungulate remains were weathered – although the intensity of bone weathering did not vary dramatically by complex. Thus, while weathering has obscured some surface modifications, it has not biased comparisons between different sedimentary complexes.

None of the animal remains from Layers H to E are burned. This evidence correlates with the lack of evidence of hearths or other combustion features at Vindija in the Pleistocene layers.

Given the relatively small ungulate assemblages from Levels G3 and G1, it is not surprising that there are relatively few modified bones from these levels. Only 2 of 19 identified bones from Level G3 show carnivore

Fig. 13.5. Reindeer phalanx 2 (Vi-418) with digestion marks from Layer G

gnawing, a red deer distal humerus and a second phalanx identified to *Bos/Bison*. From Level G1, only 1 of 18 identified bones shows carnivore gnawing, a roe deer proximal femur. There is also clear evidence of human modifications from both levels. There is a *Bos/Bison* distal tibia shaft from Level G3 (Vi-1135) with 12 cuts oblique to the long bone axis, probably produced during meat removal (Figure 13.6). From Level G1 there are two red deer metatarsal shafts with cut marks. Vi-653 has two oblique cuts on the anterior shaft, perhaps related to removal of the periosteum prior to breaking open the bone to extract marrow. The second, Vi-787, has three vertical cuts in the anterior sulcus (Figure 13.7). Numerous sediment scratches are also visible on the bone surface, underlining our point about the importance of distinguishing between marks produced by trampling as opposed to cutting.

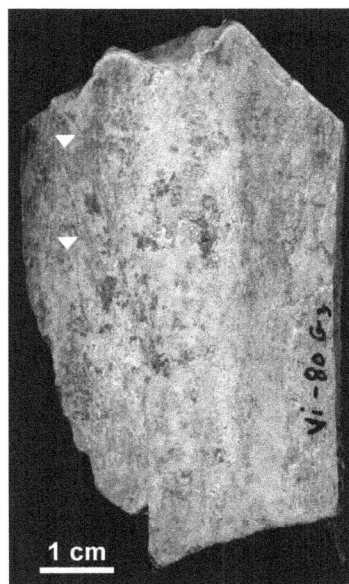

Fig. 13.6. *Bos/Bison* distal tibia shaft (Vi-1135) with cut marks from Layer G3

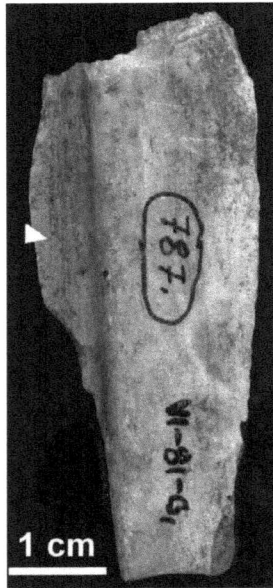

Fig. 13.7. Red deer metatarsal shaft from Layer G1 with cut marks in the anterior suclus (Vi-787)

verified. Wolves periodically visited the cave and scavenged from hominin food waste. Digested bones are relatively rare throughout the sequence, with a maximum value of 2.7% of NISP in Complex G lower. The absence of digested bones from Complex G upper may point to a somewhat greater intensity of hominin activities at Vindija when the Neandertal remains were deposited. Given the limitations of the sample this pattern is suggestive rather than conclusive. Broken down by taxon, reindeer stands out from the rest of the assemblage with 3 of 5 bones with evidence of digestion (Figure 13.5). This contrast may suggest that wolves and other carnivores were hunting prey in different biomes or at different times of the year than the hominins who visited Vindija. What we can conclude with certainty from this comparison of carnivore activity at Vindija is that there are not major contrasts between complexes associated with Neandertals in Complex G and Layer H and those presumably made by anatomically "modern" humans (AMH), i.e. Complex E/F. Likewise, the "transitional" strata associated with Complex G upper does not stand out from the remainder of the sequence.

When we examine evidence of bone modification for grouped levels at Vindija several interesting patterns emerge. There is neither carnivore gnawing nor digestion marks on bones from Layer H. In Complexes G to E/F the frequency of carnivore gnawed bones increases from 5.7% of NISP in Complex G to 11.3% of NISP in Complex E/F (Figure 13.8). Sample sizes are too small to identify strong contrasts in gnawing frequency by taxon. The size and shape of marks suggest wolf gnawing and remains of wolf are confirmed throughout these complexes at Vindija (Divjak 1998). Remains of other large carnivores are also reported from some of these complexes, although these identifications remain to be

We summarize cut mark data in Figure 13.9 with two measures: the frequency of bones with cut marks (%NISP with cut marks) and the intensity with which bones were cut (Ave CM/bone). The %NISP with cut marks falls from 17% in Layer H to 9% in Complex E/F. The average number of cuts per bone shows a similar pattern to the %NISP with cut marks. The coarse nature of our data does not support detailed interpretations. Here we simply note that the frequency of hominin interventions on ungulate remains decreases from complexes associated with Neandertals to those associated with AMH. However, if we examine these cut-marked bones in greater detail by layer and complex, some suggestive patterns emerge.

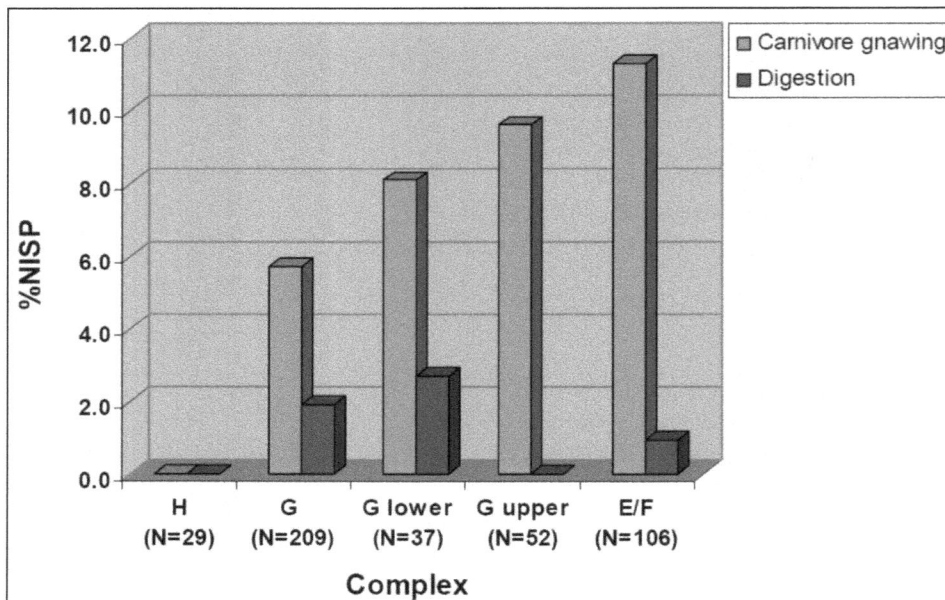

Fig. 13.8. Frequency of carnivore modification on ungulate remains at Vindija

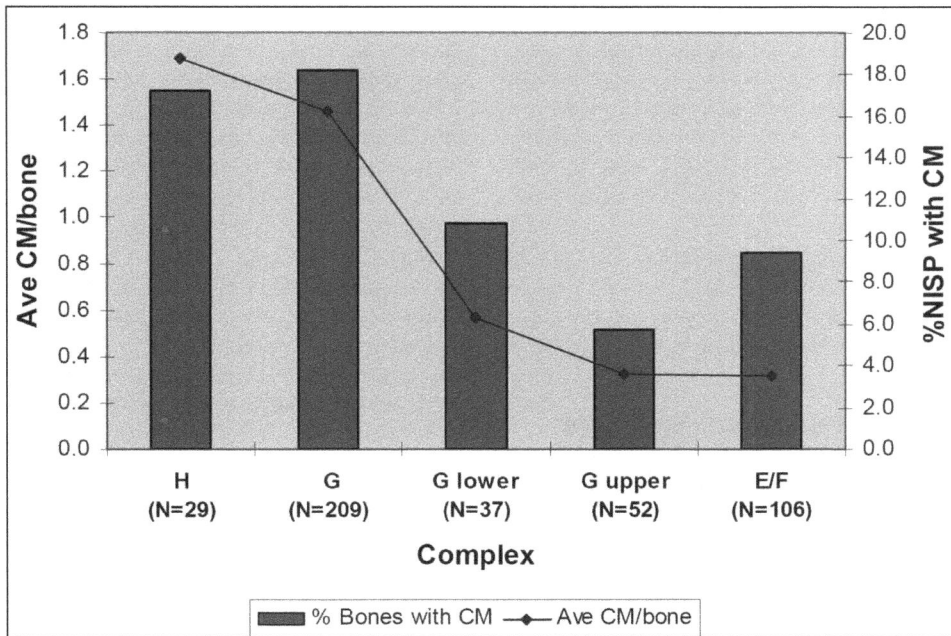

Fig. 13.9. Cut mark frequency on ungulate remains from Vindija

In Layer H cut marks are found only on metapodial bones from large cervids and bovids. These give evidence of disarticulating lower limbs (Figure 13.10) and preparing them for marrow breakage (Figure 13.11). Hominins during the deposition of Layer H butchered a few large ungulate lower limbs and cracked open a few metapodials for marrow; hominin activities at Vindija were very restricted and visits were transient.

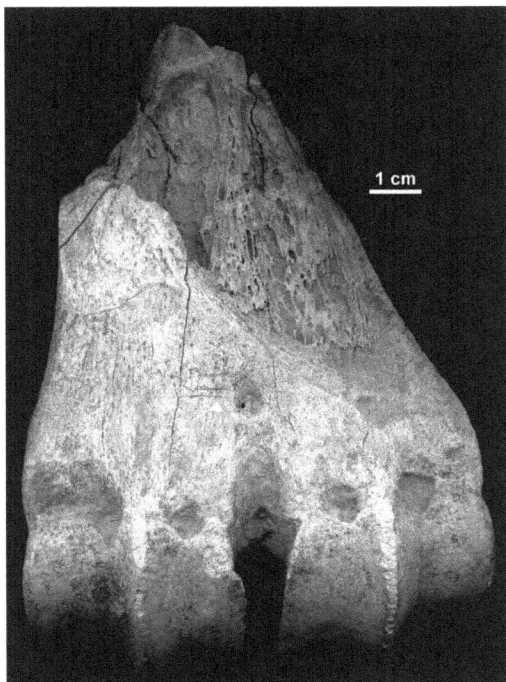

Fig. 13.11. *Megaloceros giganteus* metatarsal shaft (Vi-778) with cut marks from Layer H

Fig. 13.10. *Bos primigenius* distal metacarpal (Vi-642) with cut marks from Layer H

Although there is a trend of decreasing frequency of cut-marked bones within Complex G, this pattern is difficult to interpret given the relatively high frequency of cut-marked bones that could not be assigned to a finer stratigraphic unit than Layer "G". Nevertheless, we have cut marks on a wider range of species and elements, including mandibles, all major long bones, and metapodia. Likewise the placement of cut marks suggests both carcass disarticulation as well as meat removal (Figure 13.12). Regardless of whether the ungulate remains in G Complex were deposited in only a few discrete episodes or sporadically over a longer period of time, we have a wider range of hominin activities in G relative to H that suggest an increase in both butchery as well as meat consumption. We suspect that these activities were located in specific parts of the cave and/or the porch area in front of the cave, perhaps in a manner similar to the concentration of hominin remains near the cave entrance. Unfortunately the contextual information is too coarse to investigate intra-site spatial distributions.

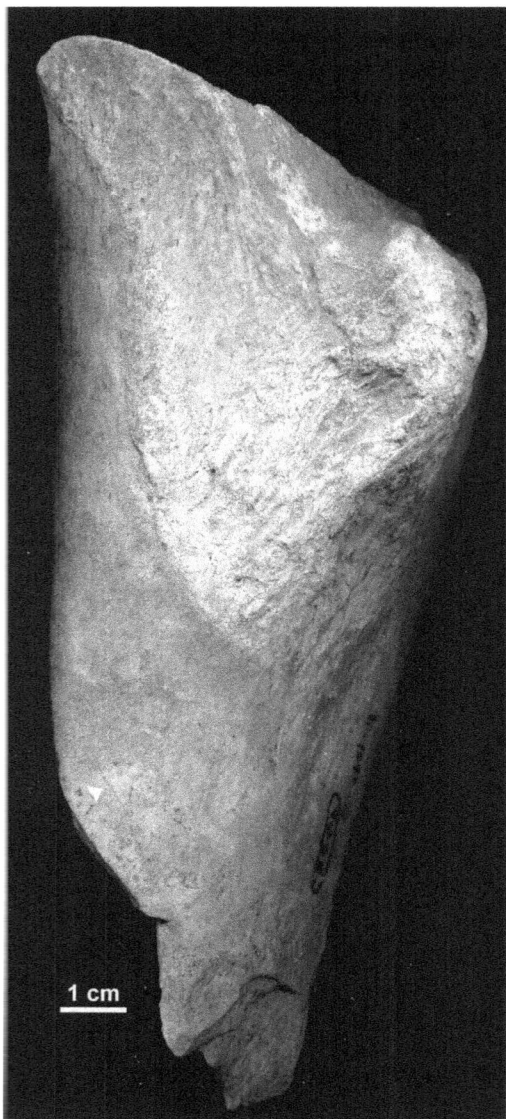

Fig 13.12. *Bos/Bison* proximal femur shaft (Vi-1075) with cut marks from meat removal from Complex G

bone midshafts. The first is a femur (Vi-1116) that preserves three light cuts (only one visible on the photograph) on the partially-eroded bone surface (Figure 13.13). The second is a distal tibia shaft (Vi-1117) with 6 cuts horizontal to the long bone axis. We interpret both instances as meat removal. The relatively low frequency of cut marks and restriction of activities to carcass dismemberment, excepting a few rhino snacks, suggests a change in carcass processing activities and food consumption in Complex E/F compared to Complex G. In Complex E/F we return to a pattern reminiscent of Layer H, hominins, presumably now "Anatomically Modern Humans" visited Vindija only rarely to process the odd chamois, elk, reindeer, or other ungulate. These activities were either restricted to selected carcass parts or the majority of remains from this dismemberment were transported/deposited away from the cave. Rhino meat would appear to have also been occasionally prepared and/or consumed. Nothing indicates major butchery activities on site. Instead, people appear to have consumed small bits of food that they brought with them to the site.

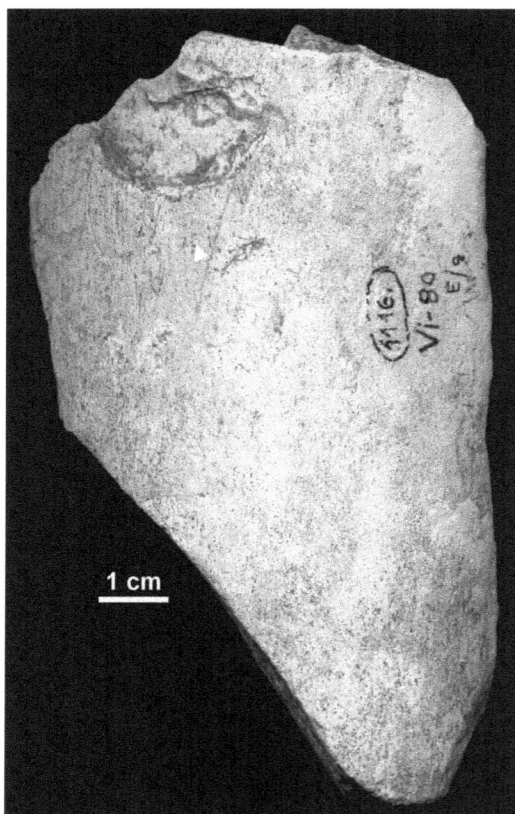

Fig. 13.13. Rhino (*Stephanorhinus* sp.) femur (Vi-1116) with cut marks from meat removal from Layer E/g

CONCLUSION

We suggest that the pattern of carcass processing at Vindija changed over time. In Layer H hominin activities were ephemeral and restricted to processing metapodials

In Complex E/F, there are relatively fewer cut-marked bones, and they are found mostly on metapodia or can be related to carcass disarticulation (e.g. *Alces* scapula Vi-851). The exceptions are cut marks on two rhino long-

114

from large bovids and cervids. In Complex G a wider range of carcass processing activities occurred, ranging from carcass dismemberment to meat removal. The lack of evidence of burning suggests that meat was either consumed raw or off site. As an aside, the lack of hearths and burned bones at Vindija suggests that such activities (and waste produced by them) were either restricted to the porch area in front of the cave or that hominins visited the cave during the warmer seasons of the year. In Complex E/F hominin visits at Vindija were again transient with relatively little carcass processing, and by inference, meat consumption. This pattern of changing carcass processing activities complements evidence presented earlier of shifts in cave bear vs. hominin use of the cave. Hominin visits were transient and activities restricted at times when ungulate remains are rare relative to cave bears. What is interesting about this pattern is that rather than seeing a progressive change in activities associated with the shift from Neandertals to Anatomically Modern Humans, we instead have a pattern whereby hominin activities at the cave appear to closely correlate with changing environmental circumstances. Local factors of ecology and environment played a much more important role than the hominin who used the cave in generating the patterns in ungulate remains that we have discussed at Vindija.

References

AHERN, J.C.M., [et al.] (2004). New discoveries and interpretations of hominid fossils and artifacts from Vindija Cave, Croatia. *Journal of Human Evolution*, 46, p. 25–65.

BINFORD, L.R., (1981). *Bones: Ancient Men and Modern Myths*. New York: Academic Press.

BLUMENSCHINE, R., [et al.] (1996). Blind tests of inter-analyst correspondence and accuracy in the identification of cut-marks, percussion marks, and carnivore tooth marks on bone surfaces. *Journal of Archaeological Science* 23, p. 493–507.

BRAJKOVIĆ, D., (2005). *Korelacija tafodema skupine ungulate iz gornjopleistocenskih sedimenata špilja Vindija, Velika pećina i Veternica u sjeverozapadnoj hrvatskoj*. Ph.D. Dissertation, Zagreb: Sveučilište u Zagrebu Prirodoslovno-Matematički Fakultet, Geološki Odsjek.

DIVJAK, S., (1998). Odredbe kranijalnih i postkranijalnih skeletnih nalaza kvartarnih kanida nekih spilja sjeverozapadne Hrvatske. B.Sc. Dissertation, Zagreb: Sveučilište u Zagrebu, Zajednički studij iz geologije, Prirodoslovno-matematički fakultet, Rudarsko-geo-loško-naftni fakultet.

FISHER, J.W.Jr., (1995). Bone surface modifications in zooarchaeology. *Journal of Archaeological Method and Theory* 2, p. 7–68.

GREEN, R.E., [et al.] (2006). Analysis of one million base pairs of Neanderthal DNA. *Nature* 444, p. 330–6.

HIGHAM, T., [et al.] (2006). Revised direct radiocarbon dating of the Vindija G1 Upper Paleolithic Neandertals. *PNAS* 103, p. 553–7.

KARAVANIĆ, I., (1995). Upper Paleolithic occupation levels and late-occurring Neandertal at Vindija cave (Croatia) in the context of Central Europe and the Balkans. *Journal of Anthropological Research* 51, p. 9–35.

KARAVANIĆ, I.; SMITH, F.H. (1998). The Middle/ Upper Paleolithic interface and the relationship of Neandertals and early modern humans in the Hrvatsko Zagorje, Croatia. *Journal of Human Evolution* 34, p. 223–48.

KARAVANIĆ, I., [et al.] (1998). Néandertaliens et Paléolithique Supérieur dans la Grotte de Vindija, Croatie: controverses autour de la couche G1. *L'Anthropologie* 102, p. 131–41.

KRINGS, M., [et al.] (2000). A view of Neandertal genetic diversity. *Nature Genetics* 26, p. 144–6.

KURTÉN, B., (1976). *The Cave Bear Story*. New York: Columbia University Press.

LYMAN, R.L., (1994). *Vertebrate Taphonomy*. Cambridge: Cambridge University Press.

MALEZ, M.; RUKAVINA, D. (1975). Krioturbacijske pojave u gornjopleistocenskim naslagama pećine Vindije kod Donje Voće u sjeverozapadnoj Hrvatskoj. *Radovi Jugoslavenske akademije znanosti i umjetnosti* 371, p. 245–65.

MALEZ, M.; RUKAVINA, D. (1979). Položaj naslaga spilje Vindije u sustavu članjenja kvartara šireg područja Alpa. *Radovi Jugoslavenske akademije znanosti i umjetnosti* 383, p. 187–218.

MALEZ, M.; ULLRICH, H. (1982). Neure paläanthro-pologische Untersuchungen am Material aus der Höhle Vindija (Kroatien, Jugoslawien). *Palaeontolo-gia Jugoslavica* 29, p. 1–44.

MALEZ, M., [et al.] (1980). Upper Pleistocene hominids from Vindija, Croatia, Yugoslavia. *Current Anthro-pology* 21, p. 365–7.

MALEZ, M., [et al.] (1984). Geološki, sedimentološki I paleoklimatski odnosi spilje Vindije i bliže okolice. *Radovi Jugoslavenske akademije znanosti i umjetnosti* 411, p. 231–64.

MIRACLE, P.T., (1991). Carnivore dens or carnivore hunts? A review of Upper Pleistocene mammalian assemblages in Croatia and Slovenia. *RAD Hrvatske akademije znanosti i umjetnosti* 458, p. 193–219.

MIRACLE, P.T., (1998). The spread of modernity in Paleolithic Europe. In OMOTO, K.; TOBIAS, P.V., eds. *Origins and Past of Modern Humans: Towards Reconciliation*. Singapore: World Scientific, p. 171–87.

MIRACLE, P.T.; STURDY, D., (1991). Chamois and the karst of Herzegovina. *Journal of Archaeological Science* 18, p. 89–108.

NOONAN, J.P., [*et al.*] (2006). Sequencing and analysis of Neanderthal genomic DNA. *Science* 314, p. 1113–8.

RICHARDS, M.P., [*et al.*] (2000). Neanderthal diet at Vindija and Neanderthal predation: the evidence from stable isotopes. *PNAS* 97, p. 7663–6.

WILD, E.M., [*et al.*] (2001). Age determination of fossil bones from the Vindija Neanderthal site in Croatia. *Radiocarbon* 43, p. 1021–8.

WOLPOFF, M.H., [*et al.*] (1981). Upper Pleistocene human remains from Vindija Cave, Croatia, Yugoslavia. *American Journal of Physical Anthropology* 54, p. 449–545.

www.ingramcontent.com/pod-product-compliance
Lightning Source LLC
Chambersburg PA
CBHW061004030426
42334CB00033B/3354